Family Circle
COOKIE & CAKE BOOK

Editorial Director	Arthur Hettich
Editor	Marie T. Walsh
Art Director	Joseph Taveroni
Associate Editor	Jean Maguire
Art Associate	Walter Schwartz
Editorial Assistant	Ceri E. Hadda
Food Consultant	Grace Manney
Production Manager	Norman Ellers

All recipes tested by Family Circle's Test Kitchen.

Created by Family Circle Magazine and published 1978 by Arno Press Inc., a subsidiary of The New York Times Company. Copyright © 1977 by The Family Circle, Inc. All rights reserved. Protected under Berne and other international copyright conventions. Title and Trademark FAMILY CIRCLE registered U.S. Patent and Trademark Office, Canada, Great Britain, Australia, New Zealand, Japan and other countries. Marca Registrada. This volume may not be reproduced in whole or in part in any form without written permission from the publisher. Printed in U.S.A. Library of Congress Catalog Card Number 76-47121. ISBN O-405-09861-8.

CONTENTS

INTRODUCTION

For generations, the smell of homemade cakes and cookies has welcomed both friends and family members across the land. Today, more and more people are returning to baking, realizing its soul-, as well as taste-satisfying benefits. The time you put into baking results in healthy eating—and says you care!

BAKING BASICS

USING BEATERS

- Beat a small amount heavy cream or one egg white in a 2-cup measure with single beater from electric hand mixer.
- To make butter-type cakes by hand, place softened butter or margarine in medium-size bowl. Beat with wooden spoon, adding sugar slowly, until well blended. Add eggs, one at a time, and beat until fluffy, then, with a wooden spoon, stir in dry ingredients alternately with liquid.
- To hand-mix one-bowl cakes, place vegetable shortening and part of liquid in medium-size bowl with dry ingredients. Beat with spoon 300 strokes. Slowly add remaining liquid, eggs and flavorings; beat 300 strokes more.
- One-bowl cakes need 150 strokes for every *minute* of electric mixer beating time.

FOLDING HINTS

- Always pour meringue, whipped cream or egg yolk mixture from smaller container into larger container, very gently, to keep as much air in eggs as possible.
- Fold egg whites into cake batter at the last moment. *Don't* beat batter afterwards—you'll decrease leavening action of the whites.
- It is better to underfold than to overfold.
- The lowest speed of certain mixers (only those with "fold" speed) may be used for folding. This keeps batter light.

PLACEMENT IN OVEN IS IMPORTANT

- When baking one cake layer or sheet of cookies, place rack in center of oven.
- Cake pans should never touch each other or the oven walls.

- When baking two cake layers, put rack in center of oven, placing layers in opposite corners.

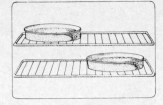

- Use 2 racks when baking three or four layers; place one rack slightly above middle of oven, the other a little below middle. Arrange pans so that they are not directly over each other.
- Bake sponge cakes and loaf cakes on the lowest shelf.
- Basic rule for oven placement is thick to the bottom of oven, thin to the top.
- Always preheat oven 10-15 minutes before baking time.
- Cookie sheets should be at least 2 inches narrower than the oven.
- Always place cookie dough on cool baking sheet; it'll spread on hot one.

USE YOUR SENSES!

- Listen to cake in oven; if it still "sings," bake it longer.
- When testing if a cake is done, watch for pulling from sides of pan. (doesn't apply to foam cakes).
- Watch for uniform shape and size when shaping cookie dough, to assure an evenly baked batch.
- To tell if sugar is dissolved in a meringue, rub a bit of the mixture through fingers. If still grainy, continue beating until smooth.

TURN OUT WELL

To remove cake from pan, cool cake in pan on wire rack 10 minutes, then loosen around edges with a knife. Tip pan on side and gently pull cake, turning all the time, until bottom of cake has loosened from pan. Place wire rack on top of cake; invert cake on rack; tap pan bottom and remove. Cool completely on wire rack.

FROSTING FOR VARIOUS SIZE CAKES

The following chart gives approximate amounts only:

BUTTER FROSTINGS

CAKE SIZE	FILLING	TOTAL
8-inch layer (2)	½ cup	2¼ cups
9-inch layer (2)	⅔ cup	2⅔ cups
8-inch square (1)		1⅓ cups
9-inch square (1)		2 cups
13x9x2-inch (1)		2⅓ cups
13x9x2-inch, cut into two 9x6½-inch layers and	⅔ cup	3 cups
9- or 10-inch angel tube		2½-3 cups
10-inch fluted tube		2½-3 cups
24 cupcakes		2¼ cups

FLUFFY FROSTINGS

CAKE SIZE	FILLING	TOTAL
8-inch layer (2)	1 cup	3¾ cups
9-inch layer (2)	1 cup	4¼ cups
8-inch square (1)		3 cups
9-inch square (1)		3⅔ cups
13x9x2-inch (1)		4¼ cups
13x9x2-inch, cut into two 9x6½-inch layers and	1 cup	4½ cups
9- or 10-inch angel tube		3½ cups
10-inch fluted tube		3½ cups
24 cupcakes		5½ cups

LIGHT, MOIST,
multi-layered cakes, rich
frostings and goodness-filled
recipes from hearty
grains, fresh fruit and
eggs distinguish American
baking. This feathery
Coconut-Lemon Cake and
Apple Harvest Cake made with
whole wheat flour are
just two of the greats
in this chapter. Recipes
start on page 6.

Chapter 1
Our
Heritage...
All-Time
American

TREASURES

COCONUT-LEMON CAKE

This triple-layer beauty includes a tart lemony filling and snowy coconut frosting. An all-time American favorite. The photograph appears on page 4.

Bake at 350° for 30 minutes.
Makes three 9-inch layers.

    3 cups cake flour
    4 teaspoons baking powder
    1 teaspoon salt
    ¾ cup vegetable shortening
    1¾ cups sugar
    3 eggs
    1 teaspoon vanilla
    ½ teaspoon lemon extract
    1¼ cups milk
      Lemon Filling (recipe follows)
      Seven-Minute Frosting (recipe
        follows)
    1 can (3½ ounces) flaked coconut

1. Grease bottoms of three 9-inch layer cake pans; line pans with wax paper; grease paper.
2. Sift cake flour, baking powder and salt onto wax paper.
3. Beat shortening with sugar until fluffy in large bowl of electric mixer at medium speed. Add eggs, one at a time, beating well after each addition; beat in vanilla and lemon extract until well blended.
4. Add sifted dry ingredients, a third at a time, alternately with milk, stirring just until blended with a wire whip. Pour into prepared pans.
5. Bake in moderate oven (350°) 30 minutes or until centers spring back when lightly touched with fingertip.
6. Cool in pans on wire racks 5 minutes; loosen around edges with a narrow spatula and turn out onto racks. Peel off wax paper; cool completely on wire racks.
7. Put layers together with LEMON FILLING: frost top and side with SEVEN-MINUTE FROSTING. Sprinkle coconut around side and over top.

LEMON FILLING

Makes enough to fill three 9-inch layers.

    ½ cup sugar
    3 tablespoons cornstarch
    ¼ teaspoon salt
    2 egg yolks
    ¾ cup water
    ⅓ cup lemon juice
    2 tablespoons butter or margarine

1. Mix sugar, cornstarch and salt in medium-size saucepan; stir in egg yolks and water with wire whip.
2. Cook, stirring constantly, until mixture thickens and bubbles 1 minute; remove from heat. Stir in lemon juice and butter or margarine until well blended; cool completely.

SEVEN-MINUTE FROSTING

Makes enough to frost three 9-inch layers.

    1½ cups sugar
    ¼ cup water
    2 egg whites
    2 tablespoons light corn syrup
    ¼ teaspoon salt
    1 teaspoon vanilla

1. Combine sugar, water, egg whites, corn syrup, salt and vanilla in top of double boiler; beat until blended.
2. Place over simmering water; cook, beating constantly with an electric mixer at high speed, 7 minutes, or until mixture triples in volume and holds firm marks of beater; remove from heat.
3. Spread on cake at once, while frosting is fluffy and light.

BAKING BASICS

ALL ABOUT FLOUR

• It isn't necessary to sift flour. Spoon it into a measuring cup, to overflowing (don't pack or tap), and level off at top with knife or spatula.
• Only use standard dry measures.
• Always make level measurements.
• Use all purpose flour for baking our recipes, unless otherwise specified.
• Whole wheat flour is generally too heavy for delicate baked goods. It contains the entire wheat grain, including bran, so use only in recipes calling for it.
• Unbleached white flour may be used in place of all purpose flour.
• Cake flour is milled from the highest grade soft wheat and suitable when you want a lighter product.
• To substitute all purpose flour for cake flour, remove 2 tablespoons from each cup of measured flour.

MEASURING DRY INGREDIENTS

Dash = under ⅛ teaspoon		
1 tablespoon = 3		teaspoons
¼ cup = 4		tablespoons
⅓ cup = 5		tablespoons
	+ 1	teaspoon
½ cup = 8		tablespoons
1 cup = 16		tablespoons

GERMAN CHOCOLATE CAKE

A real winner! After baking, layers are split and put back together with fruit filling. Photograph is on page 14.

Bake at 350° for 35 minutes.
Makes two 9-inch square layers.

    3 cups cake flour
    2½ teaspoons baking powder
    ½ teaspoon salt
    1 cup (2 sticks) butter or
      margarine
    1½ cups sugar
    2 teaspoons rum extract
    ½ teaspoon vanilla
    4 eggs
    2 packages (4 ounces each) sweet
      cooking chocolate, melted
    1¼ cups milk
      Fruit-Nut Filling (recipe follows)
      Chocolate Butter Frosting
      (recipe, page 74)

1. Grease two 9x9x2-inch pans; line with wax paper; grease paper.
2. Sift flour, baking powder and salt onto wax paper.
3. Beat butter or margarine in large bowl of electric mixer at high speed; add sugar gradually, beating until fluffy. Beat in rum extract and vanilla.
4. Beat in eggs, one at a time, until fluffy, then slowly beat in chocolate.
5. Add flour mixture, a third at a time, alternately with milk, stirring with a wire whip or beating with mixer at low speed just until blended. Pour into prepared pans, dividing evenly.
6. Bake in moderate oven (350°) 35 minutes or until centers spring back when lightly pressed with fingertip.
7. Cool in pans on wire racks 5 minutes; loosen around edges with a narrow spatula and turn out onto racks; peel off wax paper; cool layers completely.
8. While layers bake and cool, prepare FRUIT-NUT FILLING and CHOCOLATE BUTTER FROSTING.
9. Split each cake layer crosswise, with a long-bladed knife. Put back together, alternately with FRUIT-NUT FILLING and CHOCOLATE BUTTER FROSTING on a serving plate. Refrigerate cake until serving time.

FRUIT-NUT FILLING: Makes about 2 ½ cups. Beat 1 egg in the top of a double boiler; blend in 1 cup sugar, 1 tablespoon flour, 1 container (8 ounces) dairy sour cream and ½ cup chopped raisins. Cook, stirring often, over simmering water 15 minutes, or until thick. Cool about 30 minutes, then stir in 1 cup flaked coconut, ½ cup chopped pecans, ½ teaspoon vanilla, and ¼ teaspoon grated lemon rind; chill.

STRAWBERRY-RHUBARB SHORTCAKE

Fresh, sweet strawberries, whipped cream and the rhubarb you've grown in your garden make this a delightful way to end a meal.

Bake at 450° for 20 minutes.
Makes 8 servings.

    1 pound rhubarb
 1¾ cups granulated sugar
    2 tablespoons water
    1 pint strawberries
    2 cups all purpose flour
    1 tablespoon baking powder
    1 teaspoon salt
    5 tablespoons butter or margarine
 ¼ cup vegetable shortening
    1 egg
 ⅓ cup milk
    1 cup heavy cream
    2 tablespoons 10X (confectioners' powdered) sugar

1. Wash rhubarb; trim ends and cut into 1-inch pieces. (There should be about 3 cups.)
2. Combine with ¾ cup of the granulated sugar and water in a medium-size heavy saucepan; cover. Heat over low heat to boiling, then simmer 5 minutes, or until tender; remove from heat. Set aside to cool. (Rhubarb will finish cooking in heat from pan.)
3. Wash strawberries; hull and slice into a medium-size bowl; sprinkle with ½ cup of the remaining granulated sugar.
4. Sift flour, remaining ½ cup granulated sugar, baking powder and salt into a medium-size bowl; cut in 4 tablespoons of the butter or margarine and shortening with a pastry blender until mixture is crumbly.
5. Beat egg slightly with milk in a small bowl; add all at once to flour mixture; stir with a fork until evenly moist. Turn out onto a lightly floured pastry cloth or board; knead gently ½ minute. Pat into a greased 8-inch layer cake pan.
6. Melt remaining 1 tablespoon butter or margarine in a small metal cup; brush over dough; sprinkle lightly with granulated sugar, if you wish.
7. Bake in very hot oven (450°) 20 minutes, or until golden. Cool in pan on a wire rack 5 minutes; turn out onto rack.
8. Beat cream with 10X sugar until stiff in a medium-size bowl with electric mixer at medium speed.
9. Split warm shortcake with a sharp knife; place bottom layer on a serving plate. Top with half each of the rhubarb, strawberries and cream; cover with remaining shortcake layer,
fruit and soft swirls of cream.
10. Cut into wedges with a sharp knife; serve warm.

BLITZ TORTE

Meringue-topped layers are crowned with sliced almonds and filled with whipped cream in the grand tradition of pastry shops in Yorkville, N.Y.

Bake at 350° for 30 minutes.
Makes two 9-inch layers.

    2 cups cake flour
    2 teaspoons baking powder
    1 teaspoon salt
    5 eggs, separated
 1¾ cups sugar
 ⅓ cup vegetable shortening
    1 teaspoon vanilla
 ½ teaspoon almond extract
 ½ cup milk
 ¾ cup sliced almonds
    1 cup heavy cream
    2 tablespoons sugar

1. Grease two 9-inch layer cake pans; dust with flour; tap out any excess.
2. Sift flour, baking powder and salt onto wax paper; reserve.
3. Beat egg whites in small bowl of electric mixer at high speed until foamy-white and double in volume. Beat in ¾ cup of the sugar, 1 tablespoon at a time, until meringue stands in firm peaks; reserve.
4. Beat remaining 1 cup sugar, shortening, egg yolks, vanilla and almond extract in large bowl of mixer at high speed for 3 minutes.
5. Stir in flour mixture with wire whip, alternately with milk, beating after each addition until batter is smooth. Spread batter into prepared pans. Carefully spread reserved meringue over cake batter; sprinkle with sliced almonds.
6. Bake in moderate oven (350°) 30 minutes, or until meringue is golden brown and cake begins to pull from sides of pans. (Meringue may crack in baking, but don't worry, it will settle while cooling.)
7. Cool cake layers in pans on wire racks 30 minutes, or until cool enough to handle. Loosen around edges with a knife; turn out onto your hand, then gently place, meringue-side up, on wire racks to cool completely.
8. At least 2 hours before serving, beat cream and 2 tablespoons sugar in a small bowl until stiff with electric mixer at medium speed.
9. Put layers together on serving plate with part of the whipped cream. Garnish cake with remaining cream and strawberries, if you wish. Refrigerate until serving time.

HARVEST SPICE CAKE

This three-layer cake will bring back memories of dinner at grandmother's on Sunday.

Bake at 350° for 25 minutes.
Makes three 8-inch layers.

    3 cups all purpose flour
    1 tablespoon baking powder
 ½ teaspoon baking soda
    1 teaspoon salt
 ½ teaspoon ground allspice
 ½ teaspoon ground nutmeg
 ½ teaspoon ground cinnamon
 ¾ cup (1½ sticks) butter or margarine
 1½ cups firmly packed brown sugar
    3 eggs
 ¾ cup milk
 ½ cup apple cider
    1 teaspoon vanilla
       Butter Rum Frosting (recipe follows)
       Walnuts

1. Sift flour, baking powder, baking soda, salt, allspice, nutmeg and cinnamon onto wax paper.
2. Beat butter or margarine until softened in the large bowl of an electric mixer at high speed; gradually add brown sugar and continue beating until fluffy. Beat in eggs, one at a time, until smooth and creamy; turn mixer to lowest speed.
3. Combine milk, apple cider and vanilla in a 2-cup measure.
4. Stir in flour mixture, alternately with milk mixture, beginning and ending with flour, until batter is smooth. Pour batter into three 8-inch greased and floured layer cake pans.
5. Bake in moderate oven (350°) 25 minutes, or until top springs back when lightly touched with fingertip. Cool cake layers in pans on wire racks 5 minutes. Loosen layers around edges with a small spatula; invert onto racks; cool completely.
6. Put layers together with part of the BUTTER RUM FROSTING on serving plate. Frost side and top of cake. Garnish with walnuts.

BUTTER RUM FROSTING

Makes enough to fill and frost three 8-inch layers.

 ½ cup (1 stick) butter or margarine
    1 package (1 pound) 10X (confectioners' powdered) sugar, sifted
 ⅓ cup dark corn syrup
    2 teaspoons rum extract

Beat butter or margarine until soft in a medium-size bowl with electric mixer on medium speed. Gradually beat in 10X sugar, corn syrup and rum extract until smooth and creamy.

THESE BUTTERY SUGAR COOKIES
are a tradition in this country that's just
as popular today as when our ancestors
churned the butter to make them in their
country kitchens. And it's no wonder.
They're a confectioner's dream—crispy and
delicate-tasting and so adaptable to any
form. We've chosen a star shape for
ours, and we think you'll agree, they

make a sparkling display on this 19th Century miniature cook stove. Resting on the top tier are Stained Glass Stars, with melted sour balls for centers and Star Jewels gleaming with jelly. Middle tier: Gaily frosted Butterscotch-Nut Stars; Double Stars made with a simple cutout trick; tangy orange-coated California Stars. Bottom tier: Mellow Chocolate Stars topped with candies.

9

FAVORITE YELLOW CUPCAKES

Kids love having a cake all to themselves, and that's probably why mothers first made cupcakes. These are topped with one of kids' favorite candies, too. Photo is on page 11.

Bake at 350° for 20 minutes.
Makes 36 cupcakes.

    3 cups cake flour
    1¾ cups sugar
    1 tablespoon baking powder
    1 teaspoon salt
    ½ cup vegetable shortening
    2 eggs
    1 cup milk
    1 teaspoon vanilla
    1 teaspoon lemon extract
      Butter Cream Frosting (recipe
        follows)
      Colored sugar-coated
        chocolates (see Cook's Guide)

1. Sift flour, sugar, baking powder and salt into the large bowl of electric mixer; add shortening, eggs, milk, vanilla and lemon extract.
2. Beat at medium speed 4 minutes, scraping bowl often.
3. Line 36 muffin tins with paper liners; fill two-thirds full with batter.
4. Bake in moderate oven (350°) 20 minutes, or until tops spring back when lightly pressed with fingertip. Remove from tins and cool completely on wire racks.
5. Spread with BUTTER CREAM FROSTING and garnish with candies.
BAKER'S TIP: If you don't have 36 muffin tins, fill as many as you have two-thirds full, then cover bowl with plastic wrap and keep at room temperature while first batch bakes.

BUTTER CREAM FROSTING

Makes enough filling and frosting for 36 cupcakes, or two 9-inch layers.

    ½ cup (1 stick) butter or margarine
    1 package (1 pound) 10X
      (confectioners' powdered)
      sugar, sifted
    ¼ cup milk
    1½ teaspoons vanilla

1. Beat butter or margarine in a medium-size bowl until soft with electric mixer at high speed.
2. Add 10X sugar, alternately with milk and vanilla, until smooth.
Suggested Variations: LEMON BUTTER CREAM—Substitute 2 tablespoons lemon juice for 2 tablespoons of the milk in BUTTER CREAM FROSTING and add 2 teaspoons grated lemon rind. ORANGE BUTTER CREAM—Substitute 2 tablespoons orange juice for 2 tablespoons of the milk in BUTTER CREAM FROSTING and add 2 teaspoons grated orange rind. STRAWBERRY BUTTER CREAM—Substitute ⅓ cup mashed strawberries for the milk in BUTTER CREAM FROSTING. BRANDY BUTTER CREAM—Substitute 2 tablespoons brandy for 2 tablespoons of the milk in BUTTER CREAM FROSTING. RUM BUTTER CREAM—Substitute 2 tablespoons rum for 2 tablespoons of the milk in BUTTER CREAM FROSTING. MOCHA BUTTER CREAM—Substitute 3 tablespoons coffee liqueur for 2 tablespoons of the milk in BUTTER CREAM FROSTING and add 1 tablespoon instant coffee.

PENNSYLVANIA-DUTCH CAKE

It's a real beauty inspired by an old-time recipe. Apple butter makes it extra moist.

Bake at 350° for 30 minutes.
Makes three 8-inch layers.

    2½ cups all purpose flour
    1½ teaspoons baking soda
    ½ teaspoon salt
    ½ teaspoon ground cinnamon
    ½ teaspoon ground nutmeg
    1 tablespoon vinegar
    1 cup milk
    ½ cup vegetable shortening
    1 cup sugar
    4 eggs
    1 cup apple butter
      Fluffy Filling and Frosting
        (recipe, page 22)
    1 red apple
      Walnut halves

1. Grease bottom of three 8-inch layer cake pans; line pans with wax paper; grease paper.
2. Measure flour, baking soda, salt, cinnamon and nutmeg into sifter. Stir vinegar into milk in 2-cup measure.
3. Beat shortening and sugar until fluffy in large bowl of electric mixer at medium speed. Beat in eggs, 1 at a time, beating well after each addition. Stir in apple butter.
4. Sift in dry ingredients, a quarter at a time, adding alternately with milk mixture; stir with a wire whip or beat with mixer at low speed just until blended. Pour into pans.
5. Bake in moderate oven (350°) 30 minutes, or until centers spring back when lightly touched with fingertip.
6. Cool in pans on wire racks 5 minutes; loosen around edges with a narrow spatula; turn out onto racks. Peel off paper; cool layers completely.
7. Make FLUFFY FILLING AND FROSTING. Put layers together with filling; cover top and side with frosting.
8. Quarter, core, and slice apple into thin wedges. Arrange with walnuts around top and side of cake. Chill until ready to serve.

ORANGE-APPLE CAKE

Such a good keeper, if you can hide it that long. Bits of tart apple and raisins add extra moistness to a classic spice cake.

Bake at 350° for 35 minutes.
Makes three 8-inch layers.

    2½ cups all purpose flour
    1½ teaspoons pumpkin pie spice
    1 teaspoon baking powder
    1 teaspoon baking soda
    1 teaspoon salt
    ½ cup vegetable shortening
    1¾ cups sugar
    3 eggs
    2 cups grated pared apples
      (2 large)
    1 teaspoon vanilla
    ½ cup milk
    1 cup raisins
    1 cup chopped walnuts
      Orange Cream Frosting (recipe
        follows)

1. Grease bottoms of three 8-inch layer cake pans.
2. Measure flour, pumpkin pie spice, baking powder, soda and salt into sifter.
3. Beat shortening with sugar until fluffy in the large bowl of electric mixer at medium speed. Beat in eggs, 1 at a time, until fluffy again, then stir in apples and vanilla.
4. Sift in flour mixture, adding alternately with milk, and stirring just until blended; fold in raisins and walnuts. Pour into prepared pans.
5. Bake in moderate oven (350°) 35 minutes, or until centers spring back when lightly pressed with fingertip. Cool layers in pans on wire racks 5 minutes; loosen around edges with a knife; turn out onto racks. Cool layers completely on wire racks.
6. Put layers together with ORANGE CREAM FROSTING; then frost side, making deep swirls.

ORANGE CREAM FROSTING

Makes enough filling and frosting for three 8-inch layers.

    ½ cup (1 stick) butter or margarine
    1 package (3 ounces) cream cheese
    1 package (1 pound) 10X
      (confectioners' powdered)
      sugar, sifted
    ¼ cup orange juice
    4 teaspoons grated orange rind
      Dash salt
    1 teaspoon vanilla

Beat butter or margarine and cream cheese until soft in large bowl of electric mixer at high speed; gradually beat in 10X sugar, alternately with orange juice, until smooth. Stir in orange rind, salt and vanilla.

OLD-FASHIONED treats loved in every American home: Best-Ever Brownies, crunchy Toll-House Cookies, Favorite Yellow Cupcakes.

ELECTION CAKE

Also called "Hartford Election Cake," this rich yeast cake was served at election time in Connecticut 200 years ago.

Bake at 350° for 40 minutes.
Makes one 8-inch round cake.

- 1 envelope active dry yeast
- ¼ cup very warm water
- ½ cup milk
- ½ cup firmly packed brown sugar
- ¼ cup (½ stick) butter or margarine
- 2 eggs
- 3½ cups all purpose flour
- 1 teaspoon pumpkin pie spice
- 1 teaspoon salt
- ¾ cup raisins
- 8 figs, finely chopped
- ¾ cup 10X (confectioners' powdered) sugar
- 1 tablespoon hot water
- ½ teaspoon vanilla

1. Sprinkle yeast over very warm water in a large bowl. ("Very warm" water should feel comfortably warm when dropped on wrist.) Stir in 1 teaspoon sugar until dissolved. Allow to rest 10 minutes, until mixture begins to bubble.
2. Heat milk, sugar and butter or margarine in a small saucepan until butter melts; remove from heat; cool slightly.
3. Beat eggs into yeast mixture with a wooden spoon, then stir in cooled milk mixture. Stir in 2 cups of the flour, pumpkin pie spice and salt; beat until well blended; beat in raisins and figs. Beat in enough of remaining flour to make a stiff dough.
4. Turn out onto a lightly floured pastry cloth or board. Knead 5 minutes, or until dough is smooth and elastic. Place in a greased bowl; turn to coat other side; cover bowl with plastic wrap. Let rise in a warm place, away from draft, 1½ hours, or until double in bulk.
5. Punch dough down; turn out onto lightly floured pastry cloth or board; knead dough several times; shape into an 8-inch ball. Place in a greased 8-inch springform pan or a greased deep 8-inch layer cake pan. Cover with plastic wrap. Allow to rise in warm place, away from draft, 45 minutes; remove wrap.
6. Bake in moderate oven (350°) 40 minutes, or until cake gives a hollow sound when tapped; remove from pan to wire rack. Cool.
7. Beat 10X sugar, hot water and vanilla in a small bowl until smooth; spread over cake.

BAKER'S TIP: Use an alarm clock to remind you that your cake is baking in the oven.

LONG ISLAND CHOCOLATE CAKE

Eastern Long Island has always been known for its fine potatoes. Here is a cake that's even more moist and tasty because of the potatoes in the batter. Photo is on page 14.

Bake at 350° for 30 minutes.
Makes two 9-inch layers.

- 2½ cups all purpose flour
- 2 teaspoons baking powder
- ½ teaspoon baking soda
- 1 teaspoon salt
- ¾ cup vegetable shortening
- 1½ cups sugar
- 4 eggs
- 4 squares unsweetened chocolate, melted
- 1 large potato, peeled and finely shredded (1 cup)
- 2 teaspoons vanilla
- ½ cup milk
  Rich Fudge Frosting (recipe, page 13)

1. Sift flour, baking powder, baking soda and salt onto wax paper.
2. Beat shortening and sugar until fluffy in large bowl of electric mixer at high speed; beat in eggs, one at a time, beat in chocolate; fold in shredded potato and vanilla.
3. Add dry ingredients and milk, alternately. Pour into two greased and floured 9-inch layer cake pans.
4. Bake in moderate oven (350°) 30 minutes, or until cake springs back when lightly touched with fingertip. Cool in pans on wire racks 10 minutes; loosen around edges with narrow spatula; turn out onto racks; cool completely.
5. Put layers together with RICH FUDGE FROSTING; frost side and top, making deep swirls with spatula.

COFFEE CHIFFON CAKE

A special treat for coffee lovers.

Bake at 325° for 1 hour, 10 minutes.
Makes one 10-inch angel tube cake.

- 2⅓ cups cake flour
- 1⅓ cups sugar
- 1 tablespoon baking powder
- 1 teaspoon salt
- ½ cup vegetable oil
- 5 egg yolks
- ¾ cup cold water
- 1 tablespoon instant coffee powder
- 1 cup (7 to 8) egg whites
- ½ teaspoon cream of tartar
  Shiny Chocolate Glaze (recipe, page 21)

1. Sift flour, 1 cup of the sugar, baking powder and salt into a medium-size bowl. Make a well and add in order: Oil, egg yolks, water and coffee; beat with wire whip until well blended and smooth.
2. Beat egg whites and cream of tartar in large bowl of electric mixer at high speed, until foamy-white and double in volume. Beat in remaining ⅓ cup sugar, 1 tablespoon at a time, until meringue stands in firm peaks.
3. Gradually pour egg yolk mixture over beaten whites, gently folding in with wire whip until no streaks of white remain. Spoon into ungreased 10-inch angel cake tube pan.
4. Bake in slow oven (325°) 1 hour, 10 minutes, or until top springs back when lightly pressed in center.
5. Invert pan, placing tube over a quart-size bottle; let cake cool completely. When cool, loosen cake around outside edge and tube and down side with a spatula. Cover pan with serving plate; turn upside down; shake gently; lift off pan. Drizzle SHINY CHOCOLATE GLAZE over top of cake, letting it run down the side.

TUNNEL-OF-FUDGE CAKE

A past winner of the national Bake-Off® contest. This recipe began the national use of the Bundt® pan in home baking. The photograph is on page 14.

Bake at 350° for 1 hour.
Makes one 10-inch fluted tube cake.

- 1½ cups (3 sticks) butter or margarine
- 6 eggs
- 1½ cups sugar
- 2 cups all purpose flour
- 1 package (about 1 pound) double Dutch chocolate frosting mix
- 2 cups chopped walnuts

1. Grease well a 12-cup fluted tube pan, or 10-inch angel cake tube pan.
2. Beat butter or margarine in large bowl of electric mixer at high speed until creamy; beat in eggs, one at a time, until well blended; gradually beat in sugar until fluffy.
3. Stir in flour and 3⅓ cups of *dry* frosting mix and walnuts into batter with wooden spoon until well blended; pour into tube pan.
4. Bake in moderate oven (350°) 1 hour, or until top is dry and shiny. (Because the frosting mix has made a soft tunnel in center of cake, it is impossible to test the cake, using standard tests.)
5. Cool cake in pan on wire rack 1 hour; loosen cake around edge and tube; invert onto wire rack; cool.
6. Stir a few drops water into remaining frosting mix in a small bowl; spoon over cake just before serving.

IOWA CHOCOLATE CAKE

This recipe is so simple, yet delicious, it's bound to be used often.

Bake at 350° for 25 minutes.
Makes two 9-inch layers.

- 2 cups all purpose flour
- 1½ cups sugar
- ⅔ cup cocoa powder (not a mix)
- 2 teaspoons baking powder
- ½ teaspoon baking soda
- ½ teaspoon salt
- ⅔ cup vegetable shortening
- 2 eggs
- ⅔ cup milk
- ½ cup hot water
- 1 teaspoon vanilla
  Rich Fudge Frosting (recipe follows)

1. Sift flour, sugar, cocoa, baking powder, baking soda and salt into the large bowl of an electric mixer.
2. Add shortening, eggs, milk, water and vanilla to bowl. Turn speed to low and beat 1 minute, scraping side of bowl several times.
3. Turn speed to medium and beat 3 minutes, or until batter is creamy and smooth. Pour into 2 greased and floured 9-inch layer cake pans.
4. Bake in moderate oven (350°) 25 minutes, or until top springs back when lightly touched with fingertip. Cool in pans on wire racks 10 minutes; loosen around edges with a narrow spatula; invert onto wire racks; cool completely. Put together and frost WITH RICH FUDGE FROSTING, making deep swirls in frosting with back of spoon.
Suggested Variation: For WALNUT CHOCOLATE CAKE, stir ½ cup chopped walnuts into IOWA CHOCOLATE CAKE batter before pouring into prepared pans.

RICH FUDGE FROSTING

Makes enough filling and frosting for two 9-inch layers.

- ½ cup (1 stick) butter or margarine
- ½ cup cocoa powder (not a mix)
- ¼ cup water
- 1 package (1 pound) 10X (confectioners' powdered) sugar, sifted
  Dash salt
- 1 teaspoon vanilla

Melt butter or margarine with cocoa in a large saucepan over low heat, stirring often, until mixture is smooth; remove from heat. Beat in 10X sugar, salt and vanilla until smooth with electric mixer at high speed.
BAKER'S TIP: If mixture becomes too thick while frosting cake, add a few drops hot water and beat.

LUSCIOUS DEVIL'S FOOD CAKE

You'll have a hard time saving this one for company, if the kids get near it.

Bake at 350° for 30 minutes.
Makes two 9-inch layers.

- 4 squares unsweetened chocolate
- 1½ cups sugar
- 1½ cups milk
- 1 teaspoon white vinegar
- 2 cups cake flour
- 1 tablespoon baking powder
- ½ teaspoon baking soda
- ½ teaspoon salt
- 2 eggs, separated
- ½ cup (1 stick) butter or margarine
- 1 teaspoon vanilla
  Velvet Frosting (recipe follows)

1. Grease two 9-inch layer cake pans; dust with flour; tap out any excess.
2. Combine chocolate, ½ cup of the sugar, and 1 cup of the milk in a small heavy saucepan. Cook, stirring constantly, until mixture thickens and turns a deep chocolate color. Cool.
3. Stir white vinegar into the remaining ½ cup milk in a 1-cup measure to sour.
4. Sift flour, baking powder, baking soda and salt onto wax paper.
5. Beat butter or margarine, remaining 1 cup sugar and egg yolks in large bowl of electric mixer at high speed 3 minutes. Beat in cooled chocolate mixture until light and fluffy with mixer at medium speed.
6. Stir in flour mixture, alternately with soured milk and vanilla, beating after each addition until batter is smooth.
7. Beat egg whites until stiff, but not dry, in small bowl of mixer at high speed; fold into batter with wire whip; pour batter into prepared pans.
8. Bake in moderate oven (350°) 30 minutes, or until centers spring back when lightly pressed with fingertip.
9. Cool layers in pans on wire racks 10 minutes. Loosen around edges with a knife and turn out onto wire racks; cool completely.
10. Put layers together with VELVET FROSTING; frost sides and top with remaining frosting.

VELVET FROSTING

Makes enough filling and frosting for two 9-inch layers.

- 1½ cups sugar
- ⅓ cup cornstarch
- ¼ teaspoon salt
- 1½ cups boiling water
- 3 squares unsweetended chocolate
- ¼ cup (½ stick) butter or margarine
- 1 teaspoon vanilla

1. Combine sugar, cornstarch and salt in a medium-size saucepan; stir in boiling water until mixture is well blended.
2. Cook, stirring constantly, until mixture thickens. Add chocolate squares and butter or margarine; continue cooking and stirring until chocolate and butter melt; remove from heat; stir in vanilla.
3. Pour into a medium-size bowl; chill in refrigerator, stirring several times, until thick enough to spread.

BRETON CHOCOLATE POUND CAKE

Aromatic bitters bring out the deep chocolate flavor in this pound cake. The perfect dessert for a special holiday dinner.

Bake at 300° for 1 hour, 45 minutes.
Makes one 8-inch fluted tube cake.

- 5 squares unsweetened chocolate
- 1⅓ cups water
- 2 cups all purpose flour
- 2 cups sugar
- 1 teaspoon salt
- ½ cup (1 stick) butter or margarine
- 3 eggs
- 1 teaspoon aromatic bitters
- 1 teaspoon vanilla
- 2 teaspoons baking powder
  Shiny Chocolate Glaze (recipe, page 21)

1. Combine chocolate and water in a small saucepan. Heat, stirring constantly, until chocolate melts; cool until lukewarm.
2. Sift flour, sugar and salt into large bowl of electric mixer; cut in butter or margarine with a pastry blender to make a crumbly mixture.
3. Add cooled chocolate mixture. Beat at medium speed for 5 minutes. Chill batter in bowl in the refrigerator for at least 1 hour.
4. Return bowl to mixer. Beat at medium speed 1 minute. Add eggs, 1 at a time, beating 1 minute after each addition. Add aromatic bitters and vanilla and beat 2 minutes. Add baking powder and beat 2 minutes more.
5. Pour batter into a greased 8-cup fluted tube pan which has been lightly dusted with dry cocoa (or a 9x5x3-inch loaf pan).
6. Bake in slow oven (300°) 1 hour, 45 minutes, or until a toothpick inserted in center comes out clean. Cool cake in pan on wire rack 10 minutes; loosen around edges with a knife. Turn cake out of pan on wire rack and cool completely.
7. Frost with SHINY CHOCOLATE GLAZE and garnish with sliced almonds or walnuts, if you wish.

LUSCIOUS and moist, these cakes are winners: Tunnel-of-Fudge Cake, Long Island Chocolate Cake and German Chocolate Cake.

PLANTATION PRUNE CAKE

Rich with buttermilk and pecans, this cake has a Southern charm all its own.

Bake at 350° for 1 hour.
Makes one 10-inch angel tube cake.

  1 jar (1 pound) cooked prunes
2½ cups all purpose flour
  1 teaspoon baking soda
  1 teaspoon salt
  1 teaspoon ground allspice
  1 teaspoon ground cinnamon
  1 teaspoon ground nutmeg
  1 cup finely chopped pecans
  3 eggs
1½ cups sugar
  1 cup vegetable oil
 ½ cup buttermilk
   Vanilla Glaze (recipe follows)

1. Grease a 10-inch angel cake tube pan; flour, tapping out any excess.
2. Drain liquid from prunes into a cup. Pit prunes, then cut each into 3 or 4 pieces; place in a 1-cup measure. Add prune liquid to make 1 cup.
3. Sift flour, soda, salt, allspice, cinnamon and nutmeg into a medium-size bowl; stir in pecans.
4. Beat eggs well in the large bowl of electric mixer at high speed; slowly beat in sugar until mixture is fluffy. Beat in vegetable oil, then buttermilk; stir in prunes. Beat in flour mixture, a third at a time, until well blended. Pour into prepared pan.
5. Bake in moderate oven (350°) 1 hour, or until top springs back when lightly pressed with fingertip. Cool 10 minutes in pan on a wire rack. Loosen cake around edge and tube with a knife; turn out onto rack; cool.
6. Wrap cake in plastic wrap, then in heavy-duty aluminum foil; freeze up to 8 weeks.
7. The day before serving, remove cake from freezer; let stand, still wrapped, at room temperature to thaw. An hour before serving, unwrap cake and place on a deep plate.
8. Make VANILLA GLAZE. While hot, drizzle slowly over cake, spooning any that drips onto plate back over cake. Serve with ice cream, if you wish.

VANILLA GLAZE—Makes 1½ cups. Combine 1 cup sugar, ½ teaspoon baking soda, ½ cup buttermilk, 1 tablespoon light corn syrup and ½ cup (1 stick) butter or margarine in a medium-size saucepan. Heat slowly, stirring contantly, to boiling; then cook, stirring constantly, 2 minutes. Remove from heat; stir in 1 teaspoon vanilla.
BAKER'S TIP: If serving cake without freezing, cover with glaze as soon as cake is removed from pan.

PEANUT BUTTER-CHOCOLATE SQUARES

These chewy treats will remind you of the popular candy combination. They're great with a cup of hot cocoa or coffee.

Bake at 350° for 40 minutes.
Makes 16 squares.

 ¾ cup all purpose flour
 ½ teaspoon salt
 ½ teaspoon baking powder
 ¼ teaspoon baking soda
 ½ cup (1 stick) butter or margarine
 ½ cup peanut butter
 ½ cup light molasses
 ½ cup sugar
  1 egg
 ½ teaspoon vanilla
 ½ cup semi-sweet chocolate pieces

1. Sift flour, salt, baking powder and baking soda onto wax paper.
2. Beat butter or margarine, peanut butter and molasses in mcdium-size bowl until fluffy with electric mixer at medium speed; add sugar gradually, beating until mixture is well blended.
3. Beat in egg until fluffy; beat in vanilla; turn mixer speed to low.
4. Add sifted dry ingredients, a third at a time, beating just until blended; spread batter in a greased 8x8x2-inch baking pan.
5. Bake in moderate oven (350°) 40 minutes, or until top springs back when lightly touched with fingertip.
6. Sprinkle chocolate pieces over top; return to oven for 2 to 3 minutes, or until chocolate is melted; spread with knife to frost.
7. Cool completely in pan on wire rack; cut into 16 squares.

HONEY BROWNIES

Honey gives both moistness and flavor to these flavorful squares; wheat germ and rolled oats make them high in nutrition.

Bake at 325° for 55 minutes.
Makes 16 bars.

 ½ cup all purpose flour
  1 teaspoon baking powder
 ½ teaspoon salt
  1 cup honey
 ⅓ cup vegetable shortening
  1 egg
  1 teaspoon vanilla
 ½ cup ground almonds (see page 60)
 ¼ cup wheat germ
 ¼ cup old-fashioned rolled oats
 ½ cup sliced almonds

1. Sift flour, baking powder and salt onto wax paper.
2. Beat honey and vegetable shortening until fluffy in medium-size bowl

with electric mixer at high speed; add egg and beat well; beat in vanilla; turn mixer speed to low.
3. Add sifted dry ingredients, a third at a time, beating just until blended.
4. Stir in ground almonds, wheat germ and oats; spread mixture into well greased 8x8x2-inch baking pan; sprinkle sliced almonds over top, pressing in gently.
5. Bake in moderate oven (325°) 55 minutes, or until top springs back when lightly touched with fingertip.
6. Cool completely in pan on wire rack; cut into 16 squares.

DAFFODIL CAKE

Light and lemony, it's a favorite choice of dessert around Eastertime.

Bake at 325° for 50 minutes.
Makes one 10-inch angel tube cake.

1¼ cups cake flour
1½ cups sugar
 10 egg whites (1¼ cups)
1½ teaspoons cream of tartar
 ¼ teaspoon salt
  4 egg yolks
  1 teaspoon grated lemon rind
  1 teaspoon vanilla

1. Sift flour and ½ cup of the sugar onto wax paper.
2. Beat egg whites, cream of tartar and salt in large bowl of electric mixer at high speed until foamy-white and double in volume. Beat in the remaining 1 cup of sugar, 1 tablespoon at a time, until meringue stands in soft peaks.
3. Fold in flour mixture, a third at a time, with a wire whip or rubber scraper until completely blended.
4. Beat egg yolks in small bowl of mixer at high speed until thick and lemon-colored. Beat in lemon rind and vanilla.
5. Fold half of the meringue batter into egg yolks until no streaks of white or yellow remain.
6. Spoon batters by tablespoonfuls, alternating colors, into an ungreased 10-inch angel cake tube pan. (Do not stir batters in pan.)
7. Bake in slow oven (325°) 50 minutes, or until top springs back when lightly pressed with fingertip.
8. Invert pan, placing tube over a quart-size bottle; let cake cool completely. Loosen cake around the edge and tube and down the side with a spatula. Cover pan with a serving plate; turn upside down; shake gently; lift off pan. Cut into wedges and serve with lemon sherbet or vanilla ice cream, if you wish.

SOUR CREAM-BANANA CAKE

Each mouthful is a pleasure.

Bake at 350° for 40 minutes.
Makes one 13x9x2-inch cake.

¼ cup (½ stick) butter or margarine, softened
1⅓ cup sugar
2 eggs
1 teaspoon vanilla
2 cups all purpose flour
1 teaspoon baking powder
1 teaspoon baking soda
¾ teaspoon salt
1 container (8 ounces) dairy sour cream
1 cup mashed ripe banana (2 medium)
½ cup chopped pecans
Praline Topping (recipe, page 20)

1. Beat butter or margarine until fluffy in large bowl of electric mixer at high speed. Gradually add sugar; continue beating until light and fluffy. Beat in eggs, 1 at a time. Add vanilla.
2. Sift flour, baking powder, baking soda and salt onto wax paper. Add to sugar mixture alternately with sour cream. Add banana and pecans; mix just until blended. Turn into a greased and floured 13x9x2-inch baking pan.
3. Bake in moderate oven (350°) 40 minutes, or until center springs back when lightly pressed with fingertip. Cool cake in pan 10 minutes. Turn out onto wire rack; cool completely. Frost with PRALINE TOPPING. Broil, 3 inches from heat, 3 minutes.

FAMILY CIRCLE'S FAVORITE CHEESECAKE

We have tasted many, but this is the one we feel is the very best.

Bake at 350° for 1 hour, 15 minutes.
Makes one 9-inch cake.

Crust
1½ cups graham cracker crumbs
3 tablespoons sugar
½ teaspoon ground cinnamon
¼ cup (½ stick) sweet butter, melted
Filling
3 packages (8 ounces each) cream cheese, room temperature
1¼ cups sugar
6 eggs, separated
1 container (1 pint) dairy sour cream
⅓ cup all purpose flour
2 teaspoons vanilla
Grated rind of 1 lemon
Juice of ½ lemon

1. Make crust: Generously grease a 9x3-inch springform pan with butter.

Place pan in center of a 12-inch square of aluminum foil and press foil up around side of pan.
2. Combine graham cracker crumbs, sugar, cinnamon and melted butter in a small bowl until well blended. Press ¾ cup of crumb mixture into bottom and side of pan. Chill prepared pan while making filling.
3. Make filling: Beat cream cheese in a large bowl until soft with electric mixer at low speed. Gradually beat in sugar until fluffy.
4. Beat in egg yolks, one at a time, until well blended. Stir in sour cream, flour, vanilla, lemon rind and juice until smooth.
5. Beat egg whites until they hold stiff peaks in a large deep bowl with electric mixer at high speed. Fold whites into the cheese mixture with wire whip, until well blended. Pour into prepared pan.
6. Bake in moderate oven (350°) 1 hour, 15 minutes, or until top is golden; turn off oven heat and allow cake to cool in oven 1 hour.
7. Remove cake from oven and cool on wire rack at room temperature. Sprinkle remaining crumbs on top.
8. Chill overnight before serving. Dust with 10X sugar.

SEAFOAM WALNUT CAKE

Tops in the Midwest—fluffy yellow cake covered with brown sugar frosting and dotted generously with walnuts.

Bake at 375° for 30 minutes.
Makes three 9-inch layers.

3 cups cake flour
1 tablespoon baking powder
1 teaspoon salt
1 cup (2 sticks) butter or margarine
2 cups sugar
4 eggs
1 teaspoon vanilla
1 cup milk
1 cup finely chopped walnuts
1 jar (12 ounces) red currant jelly
Seafoam Frosting (recipe follows)

1. Grease three 9-inch layer cake pans; line with wax paper; grease paper.
2. Sift cake flour, baking powder and salt onto wax paper.
3. Beat butter or margarine with sugar until fluffy in large bowl with an electric mixer at high speed. Beat in eggs, one at a time, until fluffy; stir in vanilla.
4. Stir in flour mixture, a third at a time, alternately with milk; fold in walnuts. Pour batter into prepared pans, dividing evenly.
5. Bake in moderate oven (375°) 30 minutes, or until centers spring back

when lightly pressed with fingertip.
6. Cool in pans on wire racks 10 minutes. Loosen around edges with a knife; turn out onto racks; peel off paper; cool layers completely.
7. Put layers together with currant jelly on a serving plate; frost side and top of cake with SEAFOAM FROSTING. Decorate with additional chopped walnuts, if you wish.

SEAFOAM FROSTING: Makes enough to frost three 9-inch layers. Combine 1½ cups firmly packed brown sugar, ¼ cup water, 2 egg whites, 2 tablespoons light corn syrup, ¼ teaspoon salt and 1 teaspoon vanilla in the top of a double boiler; beat until blended with electric mixer at high speed. Place over simmering water. Cook 5 minutes, beating constantly with mixer, or until mixture triples in volume and holds firm marks of beater, remove from heat.

MARY GALASSO'S SOUR CREAM CAKE

"Aunt Mary's" special sour cream cake has been a family favorite for years—moist and luscious, yet light enough to top off the heartiest reunion feast.

Bake at 350° for 1 hour.
Makes one 10-inch fluted tube cake.

1 cup (2 sticks) butter or margarine
2 cups sugar
4 eggs
1 teaspoon vanilla
1 teaspoon lemon extract
3 cups all purpose flour
1 teaspoon baking powder
¾ teaspoon salt
½ teaspoon baking soda
1 container (8 ounces) dairy sour cream
1 cup raisins
¾ cup chopped walnuts or pecans

1. Beat butter or margarine and sugar until creamy in the large bowl of an electric mixer at medium speed.
2. Add eggs, one at a time, beating well after each addition. Stir in vanilla and lemon extract; turn mixer to low.
3. Sift in flour, baking powder, salt and baking soda, 1 cup at a time, adding sour cream after the second cup of flour mixture.
4. Stir in raisins and nuts with wooden spoon. Pour into a greased and floured 12-cup fluted tube pan.
5. Bake in moderate oven (350°) 1 hour, or until center springs back when lightly touched with fingertip. Cool in pan on wire rack 15 minutes; loosen around edge and tube with a narrow spatula; invert onto wire rack; cool completely.

CARROT WALNUT LOAF

We couldn't let Mrs. Chester Sibble of Manlius, N.Y., keep this recipe to herself.

Bake at 350° for 1 hour.
Makes one loaf.

> 1 **cup vegetable oil**
> ¾ **cup sugar**
> 2 **eggs**
> 1 **teaspoon vanilla**
> 1½ **cups all purpose flour**
> 1½ **teaspoons baking soda**
> 1½ **teaspoons ground cinnamon**
> ½ **teaspoon salt**
> 1½ **cups grated carrot (3 large)**
> 1½ **cups ground walnuts**
> **Citrus Glaze (recipe follows)**

1. Grease a 9x5x3-inch loaf pan; dust lightly with flour; tap out any excess.
2. Stir together vegetable oil, sugar, eggs and vanilla in a large bowl with wire whip.
3. Sift flour, baking soda, cinnamon and salt into sugar mixture; stir in carrots and walnuts; mix *just* until blended. Turn into prepared pan.
4. Bake in moderate oven (350°) 1 hour, or until center springs back when lightly pressed with fingertip. Cool cake in pan 10 minutes. Turn out onto wire rack; cool completely. Drizzle CITRUS GLAZE over top and sides of cake.

CITRUS GLAZE: Makes ¼ cup. Combine ½ cup 10X (confectioners' powdered) sugar, 1 teaspoon grated lemon rind and 1 tablespoon lemon juice in a small bowl; stir until smooth.

APPLE HARVEST CAKE

Mrs. Fred Steinbrecken of Racine, Wis., won a division first prize at the Bake-Off® with her recipe for a cake with whole wheat flour. Photograph is on page 5.

Bake at 325° for 50 minutes.
Makes one 10-inch angel tube cake.

> **Cake**
> 1¼ **cups all purpose or unbleached flour**
> 1 **cup whole wheat flour**
> 1 **cup granulated sugar**
> ¾ **cup firmly packed brown sugar**
> 1 **tablespoon ground cinnamon**
> 2 **teaspoons baking powder**
> 1 **teaspoon salt**
> ½ **teaspoon baking soda**
> ¾ **cup vegetable oil**
> 3 **eggs**
> 1 **teaspoon vanilla**
> 2 **cups finely chopped pared apples (2 large)**
> 1 **cup chopped walnuts**
> **Glaze**
> ½ **cup 10X (confectioners'**

> **powdered) sugar**
> 2 **teaspoons milk**
> ¼ **teaspoon vanilla**
> **Apple slices**
> **Walnut halves**

1. Make cake: Generously grease a 10-inch angel cake tube pan or a 12-cup fluted tube pan with butter; sprinkle with flour; tap out excess.
2. Stir flour, whole wheat flour, granulated and brown sugars, cinnamon, baking powder, salt and baking soda until well blended with wire whip in the large bowl of an electric mixer.
3. Add oil, eggs and vanilla. Beat at medium speed for 3 minutes; stir in apples and nuts with wire whip. Pour into prepared pan.
4. Bake in slow oven (325°) 50 minutes, or until a wooden pick inserted in center of cake comes out clean. Cool in pan on wire rack 15 minutes; loosen around edge and tube with spatula; invert onto wire rack; cool completely.
5. Make glaze: Combine 10X sugar, milk and vanilla in a cup; beat with a fork until smooth.
6. Place cake on serving plate; spoon glaze over cake top and allow to flow down side; garnish with apple slices and walnut halves.

BAKING BASICS

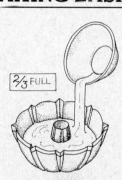

CAKE BATTER

• Only fill a cake or cupcake tin ⅔ full with batter to allow for rising.
• To adapt recipes to pans of varied sizes, use those with same batter yield.
Round pans:
• 6-inch pan holds 1¼ cups batter.
• 8-inch pan holds 2¼ cups batter.
• 9-inch pan holds 2½ cups batter.
• 10-inch pan holds 3⅔ cups batter.
• 11-inch pan holds 4¼ cups batter.
• 12-inch pan holds 5¾ cups batter.
Square pans:
• 8-inch pan holds 3½ cups batter.
• 10-inch pan holds 6 cups batter.
• 12-inch pan holds 9 cups batter.
Tube pans:
• 9-inch pan holds 5 cups batter.

• 10-inch angel tube pan holds 10 cups batter.
• 10-inch fluted tube holds 8 cups batter.
Others:
• Batter for two 8x1½-inch round pans makes 18-24 (2½-inch) cupcakes.
• Batter for three 8x1½-inch round pans fills two 9x9x2-inch pans or one 13x9x2-inch pan.
• Batter for two 9x1½-inch round pans fills two 8x8x2-inch pans or one 13x9x2-inch pan.
• Batter for one 9x5x3-inch loaf pan fills one 9x9x2-inch pan.
• Batter for two 9x5x3-inch loaf pans fills one 10-inch angel cake tube pan.
• Batter for one 8x4x3-inch loaf pan fills one 8x8x2-inch pan.
• Batter for one 9-inch angel cake tube pan fills one 10-inch fluted tube pan.
(Note: To know how big a pan is, pour water from measuring cup right to top; permanently mark capacity of pan on back with nail polish.)

SPICE CUPCAKES

Tender little spice cakes crowned with fluffy meringue.

Bake at 350° for 30 minutes.
Makes 12 cupcakes.

> 1½ **cups cake flour**
> ½ **teaspoons salt**
> ½ **teaspoon baking soda**
> 1¼ **teaspoons pumpkin pie spice**
> 1 **cup firmly packed brown sugar**
> ½ **cup (1 stick) butter or margarine, softened**
> ⅔ **cup milk**
> 2 **eggs, separated**
> ½ **teaspoon vanilla**
> ¼ **teaspoon cream of tartar**
> ¼ **cup granulated sugar**
> ¼ **cup ground pecans**

1. Sift flour, salt, baking soda and pumpkin pie spice into the large bowl of electric mixer; stir in brown sugar. Add butter or margarine and milk; beat at low speed 1½ minutes. Add egg yolks and vanilla, beat 1½ minutes longer. Fill 12 greased muffinpan cups half full with batter.
2. Bake in moderate oven (350°) for 30 minutes.
3. Beat egg whites and cream of tartar until foamy-white in small bowl of mixer at high speed. Beat in granulated sugar until meringue stands in firm peaks. Fold in nuts; spread on cupcakes.
4. Broil, 6 inches from heat, 4 minutes, or until golden.

Chapter 1 continued on page 114.

DESSERTS TO PLEASE
every taste: From the richest confections to the simplest of pound cakes.
And they're all easy on the
cook, too. For recipes
and dessert names,
turn page.

Chapter 2 FAMILY FAVORITES

APFELKUCHEN

A recipe with a dividend! You get two delicious cakes, one for now and one to freeze. The photograph appears on page 19.

Bake at 375° for 30 minutes.
Makes two 13x9x2-inch cakes.

Cake
- 2 envelopes dry yeast
- ⅔ cup warm water
- ½ cup (1 stick) butter or margarine
- 1 small can evaporated milk (⅔ cup)
- ¾ cup granulated sugar
- 1 teaspoon salt
- 2 eggs, beaten
- 4½ cups all purpose flour

Topping
- 6 medium-size tart cooking apples
- 1½ cups firmly packed brown sugar
- 1 teaspoon pumpkin pie spice
- ½ cup (1 stick) butter or margarine

1. Make cake batter: Sprinkle yeast and 1 teaspoon sugar into very warm water in a large bowl. ("Very warm" water should feel comfortably warm when dropped on wrist.) Stir until yeast dissolves; let stand until mixture bubbles, about 10 minutes.
2. Heat butter or margarine, evaporated milk, granulated sugar and salt in a small saucepan over low heat; stir until butter or margarine melts and sugar dissolves; cool. Add to yeast mixture with beaten eggs, stirring until well blended.
3. Add about half the flour; beat with a wooden spoon until smooth, about 200 strokes. Add remaining flour; beat until shiny and elastic, about 200 strokes more. Scrape down side of bowl; cover with towel. Let rise in a warm place away from draft, about 1 hour, or until double in bulk.
4. Beat dough down; divide in half. Spread dough into two greased 13x9x2-inch baking pans. Cover with a towel and set in a warm place, away from draft, to rise for 15 minutes.
5. Make topping: Pare, quarter and core apples; cut into very thin slices (about ⅛-inch). Mix brown sugar and pumpkin pie spice in a small bowl. Melt butter or margarine in a small saucepan.
6. Arrange apple slices over dough in overlapping pattern. Let rise 15 minutes longer, or until dough is almost double in bulk. Sprinkle with sugar mixture; drizzle with melted butter or margarine.
7. Bake in moderate oven (375°) 30 minutes, or until a cake tester inserted in center comes out clean. Cool in pans on wire racks at least 30 minutes. Freeze one cake, if you wish.

Shown clockwise on pages 18 and 19 are Apfelkuchen, a yeast cake topped with tart cooking apples; Grace's Half-a-Pound Cake, a new, lighter version of an old-time standard; lightly spiced and cream-topped Grandma's Ginger Cake; three simple-to-make versions of Refrigerator Cookies, and Boston Cream Pie, a cream-filled variation of an easy, one-bowl layer cake. Recipes start on this page.

PRALINE CAKE

A wholesome cake with a sweet topping.

Bake at 350° for 35 minutes.
Broil   for 3 minutes.
Makes one 13x9x2-inch cake.

- 2¾ cups cake flour
- 1⅓ cups sugar
- 1½ teaspoons baking soda
- ¼ teaspoon baking powder
- 1½ teaspoons ground cinnamon
- ½ teaspoon ground cloves
- ½ teaspoon salt
- ½ cup vegetable shortening
- 1 can (about 1 pound) applesauce
- 2 eggs
- 1½ cups raisins
- Praline Topping (recipe follows)

1. Grease a 13x9x2-inch baking pan; dust lightly with flour, tapping out any excess.
2. Sift flour, sugar, soda, baking powder, cinnamon, cloves and salt into large bowl of electric mixer.
3. Add shortening and applesauce; beat 2 minutes at medium speed, scraping down side of bowl often.
4. Add eggs; beat 2 minutes longer, or until blended; fold in raisins. Pour into prepared pan.
5. Bake in moderate oven (350°) 35 minutes, or until center springs back when lightly pressed with fingertip. Remove from oven; cool in pan on a wire rack 15 minutes. Raise oven temperature to *broil*.
6. Make PRALINE TOPPING; spread evenly over warm cake.
7. Broil, 6 inches from heat, 3 to 4 minutes, or until topping bubbles up and turns golden. Cool on a wire rack. Cut into squares and serve with whipped cream, if you wish.

PRALINE TOPPING: Makes 2 cups. Beat ½ cup (1 stick) butter or margarine with ¾ cup firmly packed brown sugar until fluffy in medium-size bowl with mixer at high speed; beat in ¼ cup cream until smooth, then stir in 1½ cups chopped pecans and ⅔ cup flaked coconut.

OLD-TIME NUT CAKE

Keep this recipe in mind for the next time the PTA is meeting and it's your turn to bring refreshments.

Bake at 350° for 1 hour.
Makes one 9-inch tube cake.

- 2¾ cups cake flour
- 2 teaspoons baking powder
- 1 teaspoon salt
- 1 cup (2 sticks) butter or margarine
- 1¾ cups sugar
- 4 eggs
- ⅔ cup milk
- 2 teaspoons vanilla
- 1 cup very finely chopped nuts (use hickory nuts, walnuts or pecans)
- Brown Butter Icing (recipe follows)

1. Grease a 9-inch tube pan or 12-cup fluted tube pan; dust lightly with flour; tap out any excess.
2. Sift flour, baking powder and salt onto wax paper.
3. Beat butter or margarine, sugar and eggs in the large bowl of electric mixer at high speed 3 minutes. Remove bowl from mixer.
4. Stir in dry ingredients, alternately with milk, beating after each addition with wooden spoon, until smooth.
5. Stir in vanilla and nuts. Pour batter into prepared pan.
6. Bake in moderate oven (350°) 1 hour, or until center springs back when lightly pressed with fingertip.
7. Cool in pan on wire rack 10 minutes; loosen cake around tube and edge with a knife; turn out onto wire rack; cool completely.
8. Frost top and side with BROWN BUTTER ICING and garnish with a ring of nuts, if you wish.

BROWN BUTTER ICING

Makes enough to frost one 9-inch tube cake.

- ½ cup (1 stick) butter or margarine
- 1 package (1 pound) 10X (confectioners' powdered) sugar, sifted
- ¼ cup milk

1. Heat butter or margarine slowly in a medium-size saucepan until liquid bubbles up, is very foamy, then settles and is lightly browned. *Remove from heat at once.* (Watch carefully to prevent over-browning; browning takes only 3 to 5 minutes.)
2. Pour browned butter over 10X sugar in large bowl; mix until crumbly.
3. Drizzle milk over; blend until smooth. Add 1 to 2 teaspoonfuls more milk, if needed, to make spreadable.

BUSY-DAY CAKE

This layer cake, made the easy, one-bowl way, is great for a trio of family desserts. Frost it to make a FAMILY CAKE, or add a few ingredients to change it into a PEAR UPSIDE-DOWN CAKE or BOSTON CREAM PIE. Photo is on page 18.

Bake at 350° for 30 to 40 minutes.
Makes one cake.

    2 cups cake flour
 1¼ cups sugar
 2½ teaspoons baking powder
    1 teaspoon salt
    ½ cup vegetable shortening
    ¾ cup milk
    2 eggs
 1½ teaspoons vanilla

1. Sift flour, sugar, baking powder and salt into the large bowl of electric mixer; add shortening; stir in milk until blended; beat at medium speed for 2 minutes; add eggs and vanilla; beat another 2 minutes. Spread batter evenly in prepared pan.
2. Bake in moderate oven (350°) 30 to 40 minutes, or until top springs back when lightly pressed with fingertip.

BOSTON CREAM PIE: Spread BUSY-DAY CAKE batter in a greased 9½-inch flavor-saver pie plate or an 8x8x2-inch baking pan. Bake, following general directions; cool in pan on wire rack 10 minutes; loosen around edge with sharp knife; invert onto wire rack and cool completely. Split cake, crosswise; place larger half on serving plate and top with RICH VANILLA FILLING (recipe follows). Place smaller layer on top. Spread with SHINY CHOCOLATE GLAZE (recipe follows).

RICH VANILLA FILLING: Makes enough filling for one 9½-inch layer. Combine 1 package (about 4 ounces) vanilla pudding mix with 1½ cups milk in a small saucepan; bring to boiling, stirring constantly; remove from heat; stir in 2 tablespoons butter or margarine and 1 teaspoon vanilla; pour into small bowl; cool completely.

SHINY CHOCOLATE GLAZE: Makes enough frosting for one 9½-inch layer. Combine 2 tablespoons butter or margarine, 3 tablespoons light corn syrup and ¼ cup water in a small saucepan; heat to boiling; remove from heat; stir in 1 package (6 ounces) semi-sweet chocolate pieces; beat until stiff enough to spread on cake layer.

PEAR UPSIDE-DOWN CAKE: Melt ⅓ cup butter or margarine in bottom of a 13x9x2-inch baking pan in oven; stir in ⅔ cup firmly packed brown sugar and ¼ teaspoon ground cloves; arrange 1 can (about 1 pound) sliced pears, drained, on top. Pour BUSY-DAY CAKE batter over pears in pan. Bake, following general directions, for 40 minutes; loosen edges of cake with knife; invert immediately onto serving plate; let stand 1 or 2 minutes; lift off pan; serve warm with cream or ice cream, if you wish.

FAMILY CAKE: Spread BUSY-DAY CAKE batter into a greased 9x9x2-inch baking pan. Bake, following general directions; cool in pan on wire rack 10 minutes; loosen around edges with sharp knife; invert onto wire rack; cool completely. Frost with COCOA FROSTING (recipe follows).

COCOA FROSTING: Makes enough to frost one 9-inch square. Beat 3 tablespoons softened butter or margarine with ⅓ cup cocoa powder (not a mix) until well blended; stir in 2 cups 10X (confectioners' powdered) sugar, alternately with 3 tablespoons milk, until smooth; stir in 1 teaspoon vanilla and ¼ teaspoon salt.

MINCE LOAF CAKE

Don't save mincemeat cakes just for the holidays. They're great for all the cold months.

Bake at 350° for 1 hour.
Makes 1 loaf.

    3 cups all purpose flour
 3½ teaspoons baking powder
    1 teaspoon salt
    ¼ teaspoon baking soda
    ¾ cup firmly packed brown sugar
 1½ cups chopped walnuts
    2 eggs
    ½ cup milk
    ⅓ cup vegetable oil
    1 cup prepared mincemeat

1. Sift flour, baking powder, salt and soda into a large bowl; stir in brown sugar and walnuts.
2. Beat eggs well in a small bowl with a wire whip; stir in milk, vegetable oil and mincemeat. Add all at once to flour mixture; stir just until evenly moist. Spoon into a greased 9x5x3-inch loaf pan; spread top evenly.
3. Bake in moderate oven (350°) 1 hour, or until a wooden pick inserted in center comes out clean. Cool in pan on a wire rack 10 minutes. Loosen around edges with a knife; turn out onto rack. Cool completely.
4. Wrap loaf in wax paper, foil or transparent wrap. Store overnight to mellow flavors.

BAKING BASICS

IF YOU'RE OUT OF SOMETHING...

INSTEAD OF	USE
Baking powder (1 teaspoon)	¼ teaspoon baking soda and ⅝ teaspoon cream of tartar,
Buttermilk (1 cup)	1 tablespoon vinegar, mixed with milk to make 1 cup; let stand 5 minutes.
Chocolate, unsweetened (1 ounce)	3 tablespoons cocoa and 1 tablespoon vegetable shortening.
Cornstarch (1½ teaspoons)	1 tablespoon flour.
Corn syrup (1 cup)	1 cup sugar and ¼ cup liquid.
Cream of tartar (¼ teaspoon)	1 teaspoon lemon juice.
Egg (1, whole)	2 egg yolks.
Honey (1 cup)	1¼ cups sugar and ¼ cup liquid OR: 1 cup maple syrup or 1 cup light molasses.
Milk, whole (1 cup)	½ cup evaporated milk and ½ cup water OR: 1 cup reconstituted non-fat milk and 2 teaspoons vegetable shortening.
Sour cream (1 cup)	1 cup undiluted milk and 1 tablespoon vinegar or lemon juice.

CARROT CAKE

You don't really taste the carrots, but they give an extra moistness to this rich spice and nut cake. Nice for a luncheon dessert.

Bake at 375° for 35 minutes.
Makes two 9-inch layers.

2½ cups all purpose flour
1 tablespoon baking powder
1 teaspoon salt
½ teaspoon ground cinnamon
½ teaspoon ground allspice
¾ cup vegetable shortening
1½ cups sugar
3 eggs
1 teaspoon vanilla
1½ cups grated carrots (4 large)
½ cup chopped pecans
½ cup hot water
Fluffy Filling and Frosting (recipe follows)

1. Measure flour, baking powder, salt, cinnamon and allspice into a sifter.
2. Beat shortening and sugar until fluffy in the large bowl of electric mixer at medium speed. Add eggs, one at a time, until blended; add vanilla.
3. Stir in carrots and nuts with a wooden spoon. Sift in flour mixture, a third at a time, blending alternately with water, to make a smooth batter. Divide batter between two greased and floured 9-inch layer cake pans.
4. Bake in moderate oven (375°) 35 minutes, or until top springs back when lightly touched with fingertip; cool in pans on wire racks 10 minutes. Loosen cakes around edges with a narrow spatula; turn onto wire racks; cool completely.
5. Fill and frost layers with FLUFFY FILLING AND FROSTING. Garnish with pecan halves, if you wish.

FLUFFY FILLING AND FROSTING

Makes enough filling and frosting for two 9-inch layers.

1 cup (2 sticks) butter or margarine
1 package (1 pound) 10X (confectioners' powdered) sugar, sifted
¼ cup orange juice
2 tablespoons dark corn syrup
1 teaspoon lemon extract
¼ teaspoon salt
1 cup (8 ounces) cream-style cottage cheese
⅓ cup chopped walnuts or pecans
1 teaspoon grated orange rind

1. Beat butter or margarine until soft in medium-size bowl with electric mixer at high speed. Beat in 10X sugar, alternately with mixture of orange juice, corn syrup, lemon extract and salt, until thick and creamy.
2. Measure ½ cup of mixture into small bowl. Set remaining aside for frosting cake. Stir cottage cheese, walnuts and orange rind into the ½ cup until well blended. Use for filling.

SWEET YEAST DOUGH

One batch of dough makes two different coffee-time treats. You can make one of each, or two of the same kind.

Bake at 375° for 15 to 25 minutes.
Makes two 9-inch squares
  OR: 36 rolls.

½ cup milk
½ cup sugar
1½ teaspoons salt
¼ cup (½ stick) butter or margarine
2 envelopes active dry yeast
½ cup very warm water
2 eggs, slightly beaten
4½ cups all purpose flour

1. Heat milk with sugar, salt and butter or margarine in a small saucepan; cool to lukewarm.
2. Sprinkle yeast and 1 teaspoon sugar into very warm water in a large bowl. ("Very warm" water should feel comfortably warm when dropped on wrist.) Stir until yeast dissolves; let stand until mixture bubbles, about 10 minutes, then stir in cooled milk mixture and beaten eggs.
3. Beat in half of the flour until smooth with a wooden spoon; add remaining to make a stiff dough.
4. Turn out onto a lightly floured pastry cloth or board; knead until smooth and elastic, adding only enough extra flour to keep dough from sticking.
5. Place in a greased large bowl; turn to coat all over with shortening; cover with a clean towel. Let rise in a warm place, away from draft, 1 hour, or until double in bulk.
6. Punch down; knead a few times.

CRISSCROSS CINNAMON SQUARES: Roll dough, half at time, to 9x8-inch rectangle on lightly floured pastry cloth or board; cut into eight 1-inch-wide strips. Place 4 of the strips, about 1 inch apart, in a greased 9x9x2-inch baking pan. Weave in remaining 4 strips, over and under, to give a lattice effect; repeat with second piece of dough. Sprinkle each cake with ½ cup raisins; cover. Let rise in a warm place, away from draft, 1 hour, or until double in bulk. Melt ¼ cup (½ stick) butter or margarine in a small metal cup; mix ½ cup sugar with 2 teaspoons ground cinnamon in a cup. Brush melted butter or margarine lightly over raised coffee cakes; sprinkle with the cinnamon-sugar mixture. Bake in moderate oven (375°) 25 minutes, or until richly browned. Loosen around edges with a knife; turn out onto a clean towel; turn right-side up. Cool on wire rack.

FROSTED CHERRY CUPLETS: Roll out dough, half at a time, to a 16-inch square; cut into rounds with a floured 4-inch cutter; reroll trimmings and cut out to make 36 rounds in all. Press rounds into greased muffin tin cups. Spoon cherry jam on top of each; cover. Let rise in warm place, away from draft, 30 minutes, or until double in bulk. Bake in moderate oven (375°) 15 minutes, or until golden; remove from pans; cool on wire racks. Combine ½ cup 10X (confectioners' powdered) sugar and 1 tablespoon water in a cup; drizzle over rolls; serve warm.

RHUBARB COBBLECAKE

Homey dessert of orange biscuits on spicy fruit, to serve warm with cream.

Bake at 425° for 25 minutes.
Makes 6 servings.

1⅓ cups sugar
2 tablespoons cornstarch
¼ teaspoon ground cloves
½ cup orange juice
½ cup (1 stick) butter or margarine
1½ pounds rhubarb, washed, trimmed, and cut in ½-inch pieces (about 5 cups)
2 cups all purpose flour
1 tablespoon baking powder
1 teaspoon salt
1 cup milk
1 tablespoon grated orange rind

1. Combine 1 cup of the sugar, cornstarch and cloves in a large saucepan; stir in orange juice. Heat slowly, stirring constantly, until sugar dissolves.
2. Stir in 2 tablespoons of the butter or margarine and rhubarb; heat to boiling; spoon into a buttered 8-cup baking dish.
3. Sift flour, baking powder, ¼ cup of the remaining sugar and salt into a large bowl; cut in remaining 6 tablespoons butter or margarine until mixture is crumbly. Add milk all at once; stir just until moist. (Dough will be soft.) Drop in 6 even mounds on top of rhubarb mixture.
4. Mix remaining sugar and orange rind in a cup; sprinkle over biscuits.
5. Bake in hot oven (425°) 25 minutes, or until topping is puffed and golden. Serve with whipped cream or ice cream, if you wish.

FABULOUS FUDGE CAKE

That's just what it is. The whole family will enjoy having this for dessert.

Bake at 375° for 25 minutes.
Makes three 9-inch layers.

- 3 squares unsweetened chocolate
- 2¼ cups cake flour
- 2 teaspoons baking soda
- ½ teaspoon salt
- ½ cup (1 stick) butter or margarine
- 2¼ cups (1 pound) firmly packed brown sugar
- 3 eggs
- 2 teaspoons vanilla
- ½ cup buttermilk
- 1 cup boiling water
- Chocolate Cream Frosting (recipe follows)

1. Grease bottoms of three 9-inch layer cake pans; line pans with wax paper; grease paper.
2. Melt chocolate in small saucepan over *very low* heat.
3. Sift cake flour, baking soda and salt onto wax paper.
4. Beat butter or margarine in large bowl of electric mixer at medium speed; gradually add sugar; beat until mixture is fluffy.
5. Beat in eggs, 1 at a time; beat until thick. Stir in vanilla and chocolate with spoon or mixer at low speed.
6. Add sifted dry ingredients, a third at a time, alternately with buttermilk, stirring with mixer at low speed just until blended; stir in boiling water. Pour into pans.
7. Bake in moderate oven (375°) 25 minutes, or until centers spring back when lightly pressed with fingertip.
8. Cool in pans on wire racks 5 minutes; loosen around edges with knife; turn out onto racks; remove wax paper; cool completely. Put layers together and frost.

CHOCOLATE CREAM FROSTING

Makes enough filling and frosting for three 9-inch layers.

- 2 squares unsweetened chocolate
- 2 tablespoons butter or margarine
- 1 cup sifted 10X (confectioners' powdered) sugar
- ¼ teaspoon salt
- 1 egg
- 1 cup heavy cream
- 1 teaspoon vanilla

1. Melt chocolate and butter or margarine in top of large double boiler over hot, *not boiling,* water; beat in sugar, salt and egg until well blended and smooth.
2. Place top of double boiler over ice in large bowl; start beating mixture with electric mixer at high speed, gradually adding cream; continue beating 3 to 4 minutes, or until fluffy; stir in vanilla.
3. Keep frosting over ice as you work. Chill cake until serving time.

CINNAMON BUNS

Mary Lou Bagdovitz's family, from Tully, N.Y., love these for breakfast—but they're delicious anytime.

Bake at 375° for 25 minutes.
Makes 18 buns.

Dough
- 2 envelopes active dry yeast
- ½ cup very warm water
- 1 teaspoon sugar
- ½ cup milk
- ½ cup sugar
- 1½ teaspoons salt
- ¼ cup (½ stick) butter or margarine
- 2 eggs
- 4½ cups all purpose flour

Filling
- ½ cup (1 stick) butter or margarine, softened
- 1 cup firmly packed brown sugar
- 1 cup raisins
- ½ cup chopped walnuts
- 1 teaspoon ground cinnamon

1. Make dough: Sprinkle yeast into very warm water in a 1-cup measure. ("Very warm" water should feel comfortably warm when dropped on wrist.) Stir in 1 teaspoon sugar and allow to stand 10 minutes, or until mixture begins to foam.
2. Heat milk, sugar, salt and butter or margarine in a medium-size saucepan, just until butter melts; pour into a large bowl; allow to cool slightly. Beat in eggs with a wire whip until well blended. (Test temperature of liquid at this time. It should be no warmer than water used with yeast.) Stir in foaming yeast.
3. Beat in 2 cups of the flour until smooth; stir in enough of the remaining flour to make a soft dough.
4. Turn dough out onto a lightly floured pastry cloth or board; knead until smooth and elastic, about 5 minutes, using only as much flour as needed to keep dough from sticking.
5. Place dough in a large greased bowl; turn over to bring greased side up. Cover. Let rise in warm place, away from draft, 1½ hours, or until double in bulk.
6. Punch dough down; knead a few times; let rest 5 minutes.
7. Make filling: Beat softened butter or margarine and brown sugar until well blended in medium-size bowl with wire whip; stir in raisins, nuts and cinnamon until well blended.
8. Divide dough in half; roll out to a 15x9-inch rectangle on a lightly floured pastry cloth or board. Spread half the raisin and nut mixture over dough. Roll up, jelly roll fashion, starting with short end. Cut into 9 equal slices.
9. Place, cut-side down, in buttered 8x8x2-inch baking pan. Repeat with remaining dough and filling to make a second pan of buns.
10. Cover pans; let rise in a warm place 45 minutes, or until it has become double in bulk.
11. Bake in moderate oven (375°) 25 minutes, or until golden brown. Invert pans immediately onto wire racks.
12. Separate buns with two forks; serve with your favorite flavor of jam.

BEACH-BALL CAKE

Make this fun cake to honor a young "beachcomber" on his or her birthday.

Bake at 325° for 55 minutes.
Makes 12 servings.

- 1 package (14½ ounces) angel food cake mix
- Water
- Seven-Minute Frosting (recipe, page 6)
- Yellow food coloring
- 1 can (7 ounces) flaked coconut
- Yellow peppermint patty

1. Prepare angel food cake mix, following label directions; pour batter into ungreased 12-cup deep ovenproof mixing bowl.
2. Bake in slow oven (325°) 55 minutes, or until top is golden and a long, thin metal skewer inserted in center comes out clean. Turn cake upside down to cool, resting edge of bowl on three cans or glasses; cool.
3. Make SEVEN-MINUTE FROSTING. Tint half of frosting yellow with food coloring in a small bowl; leave other half white.
4. Loosen cake around edge of bowl with a knife; turn out, rounded-side up, on wire rack. Mark cake into 6 wedge-shape sections with sharp point of knife; frost sections with alternating white and yellow SEVEN-MINUTE FROSTING.
5. Tint 1⅓ cups of the coconut yellow by shaking with ¼ teaspoon water and a few drops yellow food coloring in a jar with tight-fitting cover; sprinkle over yellow sections. Sprinkle remaining 1⅓ cups coconut over white sections. Decorate top with peppermint patty "button" fastened with a dot of frosting.

GRACE'S HALF-A-POUND CAKE

Grace Manney, nationally known food expert, shares her quick and easy pound cake recipe. Photo is on page 19.

Bake at 325° for 1 hour, 15 minutes.
Makes 1 loaf.

- ½ pound eggs = 5, separated
- ½ pound butter (2 sticks) = 1 cup
- ½ pound sugar = 1 cup
- ½ pound cake flour = 2¼ cups
- ½ teaspoon baking powder
- 2 teaspoons vanilla

1. Beat egg whites until they hold soft peaks in small bowl of electric mixer at high speed; reserve.
2. Beat butter and sugar until fluffy in large bowl of mixer at high speed.
3. Beat egg yolks until thick in a second small bowl with mixer at high speed; beat into butter mixture until thick and light.
4. Sift flour and baking powder over butter mixture; stir in with a wire whip; fold in egg whites and vanilla until well blended; pour into a buttered 9x5x3-inch loaf pan.
5. Bake in slow oven (325°) 1 hour, 15 minutes, or until cake is firm to the touch. Cool in pan on wire rack 10 minutes; loosen around edges with a spatula; cool completely on wire rack. Sprinkle with 10X sugar before serving, if you wish.
Suggested Variations: You can make 3 other cakes with this recipe, simply by adding a different ingredient to the batter of each. For SPICE POUND CAKE, stir in ½ teaspoon ground nutmeg; for CITRUS POUND CAKE, stir in 2 tablespoons orange rind or 2 teaspoons lemon rind; for CITRON POUND CAKE, stir in ⅓ cup finely chopped candied citron and ½ teaspoon lemon extract.

BANANA TEA BREAD

John Canfield of Syracuse, N.Y. has won ribbons with this loaf. He suggests that you let it ripen a day or two before serving.

Bake at 350° for 1 hour.
Makes one loaf.

- ½ cup (1 stick) butter or margarine
- 1 cup sugar
- 1 egg, beaten
- 1 cup mashed bananas (2 medium)
- 3 tablespoons milk
- 2 cups all purpose flour
- 1 teaspoon baking powder
- ½ teaspoon baking soda
- ½ cup chopped walnuts

1. Beat butter or margarine, sugar and egg until fluffy in a large bowl with electric mixer at high speed.
2. Mix bananas and milk in a bowl.
3. Sift flour, baking powder and baking soda onto wax paper. Stir into sugar mixture, alternately with banana-milk mixture. Add nuts. Turn into greased 9x5x3-inch loaf pan.
4. Bake in moderate oven (350°) 1 hour, or until center springs back when lightly pressed with fingertip. Cool in pan on wire rack 5 minutes. Turn out of pan. Cool completely.

POPPY SEED CAKE

Treat the family to this luscious layer cake in the middle of a tough week, and they'll remember it always.

Bake at 350° for 30 minutes.
Makes two 9-inch square layers.

- 1 cup poppy seeds
- 1½ cups milk
- 3 cups cake flour
- 1 tablespoon baking powder
- 1 teaspoon salt
- 4 egg whites
- 1½ cups sugar
- ¾ cup (1½ sticks) butter or margarine
- 1 teaspoon vanilla
  Lemon Butter Cream (recipe, page 10)

1. Grease two 9x9x2-inch cake pans; dust with flour; tap out excess.
2. Combine poppy seeds and ¾ cup of the milk in a small saucepan. Bring to boiling. Remove from heat; cover saucepan. Allow to stand until milk is absorbed, about 1 hour.
3. Sift flour, baking powder and salt onto wax paper.
4. Beat egg whites until foamy-white and double in volume in the small bowl of electric mixer at high speed; beat in ½ cup of the sugar, 1 tablespoon at a time, until meringue forms soft peaks.
5. Beat butter or margarine and remaining 1 cup sugar in large bowl of mixer at high speed for 3 minutes; blend in poppy seed mixture.
6. Stir in flour mixture, alternately with the remaining ¾ cup milk and vanilla, beating after each addition until batter is smooth.
7. Fold meringue into batter until no streaks of white remain; pour into prepared pans.
8. Bake in moderate oven (350°) 30 minutes, or until centers spring back when lightly pressed with fingertip.
9. Cool layers in pans on wire racks 10 minutes; loosen around edges with a knife; turn out onto wire racks; cool.
10. Put layers together with LEMON BUTTER CREAM; frost side and top with remaining frosting.

ZUCCHINI-NUT CAKE

It's true—grated fresh zucchini adds a special moisture to this delicious tube cake.

Bake at 350° for 1 hour.
Makes one 10-inch fluted tube cake.

- 2½ cups all purpose flour
- 2½ teaspoons baking powder
- 1½ teaspoons baking soda
- 1 teaspoon salt
- 1 teaspoon pumpkin pie spice
- ¾ cup vegetable shortening
- 2 cups sugar
- 3 eggs
- 3 squares unsweetened chocolate, melted
- ½ cup milk
- 1 teaspoon vanilla
- 1½ cups shredded raw zucchini (3 medium)
- ¾ cup chopped walnuts
  10X sugar

1. Sift flour, baking powder, baking soda, salt and pumpkin pie spice onto wax paper.
2. Beat shortening and sugar until fluffy in the large bowl of electric mixer at high speed. Beat in eggs until well blended; turn speed to low; blend in chocolate. Combine milk and vanilla in a 1-cup measure.
3. Add flour mixture, alternately with milk, until well blended. Fold in zucchini and nuts, just until blended. Spoon batter into a well greased and floured 12-cup fluted tube pan or a 9-inch angel cake tube pan.
4. Bake in moderate oven (350°) 1 hour, or until a wooden pick inserted near center comes out clean; cool in pan on wire rack 15 minutes. Loosen cake around edge and tube with a narrow spatula; invert onto wire rack. Cool completely. Allow to ripen for 1 day, if you can. Sprinkle with 10X sugar before serving.

PECAN-HONEY LOAF

Mrs. Ernest Fish of Manlius, N.Y. has won prizes at the State Fair with this moist loaf that keeps so well.

Bake at 325° 1 hour, 10 minutes.
Makes one loaf.

- 2 tablespoons butter or margarine
- 1 cup honey
- 1 egg, beaten
- 2½ cups all purpose flour
- 2½ teaspoons baking powder
- ½ teaspoon baking soda
- ½ teaspoon salt
- ¾ cup milk
- ¾ cup chopped pecans

1. Beat butter or margarine and honey until creamy in large bowl with electric mixer at high speed; add egg.

2. Sift flour, baking powder, baking soda and salt onto wax paper. Stir into honey mixture alternately with milk. Add pecans. Turn into a greased 9x5x3-inch loaf pan.

3. Bake in moderate oven (325°) 1 hour, 10 minutes, or until center springs back when lightly pressed with fingertip. Cool in pan on wire rack 5 minutes. Loosen cake around edges with a sharp knife. Turn out of pan. Cool completely.

DATE-WALNUT PUDDING

Lightly spiced and cake-like, with a fruity flavor. You "bake" it in a kettle.

Steam for 2 hours, 30 minutes.
Makes 8 servings.

    1½ cups all purpose flour
     1 teaspoon baking powder
     ¾ teaspoon baking soda
     ½ teaspoon salt
     ¼ teaspoon ground cinnamon
     ⅛ teaspoon ground mace
     1 egg
     ½ cup sugar
     3 tablespoons butter or margarine
     1 cup orange juice
     ¼ cup orange marmalade
     1 tablespoon grated lemon rind
     1 teaspoon vanilla
     1 cup chopped walnuts
     1 cup chopped dates
     ½ cup candied cherries, chopped

1. Butter a 6-cup pudding mold or heat-proof bowl; sprinkle with sugar.

2. Sift flour, baking powder, baking soda, salt, cinnamon and mace onto wax paper.

3. Beat egg in a large bowl with a wire whip; beat in sugar, butter or margarine, orange juice, marmalade, lemon rind and vanilla.

4. Combine walnuts, dates and cherries with flour mixture; stir into egg mixture. Turn into prepared mold or bowl; cover tightly with a double layer of heavy-duty aluminum foil.

5. Place on rack in a large kettle (or, make a doughnut shape of crumpled foil to fit bottom of kettle to serve as a rack); pour in boiling water to halfway point on mold. Cover kettle. Keep water gently boiling; add more boiling water, if necessary. Steam 2½ hours.

6. Cool pudding 10 minutes on wire rack; turn out onto serving plate. Serve warm with vanilla ice cream.

7. To reheat: Place pudding on sheet of heavy foil; bring foil up and gather at top, folding securely, to make pouch. Place pudding on rack in same kettle it was cooked in. Pour 2 inches of boiling water into kettle; cover; simmer for 30 minutes, or until heated through to center.

COFFEE-HONEY CAKE

It's so nice to have a spicy cake on hand when guests drop in for a cup of coffee.

Bake at 300° for 1 hour, 15 minutes.
Makes one 10-inch angel tube cake.

    1 ¾ cups honey
     1 cup strong coffee
     2 tablespoons brandy
    3 ½ cups all purpose flour
     1 tablespoon baking powder
     1 teaspoon baking soda
    1 ¼ teaspoons ground cinnamon
     ¼ teaspoons ground cloves
     ¼ teaspoon ground ginger
     ¼ teaspoon ground nutmeg
     ½ cup chopped almonds
     ½ cup chopped raisins
     1 tablespoon grated lemon rind
     4 eggs
     1 cup firmly packed brown sugar
     1 tablespoon vegetable oil

1. Heat honey and coffee to boiling in a medium-size saucepan. Cool completely. Stir in brandy.

2. Sift flour, baking powder, baking soda, cinnamon, cloves, ginger and nutmeg onto wax paper; add almonds, raisins and lemon rind.

3. Beat eggs slightly in the large bowl of electric mixer at medium speed; add honey mixture, sugar and oil. Beat until smooth and completely blended. Add flour mixture and beat until batter is smooth; pour batter into a greased 10-inch angel cake tube pan.

4. Bake in slow oven (300°) 1 hour, 15 minutes, or until center springs back when lightly pressed with fingertip and top is golden.

5. Cool in pan on wire rack for 10 minutes; loosen around edge and tube with small spatula. Turn out onto wire rack; cool completely.

BASIC TWO-EGG BUTTER CAKE

This recipe is so simple, you can keep it in your memory and make it in minutes whenever you want a cake in a hurry.

Bake at 350° for 30 minutes.
Makes two 8-inch layers.

    2 cups cake flour
    2½ teaspoons baking powder
    1 teaspoon salt
    2 eggs, separated
    ½ cup (1 stick) butter or margarine, softened
    1 cup sugar
    1 teaspoon vanilla
    ¾ cup milk

1. Sift flour, baking powder and salt onto wax paper. Beat egg whites until they form soft peaks in the small bowl of electric mixer at high speed; then, in the large bowl of mixer, beat butter

or margarine, slowly adding sugar and beating until fluffy.

2. Beat in egg yolks and vanilla. Add flour mixture, a third at a time, alternately with milk, beating just until blended. Fold in beaten whites. Pour into greased 8-inch layer cake pans.

3. Bake in moderate oven (350°) 30 minutes, or until top springs back when lightly pressed with fingertip. Cool in pans on wire racks 5 minutes; turn out on racks to cool.

SPICY PRUNE ROLL

A thick, flavorful prune filling adds the perfect touch to the spicy jelly roll.

Bake at 400° for 13 minutes.
Makes 10 servings.

    ¾ cup cake flour
    1 teaspoon baking powder
    ½ teaspoon ground cinnamon
    ½ teaspoon salt
    4 eggs
    ¾ cup granulated sugar
    1 teaspoon vanilla
       10X sugar
       Prune Filling (recipe follows)

1. Grease a 15x10x1-inch jelly roll pan; line with wax paper cut to fit; grease paper.

2. Measure flour, baking powder, cinnamon and salt into a sifter.

3. Beat eggs until foamy in the small bowl of electric mixer at high speed; gradually beat in granulated sugar until mixture is very thick and light. Stir in vanilla.

4. Sift dry ingredients over egg mixture; gently fold in until no streaks of flour remain. Spread batter evenly in prepared pan.

5. Bake in hot oven (400°) 13 minutes, or until center springs back when lightly pressed with fingertip.

6. Loosen cake around sides of pan with a sharp knife; turn upside down onto clean towel sprinkled with 10X sugar. Starting at short end, gently roll up cake with towel; cool, seam-side down.

7. To serve, unroll carefully; remove towel; spread cake with PRUNE FILL-ING; reroll. Decorate cake roll with whipped cream, if you wish. Cut crosswise into 10 slices.

PRUNE FILLING: Makes 1½ cups. Combine 2 cups pitted prunes with 1 cup water in a small saucepan; simmer, covered, 25 minutes; purée prunes with remaining cooking liquid, part at a time, in blender (or press through a sieve). Stir in 2 tablespoons sugar, 1 tablespoon lemon juice, and ½ teaspoon ground cinnamon. Chill.

Fruits from country
orchards bake with nuts,
milk and flour to make
dozens of family treats.

MAKE 480 CAKES & COOKIES

Mix and match the spices, fruits, nuts, pans and toppings from this chart and you can bake over 160 cake and 320 cookie variations. Master just two basic recipes and voilà— a repertoire of baking master-pieces.

EASY COOKIES	QUICK MIX CAKES
Bake at 375° for 8 to 10 minutes, or until golden. Makes about 3 dozen.	Bake at 350° from 30 to 50 minutes. Makes 1, 2 or 3 layers.
3 cups all purpose flour 1 tsp. baking powder 1 teaspoon salt ¾ cup (1½ sticks) butter or margarine 1¼ cups sugar 1 egg 2 tsp. vanilla	3 cups all purpose flour 4 tsp. baking powder 1 tsp. salt 1¾ cups sugar ¾ cup shortening 3 eggs 1 cup milk 1 tsp. vanilla
Beat butter or margarine and sugar until fluffy in large bowl with electric mixer at high speed. Beat in egg and vanilla. Sift in flour, baking powder and salt. Wrap in wax paper; chill. Roll to ¼-inch thickness; cut with 3-inch cookie cutters on lightly floured board.	Sift flour, baking powder, salt and sugar into a large bowl. Add shortening, eggs, milk and vanilla and beat on low speed of electric mixer for 2 minutes; increase speed to medium and beat for 2 minutes. Pour into greased and floured baking pans.
Bake in moderate oven (375°) 8 to 10 minutes, or until golden.	Bake in moderate oven (350°) 30 to 50 minutes, or until cake tests done.

VARIATIONS:
Substitute brown sugar.
Add: 1 tsp. nutmeg.
  1 cup chopped figs.
  1 tbsp. orange rind.
  ½ cup peanut butter.
  1 tsp. rum extract.
  1 cup chopped pecans.
  1 cup wheat germ.
	VARIATIONS:
	Add: ½ cup cocoa.
	  1 tsp. cinnamon.
	  1 grated apple.
	  ½ cup chopped nuts.
	  2 tsp. grated lemon.
	  ¾ cup dry currants.
	  1 grated carrot.
	  1 mashed banana.

TOPPINGS: Toasted sliced almonds Crushed dry cereal Chopped pistachio nuts Toasted sesame seeds Cinnamon-sugar Poppy seeds Colored sugars Flaked coconut	**TOPPINGS:** 1 cup coconut + ½ cup dark corn syrup 1 cup semi-sweet chocolate bits + ½ cup nuts 1 sliced, ripe pear + 1 cup cherry jam Canned vanilla frosting + 1 cup crushed mints
DROP COOKIES: Add 1 cup applesauce OR ¼ cup milk OR ¼ cup orange juice OR ½ cup light molasses OR 1 mashed banana.	**BAKING PANS:** Two 9-inch layer cake Three 8-inch layer cake One 13x9x2-inch baking Two 8x8x2-inch baking One 12-cup fluted tube
BAR COOKIES: Add 1 cup rolled oats and 1 cup chopped dates. Bake in 13x9x2-inch pan for 35 minutes.	**FOR CUPCAKES:** Spoon half the batter into 36 muffin cups. Add jelly; top with batter. Bake 20 minutes.

GRANDMA'S GINGER CAKE

An old English recipe that moved west across America with the wagon trains. It's as economical today as it was then and just as delicious. Pictured on page 18.

Bake at 350° for 30 minutes.
Makes one 13x9x2-inch cake.

- 2½ cups all purpose flour
- 1¾ teaspoons baking soda
- 1 teaspoon ground ginger
- 1 teaspoon ground cinnamon
- ¼ teaspoon ground cloves
- ¼ teaspoon salt
- 1 cup sugar
- ½ cup vegetable shortening
- 1 cup light molasses
- 1 cup boiling water
- 2 eggs, well beaten
  Orange-Cheese Topping (recipe follows)

1. Sift flour, soda, ginger, cinnamon, cloves and salt onto wax paper.
2. Beat sugar with shortening and molasses in the large bowl of electric mixer at high speed, until well blended.
3. Add sifted dry ingredients to beaten mixture, alternately with boiling water, beginning and ending with dry ingredients. Stir in eggs.
4. Pour into a well greased 13x9x2-inch baking pan.
5. Bake in moderate oven (350°) 30 minutes, or until center springs back when lightly pressed with fingertip. Cool upright in pan to room temperature. Cut in large squares and serve with ORANGE-CHEESE TOPPING.

ORANGE-CHEESE TOPPING: Makes ¾ cup. Beat 1 package (8 ounces) cream cheese until smooth in a medium-size bowl with wooden spoon. Beat in ¼ cup 10X (confectioners' powdered) sugar, 1 teaspoon orange rind and 2 tablespoons orange juice until smooth. Chill until serving.

BAKING BASICS

DON'T DISCARD LEFTOVERS

Cake and cookie crumbs can be used in many creative ways.
- Use them to roll around ice cream balls, then top with your favorite chocolate or butterscotch sauce.
- Moisten cake pieces with fruit juice, sweetened coffee, sherry or your favorite liqueur; fold into pudding, or serve topped with cream, whipped or just plain.
- Make crumb crusts for cream pies from leftover cookies.
- Use crushed cookies as a topping for puddings, fruit crisps, fruit cups or ice cream.

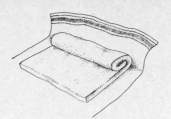

MAKING A JELLY ROLL

- To roll jelly roll more easily, sprinkle a clean towel with 10X or granulated sugar; invert hot cake on sugar and peel off wax paper; start first turn with hand, then lift towel higher and higher; cake should start to roll by itself.
- Be sure to start rolling jelly roll from the narrow end for wide rolls and long end for thin rolls.
- To cut jelly roll slices, place a piece of thread, about 18-inches long under cake; crisscross string on top of jelly roll. To cut each slice, pull thread quickly and evenly.

CINNAMON-APPLE CAKE

If you're lucky enough to have any left, reheat for a breakfast coffee cake treat.

Bake at 350° for 30 minutes.
Makes one 13x9x2-inch cake.

- 2 cups all purpose flour
- 2½ teaspoons baking powder
- 1 teaspoon salt
- ½ cup granulated sugar
- ½ cup vegetable shortening
- 2 eggs
- ½ cup milk
- 3 large apples pared quartered, cored and cut in thick slices
- ½ cup firmly packed brown sugar
- 1 teaspoon ground cinnamon
- 1 teaspoon grated lemon rind
- 2 tablespoons butter or margarine, melted

1. Sift flour, baking powder and salt into a large bowl; stir in granulated sugar; cut in shortening with a pastry blender until mixture is crumbly.
2. Beat eggs slightly with milk in 2-cup measure. Stir into flour mixture until well blended; pour into a greased 13x9x2-inch baking pan. Arrange apple slices, overlapping slightly, in rows to cover top.
3. Combine brown sugar, cinnamon, lemon rind and melted butter or margarine in small bowl; sprinkle over apples.
4. Bake in moderate oven (350°) 30 minutes, or until wooden pick inserted in top comes out clean. Cut in squares and serve warm with ice cream or whipped cream, if you wish.

SPICY BANANA CAKE

Banana-flavored cream cheese tops moist squares of this easy-to-make cake.

Bake at 350° for 45 minutes.
Makes one 13x9x2-inch cake.

- ½ cup (1 stick) butter or margarine, softened
- 1¼ cups sugar
- 2 eggs
- 1 teaspoon vanilla
- 2¼ cups all purpose flour
- 1 teaspoon baking soda
- ¼ teaspoon baking powder
- 1 teaspoon salt
- ½ teaspoon ground nutmeg
- 1 teaspoon lemon juice
- ⅓ cup milk
- 2 cups mashed ripe bananas (about 4)
- 1 large banana
- 1 teaspoon lemon juice
- 1 container (8 ounces) whipped cream cheese

1. Beat butter or margarine, sugar, eggs and vanilla in the large bowl of electric mixer at medium speed, until well blended and fluffy.
2. Sift flour, baking soda, baking powder, salt and nutmeg onto wax paper. Add 1 teaspoon of the lemon juice to the milk.
3. Turn mixer speed to very low; add sifted dry ingredients, alternately with milk mixture. Stir in mashed bananas. Fill a greased 13x9x2-inch baking pan with batter.
4. Bake in moderate oven (350°) 45 minutes, or until center of cake springs back when lightly pressed with fingertip. Cool in pan on wire rack.
5. Mash banana with remaining 1 teaspoon lemon juice in a medium-size bowl until smooth. Beat in whipped cream cheese until fluffy. Cut cake into squares in the pan. Serve with the topping.

DOUBLE-DATE CAKE

Date lovers, this is for you!

Bake at 350° for 1 hour.
Makes one 8-inch square.

- 1 package (8 ounces) pitted dates
- 1 cup boiling water
- ½ cup (1 stick) butter or margarine
- 1 cup sugar
- 1 teaspoon vanilla
- 1 egg, beaten
- 1⅔ cups all purpose flour
- 1 teaspoon baking soda
- 1 teaspoon salt
- ½ cup chopped pecans
  Date Frosting (recipe follows)

1. Chop dates; combine with boiling water, butter or margarine, sugar and

From the beginning of time cookies have been a special food. Not only because they're good to eat, but for other reasons, too. Picture an Austrian woman in the 1700's, when there were no illustrated newspapers, studying the lifelike imprints

A TREASURE CHEST OF THE WORLD'S MOST DELECTABLE
COOKIES

on cookies for fashion ideas! (That's how Springerle wafers—see opposite page—came into being.) Today, though our world is far more sophisticated, these tiny sweets continue to charm. They're great for desserts and quick snacks, and they're fun, too. The photos at left show just a few of the fanciful shapes they can be baked into. In this section you'll find a wide variety of cookies to choose from: Favorites like our sugar stars on pages 8 & 9, simple ones to make in minutes, plain ones, fancy ones, crisp, nutty rounds, rich fruit bars—and more.

AMERICAN TREASURES (CHAPTER 1)

MELLOW CHOCOLATE STARS

Aromatic bitters give a very special flavor to these cookies. Picture is on page 9.

Bake at 400° for 10 minutes.
Makes 4½ dozen.

- 3 ¼ cups all purpose flour
- ½ cup cocoa powder (not a mix)
- 1 teaspoon salt
- ½ teaspoon baking soda
- 1 cup (2 sticks) butter or margarine
- 1 ½ cups sugar
- 2 eggs
- 1 teaspoon vanilla
- ½ teaspoon bottled aromatic bitters
  White frosting from a 4-ounce tube
  Red-hot candies

1. Sift flour, cocoa, salt and baking soda onto wax paper.
2. Beat butter or margarine and sugar until fluffy in a large bowl with an electric mixer at high speed. Beat in eggs, one at a time, then vanilla and bitters until well blended.
3. Stir in flour mixture to make a stiff dough. Wrap in wax paper and chill 3 hours, or overnight.
4. Roll out dough, a quarter at a time, to a ¼-inch thickness on a lightly floured pastry cloth or board. Cut into stars with a 3-inch cutter. Place on cookie sheets.
5. Bake in hot oven (400°) 10 minutes, or until cookies are firm; remove to wire racks with spatula; cool.
6. Place the star tip on frosting tube and press a star onto center of each cookie; top each with a red-hot candy.

CRANBERRY CRUNCH BARS

A delectable mouthful with the tangy taste of fruit.

Bake at 400° for 35 minutes.
Makes 36 bars.

- 1¾ cups all purpose flour
- 1 teaspoon salt
- 1½ teaspoons ground cinnamon
- 1¼ cups firmly packed brown sugar
- 2 cups quick-cooking rolled oats
- 1 cup (2 sticks) butter or margarine
- 1 cup finely chopped walnuts
- ½ cup granulated sugar
- 2 tablespoons cornstarch
- 2 jars (14 ounces each) cranberry-orange relish
- 1 egg
- 1 tablespoon water
  10X sugar

1. Sift flour, salt and cinnamon into a large bowl; stir in brown sugar and rolled oats. Cut in butter or margarine with a pastry blender until mixture is crumbly; stir in walnuts. Press half of mixture evenly over bottom of a lightly greased 13x9x2-inch baking pan.
2. Bake in hot oven (400°) 5 minutes; cool slightly on a wire rack.
3. While layer bakes, mix granulated sugar and cornstarch in a medium-size saucepan; stir in cranberry relish. Cook slowly, stirring constantly, until mixture thickens and boils 3 minutes. Spread evenly over partly baked layer in pan. Sprinkle remaining rolled-oats mixture over top; press down firmly with hand.
4. Beat egg well in a cup; stir in water. Brush lightly over crumb mixture.
5. Bake in hot oven (400°) 30 minutes, or until firm and golden. Cool completely in pan on a wire rack. Cut into 36 bars; sprinkle with 10X sugar just before serving.

STRAWBERRY PINWHEELS

So rich they literally melt in your mouth! Whipped cream goes into the unusual pastrylike dough.

Bake at 350° for 15 minutes.
Makes 5 dozen.

- 1 cup all purpose flour
- ½ teaspoon baking powder
- ⅓ cup butter or margarine
- ½ cup heavy cream
- ⅔ cup strawberry jam

1. Sift flour and baking powder into a large bowl; cut in butter or margarine with pastry blender, until mixture is crumbly.
2. Beat cream until stiff in a small bowl with an electric mixer at high speed; stir into flour mixture, blending well to make a stiff dough. Wrap in wax paper; chill several hours, or overnight, until firm enough to roll.
3. Roll out dough, a quarter at a time, to an 8-inch square on a lightly floured pastry cloth or board; cut into 16 two-inch squares. Starting at each corner, cut diagonally through dough 1 inch in toward center.
4. Spoon a rounded ¼ teaspoonful jam in center of each square; moisten corners with water, then pick up evey other corner point and fold to center, overlapping slightly; press lightly to seal. Place, 1 inch apart, on greased cookie sheets.
5. Bake in moderate oven (350°) 15 minutes, or until firm and lightly golden. Remove from cookie sheets with spatula; cool completely on wire racks. Store in airtight container.

STAINED GLASS STARS

Sour balls melt in the centers of these cookies while baking to give a see-through effect. Picture is on page 4.

Bake at 350° for 10 minutes.
Makes 5 dozen.

- Heirloom Sugar Cookies (recipe, page 36)
- Vegetable oil
- 1 pound red sour ball candies

1. Prepare and chill HEIRLOOM SUGAR COOKIES through Step 3.
2. Roll out dough, a quarter at a time, to a ¼-inch thickness on a lightly floured pastry cloth or board. Cut into stars with a 3-inch cutter; then cut out a 1½-inch star from center of each cookie.
3. Brush cookie sheets generously with vegetable oil. (This makes cookies easier to remove from sheets.)
4. Place cookies, no more than 6 at a time, onto prepared cookie sheets. Place a sour ball into hole in center of each star. (See page 32.)
5. Bake in moderate oven (350°) 10 minutes, or until candy melts and cookies are golden. Cool on cookie sheets on wire racks 2 minutes. Gently loosen around each star with a long sharp knife, then transfer to wire racks with pancake turner to cool completely. (If candy centers become too firm, return cookies to oven for 2 minutes, or until candy melts slightly, then remove from pan at once.)
BAKER'S TIP: You can use assorted sour balls, instead of just red ones, if you wish. Bake the tiny center stars at 350° 7 minutes and put two together with frosting or jelly, if you wish.

COOKIE-CANDY SQUARES

They're a triple treat with chocolate and walnuts between butterscotch layers.

Bake at 375° for 40 minutes.
Makes 36 squares.

- ¾ cup all purpose flour
- 1 teaspoon salt
- ½ teaspoon baking soda
- ½ cup vegetable shortening
- ¾ cup firmly packed brown sugar
- 1 egg
- 1 teaspoon vanilla
- 1 cup corn flakes, crushed
- 1 cup quick-cooking rolled oats
- 1 package (6 ounces) butterscotch-flavored pieces
- 1 package (6 ounces) semi-sweet chocolate pieces
- 1 tablespoon vegetable shortening
- 1 cup walnuts, chopped
- ⅓ cup sweetened condensed milk

1. Measure flour, salt, and soda into a sifter.
2. Beat the ½ cup shortening with brown sugar until fluffy in large bowl with electric mixer at high speed; beat in egg and vanilla. Sift in flour mixture, blending to make a soft dough.
3. Stir in crushed corn flakes, rolled oats, and butterscotch-flavored pieces. Spread half of the mixture evenly over bottom of a greased 9x9x2-inch baking pan.
4. Melt chocolate pieces with the 1 tablespoon shortening in top of a double boiler over simmering water; remove from water. Stir in walnuts and sweetened condensed milk.
5. Spread over layer in pan, then spread with remaining butterscotch mixture.
6. Bake in moderate oven (375°) 40 minutes, or until firm and golden. Cool completely in pan on a wire rack. Cut into 36 squares.

DOUBLE STARS

This double-cutting trick can be used with other shapes, too. Pictured on page 9.

Bake at 375° for 10 minutes.
Makes 5 dozen.

Heirloom Sugar Cookies (recipe, page 36)
Yellow food coloring

1. Prepare HEIRLOOM SUGAR COOKIES to Step 3. Divide dough in half; tint one-half yellow with a few drops yellow food coloring. Wrap each dough separately in wax paper and chill 3 hours, or overnight.
2. Roll out white dough, half at a time, on a lightly floured pastry cloth or board to a ¼-inch thickness. Cut into stars with a 3-inch cutter; then cut out a 1½-inch star from center of each cookie; reserve smaller stars.
3. Roll out yellow dough, half at a time, on a lightly floured pastry cloth or board to a ¼-inch thickness. Cut into stars with a 3-inch cutter; then cut out a 1½-inch star from center of each cookie. Place large stars on cookie sheets; insert reserved small white stars in centers of yellow stars and place yellow centers in white.
4. Bake in moderate oven (375°) 10 minutes, or until pale golden. Remove to wire racks; cool completely.
BAKER'S TIP: If you don't have enough cookie sheets, place extra cookies on sheets of heavy-duty aluminum foil that have been cut to the size of your cookie sheet; place cookies on foil, then slide foil onto cookie sheet when ready to bake.

CHOCO-SUGAR WAFERS

These fudgy rounds are coated with a sugary coating—shaping's so easy.

Bake at 350° for 12 minutes.
Makes 4 dozen.

2 cups all purpose flour
1 teaspoon baking powder
½ teaspoon salt
¼ teaspoon baking soda
¾ cup (1½ sticks) butter or margarine
¾ cup firmly packed brown sugar
2 squares unsweetened chocolate, melted
1 egg
1 teaspoon vanilla
¼ cup milk
   Granulated sugar
   Walnut halves

1. Measure flour, baking powder, salt and baking soda into sifter.
2. Beat butter or margarine and brown sugar until fluffy in medium-size bowl with an electric mixer at high speed; beat in melted chocolate, egg, vanilla and milk. Sift in dry ingredients, a third at a time; blend to make a soft dough. Chill several hours or until firm enough to handle.
3. Roll dough, a heaping teaspoonful at a time, into marble-size balls between palms of hands; roll in granulated sugar in pie plate. Place, 3 inches apart, on ungreased cookie sheets; flatten to ¼-inch thickness with bottom of glass. Top each with a walnut half.
4. Bake in moderate oven (350°) 12 minutes, or until firm. Remove carefully from cookie sheets with spatula; cool on wire racks.

STRAWBERRY JIM-JAMS

Jam-and-walnut filling twirls inside these buttery pinwheels.

Bake at 375° for 10 minutes.
Makes 4 dozen.

2 cups all purpose flour
½ teaspoon baking powder
½ teaspoon ground nutmeg
½ teaspoon salt
½ cup (1 stick) butter or margarine
½ cup granulated sugar
¼ cup firmly packed brown sugar
1 egg
1 teaspoon vanilla
½ cup finely chopped walnuts
½ cup strawberry jam

1. Sift flour, baking powder, nutmeg and salt onto wax paper.
2. Beat butter or margarine with granulated and brown sugars until fluffy in a large bowl with an electric mixer at high speed; beat in egg and vanilla.
3. Stir in flour mixture, half at a time, blending well to make a stiff dough. Chill several hours, or overnight, until firm enough to roll.
4. Roll out dough to a 15x12-inch rectangle on a lightly floured pastry cloth or board. Mix walnuts and jam in a small bowl; spread evenly over dough; roll up, jelly roll fashion. (Be sure walnuts are chopped fine, or cookies will crack when rolled.) Wrap in wax paper or transparent wrap. Chill overnight, or until very firm.
5. When ready to bake, unwrap dough and slice into ¼-inch-thick rounds with a sharp knife; place, 1 inch apart, on greased cookie sheets.
6. Bake in moderate oven (375°) 10 minutes, or until firm. Remove from cookie sheets with spatula at once; cool completely on wire racks. Store in metal tin with tight lid.

BAKING BASICS

SHORTENING KNOW-HOW

• To measure shortening, firmly pack into dry measuring cup or spoon, making sure all air pockets are gone; level off at top with knife or spatula. Do same with peanut butter.
• Vegetable shortening comes in 1- to 3-pound cans.
• Don't use whipped butter or margarine or diet margarine in baking recipes—they have more air and less fat than regular butter or margarine.
• Vegetable shortening is not a substitute for butter or margarine, unless called for in recipe. You can, however, substitute shortening for half of the butter listed, except for cream puffs.
• Butter is often preferable to margarine in refrigerator cookies because it gets firmer when chilled; dough is easier to slice. Margarine works, too, if dough is frozen or chilled until very cold before slicing.
• When a recipe calls for melted shortening, it can be measured before or after melting.
• Only use vegetable oil when recipe, such as chiffon cake, calls for it.
• 1 stick butter or margarine = 4 ounces; 4 sticks = 1 pound, or 2 cups.

STAR JEWELS

Cookie stars sparkle with bright jelly centers. Pictured on page 9.

Bake at 400° for 10 minutes.
Makes 6 dozen.

    Heirloom Sugar Cookies (recipe follows)
⅓ **cup mint jelly**

1. Prepare and chill HEIRLOOM SUGAR COOKIES through Step 3.
2. Roll out dough, a quarter at a time, to a ⅛-inch thickness on a lightly floured pastry cloth or board. Cut into stars with a floured 3-inch star cutter; cut out centers of half the stars with a 1½-inch star cutter. (Bake little stars separately, as in our picture, or reroll along with trimmings.)
3. Place whole stars on greased cookie sheets; top with a cutout star; press edges together lightly with thumb to seal.
4. Bake in hot oven (400°) 10 minutes, or until golden. Remove to wire racks with spatula to cool.
5. Melt mint jelly in small saucepan; drop by half teaspoonfuls into star centers of cookies.
BAKER'S TIP: Strawberry jelly, grape jelly or apple jelly can be substituted for the mint jelly in this recipe.

HEIRLOOM SUGAR COOKIES

Every good baker needs a crisp, rich roll-out cookie for her files. Here's Family Circle's favorite.

Bake at 375° for 10 minutes.
Makes 5 dozen.

  5 **cups all purpose flour**
  1 **teaspoon baking powder**
  1 **teaspoon salt**
  1 **cup (2 sticks) butter or margarine**
2¼ **cups sugar**
  2 **eggs**
  2 **teaspoons vanilla**
  1 **teaspoon lemon extract**

1. Sift flour, baking powder and salt onto wax paper.
2. Beat butter or margarine and sugar until fluffy in large bowl with an electric mixer at high speed. Beat in eggs, one at a time, then vanilla and lemon extract until well blended.
3. Stir in flour mixture to make a stiff dough. Wrap in wax paper and chill 3 hours, or overnight.
4. Roll dough, a quarter at a time, on a lightly floured pastry cloth or board to a ¼-inch thickness. Cut out with 3-inch cookie cutters. Place on cookie sheets. Sprinkle with granulated sugar or colored decorating

sugar or chopped nuts, if you wish.
5. Bake in moderate oven (375°) 10 minutes, or until lightly browned; remove with spatula to wire racks to cool completely. Store in metal tin with tight-fitting cover.

WALNUT CRUNCHES

A chocolate treat with a rich, nutty flavor.

Bake at 375° for 10 minutes.
Makes 4 dozen.

2 **cups all purpose flour**
¾ **teaspoon baking soda**
½ **teaspoon salt**
1 **cup (2 sticks) butter or margarine**
½ **cup granulated sugar**
½ **cup firmly packed brown sugar**
2 **eggs**
1 **package (6 ounces) semi-sweet chocolate pieces**
1 **cup chopped walnuts**

1. Sift flour, soda and salt onto wax paper.
2. Beat butter or margarine with granulated and brown sugars until fluffy in a medium-size bowl with electric mixer at high speed; beat in eggs until well blended.
3. Stir in flour mixture, a third at a time, until well blended; fold in chocolate pieces and walnuts.
4. Drop by teaspoonfuls, 2 inches apart, on cookie sheets.
5. Bake in moderate oven (375°) 10 minutes, or until lightly golden. Remove from cookie sheets with spatula to wire racks; cool.

CALIFORNIA STARS

Orange rind and sugar make a crisp and tangy coating for this buttery cookie. It's pictured on page 9.

Bake at 375° for 10 minutes.
Makes 5 dozen.

    Heirloom Sugar Cookies (recipe, this page)
1½ **cups granulated sugar**
  3 **tablespoons finely grated California orange rind**

1. Prepare and chill HEIRLOOM SUGAR COOKIES through Step 3.
2. Roll out dough, a quarter at a time, to a ¼-inch thickness on a lightly floured pastry cloth or board. Cut into the center of each star with a 3-inch cookie cutter; place on greased cookie sheets.
3. Combine sugar and orange rind in a small bowl; press onto stars.
4. Bake in moderate oven (375°) 10 minutes, or until tops are crusty; remove to wire racks; cool.

TOLL-HOUSE COOKIES

For over thirty years this cookie, developed by Ruth Wakefield of the Toll House Restaurant in Massachusetts, has been an American favorite. Photo is on page 11.

Bake at 375° for 10 minutes.
Makes 4 dozen.

1¼ **cups all purpose flour**
½ **teaspoon baking soda**
¼ **teaspoon salt**
½ **cup (1 stick) butter or margarine**
⅓ **cup granulated sugar**
⅓ **cup firmly packed brown sugar**
1 **teaspoon vanilla**
1 **egg**
1 **package (6 ounces) semi-sweet chocolate pieces**
⅔ **cup chopped walnuts**

1. Sift flour, baking soda and salt onto wax paper.
2. Beat butter or margarine, granulated and brown sugars and vanilla until fluffy in the large bowl of electric mixer at high speed. Beat in egg.
3. Mix in flour mixture; stir in chocolate pieces and walnuts.
4. Drop by teaspoonfuls, 2 inches apart, onto greased cookie sheets.
5. Bake in moderate oven (375°) 10 minutes, or until golden brown. Remove carefully to wire racks with spatula and cool completely.

BEST-EVER BROWNIES

Cake-like bars have a sour cream chocolate frosting. They are certain to bring compliments to the baker. Photo is on page 11.

Bake at 350° for 30 minutes.
Makes 16 bars.

2 **squares unsweetened chocolate**
½ **cup (1 stick) butter or margarine**
2 **eggs**
1 **cup sugar**
1 **teaspoon vanilla**
½ **cup all purpose flour**
½ **teaspoon salt**
¾ **cup chopped walnuts**
1 **package (6 ounces) semi-sweet chocolate pieces**
½ **cup dairy sour cream**

1. Melt chocolate and butter or margarine in a small saucepan over low heat; cool.
2. Beat eggs in small bowl of electric mixer at high speed; gradually beat in sugar until mixture is fluffy. Stir in chocolate mixture and vanilla until smooth and well blended.
3. Fold in flour and salt until well blended; stir in walnuts. Spread evenly in greased 8x8x2-inch baking pan.
4. Bake in moderate oven (350°) 30 minutes, or until shiny and firm on

top. Cool in pan on a wire rack.
5. Melt chocolate pieces in top of a double boiler; stir until smooth. Remove from heat; stir in sour cream until well blended. Spread frosting on cooled brownies. Cut into 16 bars.

ORANGE SUGAR SQUARES

New angle on sugar cookies—the flavor of orange. Frost or not, as you like.

Bake at 400° for 8 minutes.
Makes 16 large cookies.

2½ cups all purpose flour
 2 teaspoons baking powder
 1 teaspoon salt
 ¾ cup (1½ sticks) butter or margarine
1¼ cups sugar
 2 eggs
 1 tablespoon grated orange rind

1. Measure flour, baking powder and salt into sifter.
2. Beat butter or margarine with 1 cup of the sugar until fluffy in a large bowl with an electric mixer at high speed; beat in eggs and orange rind. Sift in flour mixture, a third at a time, blending well. Chill until firm.
3. Roll out dough to a 16-inch square on a lightly floured pastry cloth or board; sprinkle with remaining ¼ cup sugar. Cut into 4-inch squares. Place, 1 inch apart, on large cookie sheets.
4. Bake in hot oven (400°) 8 minutes, or until firm. Remove cookies with spatula to wire racks to cool. Top with orange frosting, if you wish.

WINTER RAINBOWS

This colorful dough will keep in the refrigerator for over a week—all ready to slice and bake at a moment's notice.

Bake at 350° for 8 minutes.
Makes 4 dozen.

 2 cups all purpose flour
 ½ teaspoon baking powder
 ½ teaspoon salt
 ½ cup (1 stick) butter or margarine, softened
 ½ cup firmly packed brown sugar
 ¼ cup granulated sugar
 1 egg
 1 teaspoon vanilla
   Yellow, green and red food colorings
   Milk

1. Sift flour, baking powder and salt onto wax paper.
2. Beat butter or margarine with brown and granulated sugars until fluffy in a large bowl with electric mixer at high speed; beat in egg and vanilla. Stir in flour mixture, a third at a time, blending well to make a soft dough.
3. Divide dough into 3 equal portions; tint 1 portion yellow, 1 green and 1 pink, with food colorings.
4. Roll each portion of dough into a 9x5-inch rectangle between sheets of wax paper. Chill in freezer 10 minutes. Cut each piece of dough in half, lengthwise, cutting through wax paper. Peel off top sheets. Brush top of one strip lightly with milk; place a strip of another color, paper-side up, on top. Peel off paper. Repeat procedure with remaining dough strips, alternating colors, to make 6 layers. Press lightly together; cut finished stack lengthwise to make 2 narrow stacks. Wrap in plastic wrap or foil; refrigerate 3 hours, or overnight.
5. Unwrap dough; cut into ¼-inch slices with a sharp knife; place on cookie sheets.
6. Bake in moderate oven (350°) 8 minutes, or until edges are golden. Remove to wire racks to cool.

COCONUT FROSTIES

Crunchy squares topped with frosting.

Bake at 350° for 35 minutes.
Makes 3 dozen.

 1 cup all purpose flour
 2 tablespoons 10X (confectioners' powdered) sugar
 ½ cup (1 stick) butter or margarine
 2 eggs
 1 cup firmly packed brown sugar
 2 tablespoons all purpose flour
 ½ teaspoon baking powder
 ⅛ teaspoon salt
 1 cup coarsely chopped walnuts
 ½ cup flaked coconut
   Vanilla-Almond Cream (recipe follows)

1. Combine the 1 cup flour and 10X sugar in medium-size bowl; beat in butter or margarine with wooden spoon until well blended. Pat firmly and evenly into bottom of an ungreased 9x9x2-inch baking pan.
2. Bake in moderate oven (350°) 10 minutes; remove and let cool on wire rack 5 minutes.
3. Beat eggs slightly in medium-size bowl; stir in brown sugar until well blended, then the 2 tablespoons flour, baking powder and salt. Fold in walnuts and coconut; pour over crust
4. Bake 25 minutes longer, or until top is firm; cool completely in pan. Frost with VANILLA-ALMOND CREAM; cut into 36 tiny squares.

VANILLA-ALMOND CREAM:
Makes ¾ cup. Beat 3 tablespoons softened butter or margarine with 1¾ cups 10X (confectioners' powdered) sugar, dash salt, 2 teaspoons milk, ½ teaspoon vanilla and ¼ teaspoon almond extract in a small bowl until creamy and smooth.

MAMA'S BUTTER COOKIES

Eleanor Schwartz gave this recipe to her bachelor son with one final direction: "Eat and enjoy!"

Bake at 350° for 15 minutes.
Makes 4 dozen.

 1 cup (2 sticks) butter or margarine
 ½ cup sugar
 2 egg yolks
 ½ teaspoon vanilla
 2 cups all purpose flour
 ⅛ teaspoon salt
   Semi-sweet chocolate pieces

1. Beat butter or margarine and sugar until fluffy in a large bowl with an electric mixer at medium speed.
2. Beat in egg yolks and vanilla until well blended; turn mixer speed to low; blend in flour and salt.
3. Pack dough into a cookie press; press out onto ungreased cookie sheets, or shape into small balls; place on cookie sheets and pat down center with thumb. Place a chocolate piece, point down, in center of each cookie.
4. Bake in moderate oven (350°) 15 minutes, or just until lightly browned. Carefully remove from cookie sheets with spatula to large platter or foil.

COFFEE-DATE BARS

Chewy bars with a pleasant coffee flavor.

Bake at 350° for 35 minutes.
Makes 36 bars.

1¼ cups all purpose flour
 2 tablespoons instant coffee powder
 1 teaspoon baking powder
 ¼ teaspoon salt
 3 eggs
 1 cup sugar
 ½ cup finely chopped pitted dates
 ½ cup coarsely chopped walnuts

1. Measure flour, instant coffee, baking powder and salt into a sifter.
2. Beat eggs until light in medium-size bowl with electric mixer at high speed; beat in sugar slowly until thick; stir in dates and walnuts. Sift flour mixture over and fold in. Spread in a 13x9x2-inch baking pan.
3. Bake in moderate oven (350°) 35 minutes, or until a wooden pick inserted in center comes out clean. Cool in pan on wire rack; cut into 36 bars.

MAKE YOUR COOKING MORE FUN AS WELL AS SUCCESSFUL

1. Bundt® or 12-cup fluted tube pan is the best selling special-shaped pan. Check pan instructions for baking directions, since some non-stick surfaces use a lower baking temperature.

2. Bowls come in many sizes and it's wise to choose the right one for each recipe. Select a nest of bowls and you'll have the best bowl for each recipe.

3. Batches of cookies and baking ingredients are too pretty to keep hidden. Purchase some handsome glass jars and let them be part of your kitchen or family room decorations.

4. Cakes can be baked in a variety of metal and glass pans; try fluted and plain, plus those with removable bottoms.

5. Electric toaster ovens make it possible to bake up batches of cakes and cookies, even when your oven's busy with other baking or cooking.

6. Party time is more fun with an extra special cake. Choose the pan, then follow the specific directions for batter and baking that come with it, then see pages 66-67 for decorating ideas.

7. Newest of the unusual appliances designed to make the baker's job easier is an electric cookie-maker. This tool can also be used to fill deviled eggs, stuff cannelloni or manicotti.

SACRAMENTO SUES

Susan Goff combined two of her favorite flavors, coffee and chocolate, to produce a sophisticated version of Toll-House cookies.

Bake at 350° for 10 minutes.
Makes 4 dozen.

1 ¼ cups all purpose flour
  ½ teaspoon salt
  ½ teaspoon baking powder
  ½ cup (1 stick) butter or margarine
  ⅓ cup firmly packed brown sugar
  ⅓ cup granulated sugar
  1 egg
  ½ teaspoon vanilla
  3 tablespoons instant coffee powder
  1 square unsweetened chocolate, melted and cooled
  1 package (6 ounces) semi-sweet chocolate pieces
  ½ cup chopped walnuts

1. Sift flour, salt and baking powder onto wax paper.
2. Beat butter or margarine, brown and white sugars until fluffy in medium-size bowl with electric mixer at high speed; beat in egg, then vanilla, until well blended.
3. Beat in instant coffee and melted chocolate until well blended; add flour mixture, a third at a time, beating just until blended; stir in chocolate pieces and walnuts.
4. Drop by rounded teaspoons, 2 inches apart, onto cookie sheets.
5. Bake in moderate oven (350°) 10 minutes, or until golden. Remove to wire racks with spatula; cool.

BUTTERSCOTCH-NUT STARS

Brown sugar and almonds give a special flavor to roll-out cookies. The photograph appears on page 8.

Bake at 400° for 10 minutes.
Makes 4 dozen.

3¼ cups all purpose flour
  1 teaspoon salt
  ½ teaspoon baking soda
  ¾ cup (1½ sticks) butter or margarine
  2 cups firmly packed brown sugar
  2 eggs
  1 cup ground almonds (see page 60)
  1 teaspoon vanilla
  Pink frosting from a 4-ounce tube

1. Sift flour, salt and baking soda onto wax paper.
2. Beat butter or margarine and brown sugar until fluffy in a large bowl with an electric mixer at high speed. Beat in eggs, one at a time, ground almonds and vanilla.
3. Stir in flour mixture to make a stiff

dough. Wrap in wax paper and chill 3 hours, or overnight.
4. Roll out dough, a quarter at a time, to a ¼-inch thickness on a lightly floured pastry cloth or board. Cut into stars with a 3-inch cutter. Place, 1 inch apart, on cookie sheets.
5. Bake in hot oven (400°) 10 minutes, or until cookies are golden; remove to wire racks with spatula; cool completely.
6. Place star tip on frosting tube and pipe lines, following picture on page 8, or as you wish.

PEAR LEMON WAFERS

These cookies are rich enough to be dessert, all by themselves.

Bake at 375° for 8 minutes.
Makes about 3 dozen.

1 can (16 ounces) pear halves
  Water
¾ cup sugar
3 tablespoons cornstarch
2 egg yolks
1 tablespoon butter or margarine
1 teaspoon grated lemon rind
2 tablespoons lemon juice
1 cup (2 sticks) butter or margarine
2 cups all purpose flour
⅓ cup heavy cream

1. Drain pear syrup into a 1-cup measure, adding water to make ¾ cup. Chop pears into tiny pieces.
2. Combine sugar and cornstarch in a small saucepan; stir in pears, pear syrup and egg yolks.
3. Cook over low heat, stirring constantly, until mixture thickens and bubbles 1 minute; remove from heat; stir in the 1 tablespoon butter or margarine, lemon rind and juice. Spoon into a glass jar with a screw top; cool, uncovered, to room temperature; cover jar; chill at least 4 hours, or overnight.
4. Beat the 1 cup butter or margarine until soft in a large bowl with electric mixer at medium speed; turn speed to low; blend in flour, alternately with cream, to make a smooth dough. Wrap dough in wax paper. Chill at least 4 hours.
5. Roll out dough, a quarter at a time, to a ¼-inch thickness on a lightly floured pastry cloth or board. Cut with 3-inch fancy cookie cutters. Place on cookie sheets. Prick with a fork in several places.
6. Bake in moderate oven (375°) 8 minutes, or until golden. Remove to wire racks with pancake turner. Cool completely. Spread with pear mixture just before serving.

SUGAR SPARKLERS

They're buttery old-fashioned sugar cookies with a speedy up-to-date rolling trick.

Bake at 350° for 10 minutes.
Makes 6 dozen.

3 cups all purpose flour
1 teaspoon baking powder
½ teaspoon salt
¾ cup (1½ sticks) butter or margarine
1 cup sugar
2 eggs
1 teaspoon vanilla
  Coarse sugar

1. Measure flour, baking powder and salt into sifter.
2. Beat butter or margarine with sugar until fluffy in large bowl with electric mixer at high speed; beat in 1 egg. Separate remaining egg and beat in yolk, then vanilla.
3. Sift in dry ingredients, a quarter at a time, blending well to make a stiff dough. Chill 1 hour, or until firm enough to roll.
4. Divide dough into quarters; roll, one at a time to ⅛-inch thickness on greased cookie sheet. (Set cookie sheet on damp towel to keep it from slipping.) Brush with saved egg white, slightly beaten; sprinkle with sugar.Cut into diamonds with pastry wheel or sharp knife.
5. Bake in moderate oven (350°) 10 minutes, or until firm. Separate and remove from cookie sheets with spatula; cool on wire racks.

RUM CRISPS

You can count on these buttery drops, so rich with brown sugar and bits of chocolate, to disappear fast.

Bake at 350° for 10 minutes.
Makes 5 dozen.

2¼ cups all purpose flour
1 teaspoon baking soda
1 teaspoon salt
½ cup (1 stick) butter or margarine
½ cup vegetable shortening
1 cup firmly packed brown sugar
½ cup granulated sugar
2 eggs
1 tablespoon rum extract
1 package (12 ounces) semi-sweet chocolate pieces

1. Measure flour, soda and salt into a sifter.
2. Beat butter or margarine and shortening with brown and granulated sugars until fluffy in large bowl with an electric mixer at high speed; beat in eggs and rum extract.
3. Sift in flour mixture, a third at a

time, blending well to make a soft dough. Stir in chocolate pieces. Drop by rounded teaspoonfuls, about 2 inches apart, on cookie sheets.

4. Bake in moderate oven (350°) 10 minutes, or until lightly golden. Remove from cookie sheets with spatula; cool completely on wire racks. Store in metal tin with tight-fitting lid.

FAMILY FAVORITES (CHAPTER 2)

REFRIGERATOR COOKIES

These simple, yet tasty cookies are high on convenience—just store the shaped dough in your refrigerator or freezer and when you're ready, remove, cut into the pretty shapes below and bake. Photo is on page 18.

Bake at 350° for 10 minutes.
Makes 6 dozen.

4 cups all purpose flour
1 teaspoon baking powder
1 teaspoon salt
¼ teaspoon baking soda
1¼ cups (2½ sticks) butter or margarine
1 cup firmly packed brown sugar
½ cup granulated sugar
2 eggs
2 teaspoons vanilla

1. Sift flour, baking powder, salt and baking soda onto wax paper.
2. Beat butter or margarine with brown and granulated sugars until fluffy in a large bowl with electric mixer at high speed; beat in eggs and vanilla. Stir in flour mixture, a third at a time; blend to make soft dough.
3. Divide dough evenly into 3 parts. Flavor, shape and decorate each, following individual directions.
4. Bake in moderate oven (350°) 10 minutes, or until golden. Remove from cookie sheets with spatula to wire racks; cool completely.

RIBBON FANCIES: Divide one part of dough in half. Tint one half green with a few drops of green food coloring; leave other half plain. Roll out each half to a 9x3-inch rectangle between sheets of wax paper; chill in freezer 10 minutes; halve each rectangle, lengthwise, cutting through wax paper; peel off top sheets. Lay one plain strip, paper-side up, on top of green strip and peel off paper; repeat with remaining strips, alternating colors, to make 4 layers. Wrap in wax paper or aluminum foil; chill several hours, or freeze until very firm. When ready to bake, unwrap dough and cut into ¼-inch thick slices; place on cookie sheets. Bake

and cool as in general directions.

PINWHEEL TWIRLS: Divide a second part of dough in half. Tint one half deep pink with a few drops red food coloring; leave other half plain. Roll out each half to a 9x9-inch square between sheets of wax paper; peel off top sheets. Lay pink-tinted dough, paper-side up, on top of plain dough; peel off paper. Roll up doughs tightly, jelly roll fashion. Wrap in wax paper or aluminum foil; chill or freeze until very firm. When ready to bake, unwrap dough and slice into ¼-inch-thick rounds with a sharp knife; place on cookie sheets. Bake and cool, following general directions.

CHECKERBOARDS: Divide third part of dough in half. Blend 1 square unsweetened chocolate, melted and cooled, into one half; leave other half plain. Roll out each half to a 9x3-inch rectangle between sheets of wax paper; chill. Peel off top sheets. Cut each rectangle, lengthwise, into 6 strips, each ⅜-inch wide. Carefully lift a chocolate strip with a long-bladed spatula and place on a clean sheet of wax paper or aluminum foil; lay a plain strip close to it, then repeat with a chocolate and plain strip to make a four-strip ribbon, about 1½-inches wide. Build a second and third layer, alternating plain and chocolate strips each time. Wrap in wax paper or aluminum foil; chill or freeze until very firm. When ready to bake, unwrap dough and slice into ¼-inch rectangles with a sharp knife; place on cookie sheets. Bake and cool, following general directions.

WALNUT CHOCOLATE COOKIES

No cookie file is complete without this delicious chocolate drop cookie recipe.

Bake at 350° for 10 minutes.
Makes 3½ dozen.

1 cup firmly packed brown sugar
½ cup vegetable shortening
1 egg
1 teaspoon vanilla
½ cup milk
2 teaspoon vinegar
1⅔ cups all purpose flour
½ teaspoon salt
½ teaspoon baking soda
2 squares unsweetened chocolate, melted
½ cup chopped walnuts

1. Beat sugar and shortening until fluffy in large bowl with electric mixer at medium speed. Add egg and vanilla and beat well. Combine milk and

vinegar in a 1-cup measure.
2. Sift flour, salt and baking soda onto wax paper. Turn mixer speed to low; add milk and flour mixtures, alternately, to make a smooth batter; stir in melted chocolate and walnuts.
4. Drop by teaspoonfuls, 2 inches apart, onto cookie sheet.
5. Bake in moderate oven (350°) 10 minutes, or until cookies are set when touched lightly with finger. Remove from cookie sheet with spatula and cool on wire racks.

CURRANT-SPICE DROPS

This basic soft drop cookie dough can be varied endlessly for different effects; try our chocolate or oatmeal variations that follow.

Bake at 350° for 12 minutes.
Makes 5 dozen.

3 cups all purpose flour
1½ teaspoons baking powder
1 teaspoon salt
½ teaspoon baking soda
½ teaspoon ground allspice
1 cup vegetable shortening
1 cup sugar
2 eggs
⅓ cup milk
1 teaspoon vanilla
1 cup dried currants

1. Sift flour, baking powder, salt, baking soda and allspice together onto wax paper.
2. Beat shortening and sugar until fluffy in a large bowl with electric mixer at high speed; beat in eggs, milk and vanilla until well blended. Stir in flour mixture, a third at a time, blending well to make a soft dough; stir in currants. Drop by rounded teaspoonfuls, 2 inches apart, onto greased cookie sheets.
3. Bake in moderate over (350°) 12 minutes, or until centers are firm when lightly touched with fingertip; remove to wire racks with spatula; cool completely.

Suggested Variations: CHOCOLATE-WALNUT DROPS—prepare batter as in CURRANT-SPICE DROPS, adding ½ cup dry cocoa with the flour. Omit the allspice; substitue ⅔ cup buttermilk for regular milk and 1 cup chopped walnuts for the currants. OATMEAL-APPLESAUCE DROPS—prepare batter as in CURRANT-SPICE DROPS, omitting allspice, substituting firmly packed light brown sugar for the granulated sugar, ⅔ cup applesauce for the milk and 1 cup quick-cooking rolled oats in place of the currants. COCONUT-SPICE DROPS—prepare batter as in CURRANT-SPICE DROPS and add 1 cup flaked coconut to the dough.

SOUR-CREAM SOFTIES

Cinnamon-sugar "frosts" the tops of these big, old-fashioned puffs.

Bake at 400° for 12 minutes.
Makes 3½ dozen.

- 3 cups all purpose flour
- 1 teaspoon salt
- ½ teaspoon baking powder
- ½ teaspoon baking soda
- ½ cup (1 stick) butter or margarine
- 1½ cups sugar
- 2 eggs
- 1 teaspoon vanilla
- 1 container (8 ounces) dairy sour cream
  Cinnamon-sugar

1. Measure flour, salt, baking powder and soda into a sifter.
2. Beat butter or margarine with sugar until well blended in a large bowl with an electric mixer at high speed; beat in eggs and vanilla. Sift in flour mixture, adding alternately with sour cream and blending well to make a thick batter.
3. Drop by rounded tablespoonfuls, 4 inches apart, on greased cookie sheets; spread into 2-inch rounds; sprinkle with cinnamon-sugar.
4. Bake in hot oven (400°) 12 minutes, or until lightly golden around edges, Remove from cookie sheets with spatula; cool completely on wire racks.

BAKING BASICS

NOTES ON CHOCOLATE

• The kinds of chocolate used in our recipes:
1. 1-ounce squares—individually wrapped and sold in 8-ounce packages; grooved to break into ½-ounce pieces; available unsweetened and semisweet.
2. German sweet—a sweet cooking chocolate sold in 4-ounce bars; also suitable for snacking.
3. Cocoa—unsweetened powder, for use in cake and cookie baking when you want a deep, chocolate flavor. Be sure to use when called for.
4. Instant cocoa mix—already sweet-ened powder sometimes used in baking; a good garnish, too. (*Not* a substitute for cocoa).
• For chocolate cakes, dust greased pans with cocoa instead of flour.

PENNY WAFERS

A recipe your friends will ask for.

Bake at 425° for 5 minutes.
Makes 5 dozen.

- 2 tablespoons currants
- 1 tablespoon hot water
- 2 teaspoons rum extract
- ¼ cup (½ stick) butter or margarine
- ¼ cup sugar
- 1 egg
- ⅓ cup all purpose flour

1. Combine currants, hot water, and rum extract in small bowl; let stand about 1 hour to blend flavors.
2. Beat butter or margarine until soft in medium-size bowl with electric mixer at high speed; beat in sugar, then egg, beating until fluffy; stir in flour and currant mixture.
3. Drop batter by teaspoonfuls, about 1½ inches apart, on well greased cookie sheet.
4. Bake in hot oven (425°) 5 minutes, or until edges are golden.
5. Remove from cookie sheet with spatula; cool on wire cake racks.

SCOTCH OAT CAKES

Down East, in Maine, these cookies are often served at breakfast.

Bake at 350° for 12 minutes.
Makes 5 dozen.

- 3 cups all purpose flour
- 3 cups quick-cooking rolled oats
- 1 cup sugar
- 2 teaspoons salt
- 1 teaspoon baking soda
- 1 cup (2 sticks) butter or margarine
- ½ cup vegetable shortening or lard
- ½ cup cold water

1. Combine flour, rolled oats, sugar, salt and baking soda in a large bowl. Work in butter or margarine and shortening with fingers until mixture is crumbly. Stir in cold water until well blended.
2. Sprinkle oats on pastry cloth or board; roll out dough, a quarter at a time, to a ¼-inch thickness; cut into 2-inch squares. Place on cookie sheets.
3. Bake in moderate oven (350°) 12 minutes, or until golden; remove to wire racks with spatula; cool completely. Store in a metal tin with a tight-fitting lid.

SESAME WAFERS

Sesame seeds taste good on just about anything, but make this delicate cookie an extra-special treat.

Bake at 350° for 10 minutes.
Makes 8 dozen.

- 2 cups all purpose flour
- ½ teaspoon baking soda
- ½ teaspoon salt
- 1 cup (2 sticks) butter or margarine
- 1 cup sugar
- 1 egg
- 1 teaspoon vanilla
- ½ cup sesame seeds

1. Sift flour, soda and salt onto wax paper.
2. Beat butter or margarine with sugar until fluffy in a large bowl with electric mixer at high speed; beat in egg and vanilla.
3. Stir in flour mixture, half at a time, blending well to make a soft dough. Chill several hours, or overnight, until firm enough to handle.
4. Roll dough, a teaspoonful at a time, into balls between palms of hands, then roll in sesame seeds in a pie plate to coat lightly. Place, 2 inches apart, on lightly greased large cookie sheets.
5. Bake in moderate oven (350°) 10 minutes, or until delicately golden. Remove from cookie sheets to wire racks with spatula; cool completely.

BANANA-DATE PUFFS

Soft, moist, and spicy, they'll remind you somewhat of little cakes.

Bake at 375° for 10 minutes.
Makes 5 dozen.

- 3 cups all purpose flour
- 1 teaspoon baking soda
- 1 teaspoon pumpkin pie spice
- ½ teaspoon salt
- ¾ cup (1½ sticks) butter or margarine
- ¾ cup firmly packed brown sugar
- 1 egg
- 2 medium-sized ripe bananas, mashed (1 cup)
- 1 teaspoon vanilla
- 1 cup chopped dates

1. Sift flour, soda, pumpkin pie spice, and salt onto wax paper.
2. Beat butter or margarine with brown sugar until fluffy in large bowl with an electric mixer at high speed; beat in egg, mashed bananas and vanilla. Stir in flour mixture, half at a time, until well blended; stir in dates. Drop by rounded teaspoonfuls onto lightly greased cookie sheets.
3. Bake in moderate oven (375°) 10

minutes, or until firm and lightly golden around edges. Remove from cookie sheets to wire racks; cool.

DATE MATES

The flavor of Southern California, one of the largest date-growing areas in the world.

Bake at 350° for 8 minutes.
Makes 2½ dozen.

- ⅓ cup butter or margarine
- ¾ cup firmly packed brown sugar
- 1 egg
- 1 teaspoon vanilla
- 1 cup whole wheat flour
- ½ teaspoon baking soda
- ¼ teaspoon salt
- ⅔ chopped pitted dates

1. Beat butter or margarine in a large bowl with an electric mixer at high speed; gradually add sugar and continue beating until well blended. Beat in egg and vanilla.
2. Add whole wheat flour, baking soda and salt to butter mixture; mix well. Stir in dates. Drop by teaspoonfuls, 2 inches apart, onto greased cookie sheets.
3. Bake in moderate oven (350°) 8 minutes, or until cookies are lightly browned. Remove to wire racks with spatula to cool.

ZAMBONIES

Nutritious, good-tasting and easy to prepare, they're perfect for after-school snacks.

Bake at 350° for 8 minutes.
Makes 3 dozen.

- ½ cup (1 stick) butter or margarine
- 1 cup firmly packed brown sugar
- 1 egg
- 1 teaspoon vanilla
- 1¼ cups unbleached flour
- 2 tablespoons soya flour
- ¾ teaspoon baking soda
- ½ teaspoon salt
- ½ cup raisins
- ⅓ cup sliced blanched almonds

1. Beat butter or margarine in a large bowl with an electric mixer at high speed; gradually add sugar and continue beating until well blended. Beat in egg and vanilla.
2. Sift flour, soya flour, baking soda and salt into mixture; mix well. Stir in raisins and almonds. Drop by teaspoonfuls, 2 inches apart, onto cookie sheets.
3. Bake in moderate oven (350°) 8 minutes, or until cookies are lightly browned. Remove from cookie sheets with spatula. Cool on wire racks. Store in metal tin with tight lid.

POLKA DOTS

Tiny marshmallows dot butterscotch rounds; bake just long enough to melt.

Bake at 375° for 12 minutes.
Makes 1½ dozen.

- 2¼ cups all purpose flour
- ¾ teaspoon baking soda
- ½ teaspoon salt
- 1 cup (2 sticks) butter or margarine
- 1 cup firmly packed brown sugar
- ½ cup granulated sugar
- 2 eggs
- 1½ teaspoons vanilla
- 1 package (6 ounces) butterscotch-flavored pieces
- 1 cup tiny marshmallows

1. Measure flour, soda and salt into sifter.
2. Beat butter or margarine with brown and granulated sugars until fluffy in large bowl with electric mixer at high speed; beat in eggs and vanilla. Sift in flour mixture, a third at a time, blending well; stir in butterscotch pieces.
3. Drop dough, a scant ¼ cupful at a time, 6 inches apart, on large cookie sheets; spread into 4-inch rounds.
4. Bake in moderate oven (375°) 10 minutes; place several marshmallows on top of each cookie. Bake 2 minutes longer, or just until marshmallows melt. Remove to wire racks with spatula to cool.

ALMOND SQUARES

A special treat for a family picnic.

Bake at 325° for 25 minutes.
Makes 16 squares.

- 1 cup dates, chopped
- ½ cup water
- ¾ cup firmly packed brown sugar
- 1 cup whole wheat flour
- ¾ cup chopped almonds
- ¾ cup quick-cooking rolled oats
- 1 teaspoon soda
- ¼ teaspoon salt
- ½ cup (1 stick) butter or margarine, melted

1. Combine dates, water and ½ cup of the sugar in a medium-size saucepan; bring to boiling; lower heat; simmer 15 minutes, or until mixture thickens; remove from heat.
2. Combine whole wheat flour, almonds, oats, remaining ¼ cup sugar, baking soda and salt in a medium-size bowl; toss in melted butter or margarine until well blended.
3. Pat half the crumb mixture into a well greased 9x9x2-inch baking pan; spread date mixture over; sprinkle with remaining crumbs.

4. Bake in slow oven (325°) 25 minutes, or until topping is set; cool in pan on wire rack; cut into 16 squares.

MIX-IN-THE-PAN BROWNIES

Fudgy-rich and made right in the pan.

Bake at 350° for 30 minutes.
Makes 16 squares.

- ⅔ cup vegetable shortening
- 1 cup sugar
- 2 eggs
- 1 teaspoon vanilla
- 1 cup all purpose flour
- ½ teaspoon baking powder
- ½ teaspoon salt
- ½ cup cocoa powder (not a mix)
- ½ cup chopped walnuts

1. Melt shortening in 8x8x2-inch baking pan over low heat. Stir in sugar. Cool for 5 minutes.
2. Break eggs into pan with vanilla; beat with fork until blended.
3. Measure flour, baking powder, salt and cocoa into sifter. Sift into mixture in baking pan. Mix thoroughly with fork. Add walnuts. Smooth top.
4. Bake in a moderate oven (350°) 30 minutes, or until center springs back when lightly pressed with fingertip. Cool on wire rack. Cut into 16 squares.

MARMALADE SQUARES

Crunchy bars have a tart citrus filling.

Bake at 350° for 45 minutes.
Makes 24 squares.

- 2 cups quick-cooking rolled oats
- ¾ cup all purpose flour
- ½ cup chopped walnuts
- ½ cup firmly packed brown sugar
- 1 teaspoon baking powder
- ½ cup (1 stick) butter or margarine, melted
- 1 can (about 14 ounces) sweetened condensed milk (not evaporated)
- 1 cup orange marmalade
- ¼ cup lemon juice

1. Combine oats, flour, nuts, brown sugar and baking powder in a medium-size bowl. Stir in butter or margarine to make a crumbly mixture. Pat two-thirds of the mixture in bottom of a 13x9x2-inch baking pan.
2. Combine sweetened condensed milk, marmalade and lemon juice in a small bowl; spread over crumb layer. Sprinkle crumbs on top.
3. Bake in moderate oven (350°) 45 minutes, or until crumbs are golden. Cool in pan on wire rack. Cut into 24 squares. Refrigerate until serving.

CARROT COOKIES

Carrots are too good for just vegetable dishes. See how they give moistness to this cookie jar filler.

Bake at 350° for 15 minutes.
Makes 3 dozen.

- 2 cups all purpose flour
- 2 teaspoons baking powder
- ½ teaspoon salt
- ½ cup (1 stick) butter or margarine
- ¾ cup sugar
- 1 egg
- 1 cup mashed cooked carrots
- 2 teaspoons grated orange rind
- 1 teaspoon vanilla
- 1 package (6 ounces) butterscotch-flavored pieces

1. Sift flour, baking powder and salt onto wax paper.
2. Beat butter or margarine and sugar until fluffy in a large bowl with electric mixer at medium speed; beat in egg until smooth.
3. Turn mixer to lowest speed; blend in carrots, orange rind and vanilla until smooth; stir in butterscotch pieces until well blended.
4. Drop by rounded teaspoonfuls, 2 inches apart, onto cookies sheets.
5. Bake in moderate oven (350°) 15 minutes, or until golden brown. Remove from cookie sheets to wire racks with wide spatula or pancake turner. Cool completely before storing in metal tin between layers of wax paper.

AFTER-SCHOOL COOKIES

Chocolate drop cookies make a delicious way to say "welcome" at the end of a hard day at school.

Bake at 400° for 10 minutes.
Makes 6 dozen.

- 1 package (6 ounces) semi-sweet chocolate pieces
- 2¼ cups all purpose flour
- 2 teaspoons baking powder
- 1 teaspoon salt
- ¼ teaspoon baking soda
- ¾ cup vegetable shortening
- 1 cup firmly packed brown sugar
- 2 eggs
- 1 cup chopped walnuts
- 1 cup mashed banana (2 medium-size)
- 1 teaspoon grated lemon rind

1. Melt chocolate pieces in a small metal bowl placed in a skillet of hot (not boiling) water; remove from skillet and let cool.
2. Sift flour, baking powder, salt and baking soda onto wax paper.
3. Beat shortening and brown sugar until fluffy in a large bowl with electric mixer at medium speed; beat in eggs until smooth.
4. Stir in flour mixture until smooth with a wooden spoon; blend in melted chocolate, nuts, bananas and lemon rind until well blended.
5. Drop by rounded teaspoonfuls, 2 inches apart, onto lightly greased cookie sheets.
6. Bake in hot oven (400°) 10 minutes, or until tops spring back when lightly touched with fingertip. Remove from cookie sheets to wire racks with wide spatula or pancake turner. Cool completely before storing in metal tin between layers of wax paper or transparent wrap.

AUTUMN PICNIC BARS

The warming taste of nutmeg, cloves and apples—suitable accompaniment to a gathering around the campfire.

Bake at 375° for 35 minutes.
Makes 24 bars.

- 1¾ cups all purpose flour
- 1½ teaspoons baking soda
- ¾ teaspoon ground cinnamon
- ¼ teaspoon ground cloves
- ¼ teaspoon ground nutmeg
- ½ cup (1 stick) butter or margarine
- 1 cup firmly packed brown sugar
- 2 eggs
- 1 teaspoon vanilla
- 1 cup applesauce
- 1½ cups quick-cooking rolled oats
- 1 package (8 ounces) pitted dates, finely chopped
- ½ cup chopped walnuts
- Citrus Glaze (recipe follows)

1. Sift flour, soda, cinnamon, cloves and nutmeg onto wax paper.
2. Beat butter or margarine with brown sugar until fluffy in large bowl with an electric mixer at high speed; beat in eggs, one at a time; add vanilla. Stir in flour mixture, half at a time, alternately with applesauce, just until blended; stir in rolled oats, dates and walnuts. Spoon into a greased 13x9x2-inch pan; spread top evenly.
3. Bake in moderate oven (375°) 35 minutes, or until center springs back when lightly pressed with fingertip. Cool completely in pan on wire rack.
4. Drizzle CITRUS GLAZE over top; let stand until firm. Carry in baking pan, uncut, and cut into serving-size bars at the picnic. Store uneaten bars in metal container.

CITRUS GLAZE: Blend ½ cup 10X (confectioners' powdered) sugar with 2 teaspoons water and 2 teaspoons lemon juice until smooth in a small bowl with a wooden spoon.

TOFFEE-RAISIN BARS

Lots of sugar, spice and fruit go into these chewy cookies. They save time on busy days, for they take no fancy shaping.

Bake at 375° for 20 minutes.
Makes 30 bars.

- 2 cups all purpose flour
- ½ teaspoon baking soda
- ½ teaspoon ground nutmeg
- ½ teaspoon ground cinnamon
- ¼ teaspoon ground cloves
- 1 cup (2 sticks) butter or margarine
- 1¼ cups firmly packed brown sugar
- 2 eggs
- 2 tablespoons milk
- 1½ cups raisins

1. Measure flour, soda, nutmeg, cinnamon and cloves into sifter.
2. Beat butter or margarine with brown sugar until fluffy in large bowl with an electric mixer at high speed; beat in eggs and milk until well blended.
3. Sift in dry ingredients, a third at a time, blending well to make a thick batter; stir in raisins. Spread evenly in lightly greased 15x10x1-inch jelly roll pan.
4. Bake in moderate oven (375°) 20 minutes, or until browned around edges and top springs back when lightly pressed with fingertip. Cool in pan on wire rack 15 minutes; cut into 30 bars. Top with sweetened whipped cream or ice cream, if you wish.

GINGER WAFERS

An old-fashioned favorite.

Bake at 350° for 13 minutes.
Makes 4 dozen.

- 2 cups all purpose flour
- 2 teaspoons ground ginger
- 2 teaspoons baking soda
- 1 teaspoon ground cinnamon
- ½ teaspoon salt
- ¾ cup (1½ sticks) butter or margarine
- 1 cup sugar
- 1 egg
- ¼ cup light molasses
- Sugar

1. Sift flour, ginger, soda, cinnamon and salt onto wax paper.
2. Beat butter or margarine with the 1 cup sugar until fluffy in medium-size bowl with electric mixer at high speed; beat in egg and molasses.
3. Stir in flour mixture, a third at a time, until well blended.
4. Roll dough, a teaspoonful at a time, into small balls between palms; roll each in sugar to coat well. Place on cookie sheets.

5. Bake in moderate oven (350°) 13 minutes, or until tops are crackled. Remove to wire racks; cool.

LEMON CRINKLES

These light, lemony mouthfuls actually decorate themselves—they crackle as they bake. Great with a cup of tea.

Bake at 350° for 8 minutes.
Makes 5 dozen.

- ¾ cup (1½ sticks) butter or margarine
- 1¼ cups sugar
- 1 egg
- ½ teaspoon vanilla
- ½ teaspoon lemon extract
- ¼ cup milk
- 2 cups all purpose flour
- 1 teaspoon baking powder
- ½ teaspoon salt
- ¼ teaspoon baking soda
- 1 tablespoon grated lemon rind

1. Beat butter or margarine with ¾ cup of the sugar until fluffy in medium-size bowl with electric mixer at high speed. Beat in egg, vanilla, lemon extract and milk.
2. Sift in flour, baking powder, salt and baking soda, a little at a time, blending after each addition; chill dough several hours, or until firm.
3. Form into marble-size balls (about 1 teaspoonful for each) by rolling lightly between palms of hands. Coat balls by rolling in a mixture of remaining ½ cup sugar and lemon rind; carefully place, 2 inches apart, on cookie sheets.
4. Bake in moderate oven (350°) 8 minutes, or until tops are crackled and edges are lightly browned; cool completely on wire racks.

APPLE-OATMEAL CHEWS

These spicy-chewy, three-layer bars from Johnny Appleseed country are nutritious and great-tasting.

Bake at 350° for 30 minutes.
Makes 16 bars.

- 1 cup all purpose flour
- ½ teaspoon baking soda
- ½ teaspoon salt
- 1 teaspoon ground cinnamon
- ⅛ teaspoon ground allspice
- ⅛ teaspoon ground mace
- 1 teaspoon grated orange rind
- 1⅓ cups quick-cooking rolled oats
- ⅔ cup firmly packed brown sugar
- ½ cup vegetable shortening, melted
- 1 egg
- ¼ teaspoon vanilla
- 2 cups very thinly sliced pared apples
- 10X sugar

1. Sift flour, soda, salt, cinnamon, allspice and mace into a bowl. Add orange rind, oats, brown sugar, melted shortening, egg and vanilla; knead with the hands to mix well.
2. Pat half the dough firmly over the bottom of a greased 9x9x2-inch baking pan. Arrange apples evenly on top. Roll remaining dough between two sheets of wax paper into a 9-inch square. Peel off top sheet and invert dough on apples. Press firmly into apples, evening up ragged edges and piecing as needed so that apples are well covered.
3. Bake in a moderate oven (350°) for 30 minutes, or until cookie top begins to pull from sides of pan. Cool in pan until warm to the touch on wire rack; then press top layer firmly into apple layer. Dust top lightly with 10X sugar,

then cool to room temperature. Cut into 16 bars and serve. Store leftover bars in metal tin.

HAWAIIAN COOKIES

Crushed pineapple and butterscotch pieces star in this simple drop cookie.

Bake at 375° for 10 minutes.
Makes 3 dozen.

- 1¾ cups all purpose flour
- 2 teaspoons baking powder
- 1 teaspoon salt
- ½ cup (1 stick) butter or margarine
- 1 cup firmly packed brown sugar
- 2 eggs
- 1 teaspoon vanilla
- 1 can (8¾ ounces) crushed pineapple in pineapple juice
- 1 package (6 ounces) butterscotch-flavored pieces
- ½ cup chopped walnuts
- ½ teaspoon grated orange rind

1. Sift flour, baking powder and salt onto wax paper.
2. Beat butter or margarine and brown sugar until fluffy in a large bowl with electric mixer at medium speed; beat in eggs and vanilla.
3. Stir in flour mixture, alternately with pineapple and juice, with a wooden spoon until smooth. Stir in butterscotch pieces, walnuts and orange rind until well blended.
4. Drop by rounded teaspoonfuls, 2 inches apart, onto greased cookie sheets.
5. Bake in hot oven (375°) 10 minutes, or until golden brown. Remove from cookie sheets to wire racks with wide spatula or pancake turner. Cool completely before storing in metal tin between layers of wax paper.

MORE BAKER'S TOOLS

Color in cake carriers, stackable canisters and dry measures add a decorative touch. Choose an assortment of sizes and colors. Select a long spatula, narrow rolling pin, wire whip, pancake turner, wider spatula and rubber scraper to be among the first equipment you buy for your kitchen.

SEMISWEET ORANGE BARS

Brown sugar bar cookies are brimming with chocolate pieces and topped with glaze.

Bake at 375° for 30 minutes.
Makes 48 bars.

- 1½ cups all purpose flour
- 1½ teaspoons baking powder
- ½ teaspoon salt
- ½ cup vegetable shortening
- ⅔ cup firmly packed brown sugar
- 1 egg
- 2 tablespoons grated orange rind
- ¾ cup orange juice
- 2 teaspoons vanilla
- 1 package (6 ounces) semi-sweet chocolate pieces
- 1 cup 10X (confectioners' powdered) sugar
- 2 tablespoons orange juice

1. Sift flour, baking powder and salt onto wax paper.
2. Beat shortening and brown sugar until fluffy in a large bowl with electric mixer at medium speed; beat in egg, 1 tablespoon of the orange rind, ¾ cup orange juice and vanilla until creamy and smooth.
3. Stir in flour mixture with a wooden spoon until smooth; stir in chocolate pieces until well blended. Spread into a greased and floured 13x9x2-inch baking pan.
4. Bake in moderate oven (375°) 30 minutes, or until golden brown. Cool in pan on wire rack for 10 minutes.
5. While cake cools, combine 10X sugar, remaining 1 tablespoon orange rind and 2 tablespoons orange juice in a small bowl until well blended. Drizzle over cake. Cool completely in pan. Cut into 48 bars.

BROWN-EDGE SPICIES

Their pungent flavor carries you back to the days when ships bearing spices and whale oil returned from the Indies.

Bake at 350° about 12 minutes.
Makes 3 dozen.

- 2 cups all purpose flour
- 1 teaspoon baking powder
- ½ teaspoon baking soda
- ½ teaspoon salt
- ½ teaspoon ground cinnamon
- ½ teaspoon ground nutmeg
- ¼ teaspoon ground cloves
- ½ cup vegetable shortening
- 1 cup sugar
- 1 egg
- 1 teaspoon vanilla
- 1 cup canned applesauce

1. Measure flour, baking powder, baking soda, salt, cinnamon, nutmeg and ground cloves into sifter.

2. Beat shortening until soft in medium-size bowl with electric mixer at high speed; add sugar gradually, beating after each addition until well blended.
3. Stir in egg and vanilla; beat until mixture is fluffy.
4. Sift and add dry ingredients, alternately with applesauce, blending well after each addition.
5. Drop batter by heaping teaspoonfuls, 2 inches apart; onto lightly greased cookie sheets.
6. Bake in moderate oven (350°) about 12 minutes, or until cookies are lightly browned around edges.
7. Loosen at once from cookie sheet by running spatula under each cookie; cool on wire cake racks.
8. Store cookies in cookie jar or airtight container with an apple wedge in it to keep them soft.

SPECIAL OCCASIONS (CHAPTER 3)

VALENTINE COOKIE HEARTS

Make the day special for the whole family with heart-shaped sour cream cookies.

Bake at 350° for 10 minutes.
Makes 4 dozen.

- 1 cup (2 sticks) butter or margarine
- 1½ cups sugar
- 2 eggs
- 1 teaspoon vanilla
- ½ teaspoon almond extract
- 4¼ cups all purpose flour
- 1 teaspoon baking powder
- 1 teaspoon salt
- 1 teaspoon baking soda
- 1 container (8 ounces) dairy sour cream
- Red decorating sugar

1. Beat butter or margarine and sugar in a large bowl with an electric mixer at medium speed until light and fluffy.
2. Beat in eggs, vanilla and almond extract until well blended.
3. Sift flour, baking powder, salt and baking soda onto wax paper. Using a wooden spoon, stir into bowl, alternately with sour cream until well blended. Wrap in wax paper. Chill 2 hours, or until firm.
4. Roll out dough, a quarter at a time, to a ¼-inch thickness on a lightly floured pastry cloth or board. Cut with a 3-inch heart-shaped cutter. Place on cookie sheets; sprinkle with red sugar.
5. Bake in moderate oven (350°) 10 minutes, or until edges are golden. Remove to wire racks with pancake turner; cool completely.

FRUIT CAKE DROPS

Rich with assorted nuts and fruits, the perfect ending to Thanksgiving dinner.

Bake at 350° for 12 minutes.
Makes 12 dozen.

- 1 cup all purpose flour
- ¼ teaspoon baking soda
- ¼ teaspoon salt
- ½ teaspoon ground cinnamon
- ¼ cup (½ stick) butter or margarine
- ½ cup sugar
- 1 egg
- 2 tablespoons brandy
- 1 package (8 ounces) pitted dates, chopped
- 1 container (4 ounces) mixed candied fruits, chopped
- 1 container (4 ounces) candied red cherries, chopped
- 1 container (4 ounces) candied pineapple, chopped
- ½ cup chopped blanched almonds
- ½ cup chopped walnuts

1. Sift flour, baking soda, salt and cinnamon onto wax paper.
2. Beat butter or margarine with sugar until fluffy in medium-size bowl with electric mixer at high speed; beat in egg and brandy.
3. Stir in flour mixture, half at a time, blending well to make a soft dough. Stir in dates, candied fruits, almonds and nuts.
4. Drop batter, a rounded teaspoonful at a time, 1 inch apart, onto lightly greased cookie sheets.
5. Bake in moderate oven (350°) 12 minutes, or until firm and lightly browned. Remove from cookie sheets to wire racks with spatula; cool completely. Store in airtight containers.

MUSHROOM MERINGUES

Use a pastry bag to shape this classic accompaniment to Bûche de Noël. They are in the photo on page 71.

Bake at 250° for 30 minutes.
Makes 2 dozen.

- 2 egg whites
- ⅛ teaspoon cream of tartar
- ½ teaspoon almond extract
- ⅔ cup sugar
- ¼ cup semi-sweet chocolate pieces

1. Grease two large cookie sheets; flour lightly tapping off any excess.
2. Beat egg whites, cream of tartar and almond extract until foamy-white and double in volume in a small bowl with electric mixer at high speed.
3. Sprinkle in sugar, 1 tablespoon at a time, beating until sugar dissolves completely and meringue stands in

firm peaks when beaters are lifted.

4. Attach a # 10 plain tip to a pastry bag; spoon meringue into bag. To make mushroom caps: Press out meringue in 1½-inch rounds; smooth top of each, if needed, with knife but do not flatten. To make stems: Hold pastry bag upright, then press out meringue, pulling straight up on bag for about 1½ inches.

5. Bake in very slow oven (250°) 30 minutes or until firm, but not brown. Let stand several minutes on cookie sheets. Loosen carefully with a small knife; remove to wire racks with spatula; cool completely.

6. Melt chocolate in a cup placed in a small skillet of hot water.

7. Working carefully, make a small hollow in the underside of each cap with the tip of a wooden spoon handle. Fill hollow with melted chocolate; press stem into hollow. Let stand until chocolate is firm. Sprinkle tops with cocoa, if you wish. Store in a tightly covered container in a dry place.

LEMON CURD TARTS

Tangy lemon in rich pastry cups make a lovely addition to a pastry tray.

Bake at 350° for 15 minutes.
Makes 2 dozen.

  1 cup all purpose flour
  ½ cup (1 stick) butter or margarine
  1 package (3 ounces) cream cheese
  4 teaspoons lemon rind
  ½ cup lemon juice
  2 cups sugar
  1 cup (2 sticks) butter or margarine
  4 eggs, well beaten

1. Place flour in a medium-size bowl; cut in the ½ cup butter or margarine and cream cheese with a pastry blender until crumbly. Work into a ball with hands. Divide into 24 parts.

2. Press one ball into each of 24 tiny muffin cups; chill while mixing filling.

3. Combine lemon rind, lemon juice and sugar in top of double boiler until well blended. Cut the 1 cup butter into mixture with pastry blender.

4. Cook over simmering water, stirring constantly, until butter melts; beat in eggs. Cook 15 minutes, stirring constantly, until mixture thickens.

5. Fill each prepared muffin cup two-thirds full.

6. Bake in moderate oven (350°) 15 minutes, or until filling is set; cool in tins on wire racks 15 minutes; loosen pastry around muffin cups with a sharp knife; cool tarts completely on wire racks. Serve with a dollop of whipped cream, if you wish.

CANDY-STRIPE TWISTS

These fun-to-make cookies taste like old-fashioned licorice sticks.

Bake at 350° for 10 minutes.
Makes 5 dozen.

  3¼ cups all purpose flour
  4 teaspoons baking powder
  1 teaspoon salt
  ½ cup (1 stick) butter or margarine
  1¼ cups sugar
  1 egg
  ½ teaspoon oil of anise
  ¼ cup milk
     Red food coloring

1. Measure flour, baking powder and salt into sifter.

2. Beat butter or margarine and sugar until fluffy in large bowl with electric mixer at high speed; beat in egg and oil of anise.

3. Sift in dry ingredients, a third at a time, adding alternately with milk; stir until well blended.

4. Spoon half of dough into a medium-size bowl; blend in a few drops red food coloring to tint pink; leave other half plain.

5. Pinch off about a teaspoonful each of pink and white doughs at a time, and roll each into a pencil-thin strip about 5-inches long on lightly floured pastry cloth or board. Place strips side by side, pressing ends together, then twist into a rope. Place, 1 inch apart, on cookie sheets.

6. Bake in moderate oven (350°) 10 minutes or until firm. Remove carefully from cookie sheets; cool on wire racks. Store in airtight container between layers of wax paper or transparent wrap.

BUTTERNUTS

Cookie-lovers will favor these buttery, nut-laced rounds topped with rum frosting and candied cherries.

Bake at 325° for 15 minutes.
Makes 8 dozen.

  ¾ cup (1½ sticks) butter or margarine
  ½ cup 10X (confectioners' powdered) sugar
  ¼ teaspoon salt
  1¾ cups all purpose flour
  1 package (6 ounces) butterscotch-flavored pieces
  1 cup finely chopped pecans
     Rum Glaze (recipe follows)
     Pecan halves
     Candied red cherries, halved

1. Beat butter or margarine with 10X sugar and salt in medium-size bowl with electric mixer at high speed;

blend in flour until smooth. Stir in butterscotch pieces and pecans.

2. Shape dough, a scant teaspoonful at a time, into balls between palms of hands; place, 1 inch apart, on large cookie sheets.

3. Bake in slow oven (325°) 15 minutes, or until firm but not brown. Remove from cookie sheets to wire racks with spatula; cool completely.

4. Make RUM GLAZE. Place cookies in a single layer on wire racks set over wax paper; spoon glaze over each to cover completely. (Scrape glaze that drips onto paper back into bowl and beat until smooth before using again.) Decorate each with a pecan or candied cherry half. Let cookies stand until glaze is firm.

RUM GLAZE: Makes ¾ cup. Combine 2 cups sifted 10X (confectioners' powdered) sugar and ¼ cup light rum in medium-size bowl with an electric mixer at high speed; beat until well blended and smooth.

BUTTON MACAROONS

Crisp and chewy, these sweets keep well.

Bake at 325° for 15 minutes.
Makes 3 dozen.

  1 egg, separated
  ⅓ cup sugar
  1 teaspoon baking powder
  ⅛ teaspoon salt
  ¼ teaspoon vanilla
  ¾ cup quick-cooking rolled oats
  ½ cup coconut
  1 tablespoon butter or margarine, melted
     Candied red and green cherries, cut in slivers

1. Beat egg white until foamy-white and double in volume in small bowl with electric mixer at high speed; beat in 3 tablespoons of the sugar, 1 tablespoon at a time, until meringue stands in firm peaks.

2. Beat egg yolk well in a medium-size bowl with electric mixer at high speed; beat in remaining sugar until fluffy. Stir in baking powder, salt, vanilla, rolled oats, coconut and melted butter or margarine; fold in meringue.

3. Drop by teaspoonfuls, 1 inch apart, onto greased cookie sheets; decorate each with slivered red and green cherries.

4. Bake in slow oven (325°) 15 minutes, or until firm and lightly golden. Remove from cookie sheets with spatula; cool completely on wire racks. Store in airtight container.

ALMOND MACAROONS

Puffy, crunchy little cookies made from almond paste.

Bake at 325° for 20 minutes.
Makes 3 dozen.

1 can (8 ounces) almond paste
2 egg whites
  Dash salt
1 teaspoon vanilla
1 cup 10X (confectioner's powdered) sugar
  Granulated sugar
  Sliced almonds
  Red candied cherries, quartered

1. Grease a large cookie sheet; dust with flour; tap off any excess.
2. Break up almond paste with fingers and drop into a large bowl.
3. Add egg whites, salt and vanilla. Beat at low speed with an electric mixer until mixture is smooth and well blended.
4. Add confectioners' sugar slowly, continuing to beat at low speed, until a soft dough forms.
5. Fit a pastry bag with a #12 writing tip. Fill bag with dough.
6. Pipe dough out in 2½-inch rounds, or drop by teaspoonfuls on prepared cookie sheet. (Macaroons will spread very little when they bake.)
7. Dip fingertip into water; pat over tops; sprinkle with granulated sugar. Decorate cookies with sliced almonds and cherries.
8. Bake in slow oven (325°) for 20 minutes, or until golden brown.
9. Remove to wire racks with a spatula; cool; store between layers of wax paper in airtight metal tin. Serve with demitasse, if you wish.

BAKING BASICS

SUPER SWEETENERS

• To measure brown sugar, firmly pack into dry measuring cup; level off with knife or straight-edged spatula. Sugar should hold shape when turned out of cup.
• Use light, not dark, brown sugar for making our recipes.

• Use granulated (ordinary table) sugar unless another kind is specified.
• Superfine (very finely granulated) sugar is great for meringues or syrups.
• 10X (confectioners' powdered) sugar is powdered, with cornstarch added. It should be free of lumps before measuring. Measure like flour.
• For lumpy brown or confectioners' sugar, rub through sieve.
• To keep brown sugar soft, refrigerate with a piece of bread or apple in plastic bag or glass jar—not in a metal tin.
• Have hard brown sugar? Place approximate amount you'll need in 300° oven 15 minutes; use immediately.
• Corn syrup, made of cornstarch and sugar, comes in light, maple-flavored and dark forms.
• Use light molasses when you bake.
• Honey is not a quantity-for-quantity substitute for sugar; it adds liquid, too, so only use when called for.
• Use a liquid measuring cup for honey, molasses or corn syrup.

KRANSEKAGE

"Wreath cake" is the traditional Scandinavian party cake that's actually a large cookie! It's made with almond cookie rings and topped with a festive crown. Photograph is on page 72.

Bake at 350° for 15 minutes.
Makes 8 rings and one crown.

3¼ cups all purpose flour
1¼ cups (2½ sticks) butter or margarine
1 egg
2 cans (8 ounces each) almond paste*
  Ornamental Frosting (recipe follows)

1. Place flour in a large bowl; cut in butter or margarine with pastry blender until mixture forms small balls when pressed between fingers; beat in egg and almond extract with wooden spoon.
2. Turn dough out onto pastry board; top with almond paste; press together and knead about 5 minutes, or until dough is smooth.
3. Make rings: Pack a small amount of dough at a time into a pastry bag fitted with a ¾-inch metal tip (#9 B is a good size); press out 8 graduated-length strips onto ungreased cookie sheets, using a ruler to measure each accurately. The first strip, for smallest ring, should be 4-inches long; each succeeding strip 1½-inches longer, until the eighth measures 14½ inches. For the longest strips, press shorter strips together. (If strips break, gently

press to join again.)
4. Shape each strip into a ring; press ends with fingers to join. Shape and bake each large ring on a separate cookie sheet; shape 2 or 3 smaller rings on one sheet, allowing at least 3 inches between.
5. Bake in moderate oven (350°) 15 minutes, or until lightly browned; cool 10 minutes on cookie sheet; gently loosen and slide onto wire racks to cool completely.
6. Make crown: Flatten a 2-inch strip of dough with palm of hand; cut out a star with a 3-inch star cutter; center over 6-ounce juice can or ¼-cup metal measuring cup; bake 15 minutes, or until lightly browned.
7. Assemble and decorate cake: Slide largest ring onto serving plate; decorate with loops of ORNAMENTAL FROSTING, using #7 writing tip; place next largest ring on top before frosting has set; continue until smallest ring has been decorated. Outline crown with same tip; place on top of cake.
8. To serve: Gently pry rings apart with spoon or fork.
*BAKER'S TIP: To make your own almond paste, follow this recipe:

ALMOND PASTE: Makes 2 cups. Put 2 cans (4 ounces each) blanched almonds in electric blender, following directions on page 60. Place in large bowl; blend in 2¼ cups 10X (confectioners' powdered) sugar with a wooden spoon or with fingers, then work in ½ cup granulated sugar until well mixed. Add 2 egg yolks and 1 tablespoon water and work again until paste is stiff.

ORNAMENTAL FROSTING

Makes about 2½ cups.

3 egg whites
½ teaspoon cream of tartar
1 package (1 pound) 10X (confectioners') sugar, sifted

Beat egg whites and cream of tartar until foamy in a small bowl with electric mixer at high speed; turn mixer to low speed; slowly beat in 10X sugar until frosting stands in firm peaks and is stiff enough to hold a sharp line when cut through with a knife. Keep bowl of frosting covered with damp paper towels while working, to keep frosting from drying out. Store any leftover frosting in a tightly covered jar in the refrigerator for another day's baking. (Note: For ½ recipe, use 2 egg whites, ½ teaspoon cream of tartar and 3 cups 10X sugar.)

MEXICAN WEDDING CAKES

They'll remind you of lacy mantillas and colorful ceremonial dancers.

Bake at 325° for 25 minutes.
Makes 4 dozen.

- 1 cup (2 sticks) butter or margarine
- ¾ cup 10X (confectioners' powdered) sugar
- 2 cups all purpose flour
- 1 teaspoon vanilla
- 1 cup finely chopped pecans
- 10X sugar

1. Beat butter or margarine until fluffy in large bowl with electric mixer at high speed. Add the ¾ cup 10X sugar, flour and vanilla. Mix well. Blend in pecans.
2. Shape dough into 1-inch balls. Place, 1 inch apart, on cookie sheet.
3. Bake in slow oven (325°) 25 minutes, or until pale golden brown.
4. Roll in 10X sugar while still hot. Cool on wire racks; roll in sugar to coat evenly.

CANDY CANES

Simple to make, and a merry sight hanging on the Christmas tree.

Bake at 350° for 10 minutes.
Makes 4 dozen.

- 3¼ cups all purpose flour
- 1 teaspoon baking powder
- 1 teaspoon salt
- ½ cup (1 stick) butter or margarine, softened
- 1¼ cups sugar
- 1 egg
- ½ teaspoon peppermint extract
- ¼ cup milk
- Red food coloring

1. Sift flour, baking powder and salt onto wax paper.
2. Beat butter or margarine and sugar until fluffy in a large bowl with electric mixer at high speed; beat in egg and peppermint extract. Stir in flour mixture, alternately with milk.
3. Spoon half of dough into a medium-size bowl; tint pink with red food coloring. Leave remaining dough plain.
4. Pinch off about a teaspoonful of each dough; roll each into a pencil-thin strip 5-inches long. Place strips side by side, pressing ends together; twist. Place on cookie sheets, 1 inch apart, bending into cane shape.
5. Bake in moderate oven (350°) 10 minutes, or until firm. Cool a few minutes on cookie sheets. Carefully remove to wire racks with spatula; cool completely. Hang some on your tree; store the rest in metal tin.

MOLASSES CUTOUTS

These spicy cookies, cut out in favorite animal shapes, are sure to catch the children's fancy.

Bake at 350° for 8 minutes.
Makes 6 dozen.

- 3¾ cups all purpose flour
- 1 teaspoon baking soda
- ½ teaspoon salt
- 2 tablespoons cocoa
- 1 teaspoon ground ginger
- 1 teaspoon ground cinnamon
- 1 teaspoon ground cloves
- 1 cup (2 sticks) butter or margarine, softened
- 1 cup sugar
- 1 egg
- ½ cup light molasses
- Ornamental Frosting (recipe, page 48)

1. Sift flour, baking soda, salt, cocoa, ginger, cinnamon and cloves onto wax paper.
2. Beat butter or margarine until fluffy in a large bowl with electric mixer at high speed; add sugar gradually, beating well after each addition. Add egg and molasses; beat well. Stir in flour mixture; blend well. Wrap in plastic wrap or aluminum foil; refrigerate several hours, or overnight.
3. Roll out dough, a quarter at a time, on a floured pastry cloth or pastry board; cut into animal shapes with 3-inch cookie cutters. Place on cookie sheets.
4. Bake in moderate oven (350°) for 8 minutes, or until edges are browned. Let cookies cool a few minutes on cookie sheets. Remove to wire racks with spatula; cool.
5. Decorate the cookies with ORNA-MENTAL FROSTING, following directions on page 67. Store them in an airtight metal container.

ORANGE BELLS

Ring in springtime with these tangy, bell-shaped wafers.

Bake at 350° about 10 minutes.
Makes 3 dozen.

- 2¼ cups all purpose flour
- 1 tablespoon baking powder
- ½ teaspoon salt
- ½ cup (1 stick) butter or margarine
- 1⅓ cups sugar
- 1 egg
- 1 tablespoon cream
- 1½ teaspoons orange extract
- 1 egg yolk
- 1 tablespoon water
- ¼ cup finely chopped pistachio nuts
- 1½ teaspoons grated orange rind

1. Sift flour, baking powder and salt onto wax paper.
2. Beat butter or margarine and 1 cup of the sugar until fluffy in a large bowl with electric mixer at high speed; beat in egg, cream and orange extract.
3. Stir in flour mixture, a third at a time, blending well to make a soft dough. Chill several hours, or overnight, until firm enough to roll.
4. Roll out, a quarter at a time, ¼-inch thick, on a lightly floured pastry cloth or board. Cut into bell shapes with 2-inch cookie cutter. Place on greased large cookie sheets.
5. Mix egg yolk with water in a cup. Mix the remaining ⅓ cup sugar, pistachio nuts and grated orange rind in a second cup. Brush cookies with egg yolk mixture, then sprinkle with orange mixture.
6. Bake in moderate oven (350°) 10 minutes, or until firm but not brown. Remove carefully from cookie sheets to wire racks with spatula; cool completely. Store in metal tin.

FRUIT SPRITZ

Great for hungry little witches and goblins at trick-or-treating time.

Bake at 375° for 10 minutes.
Makes 10 dozen.

- 4½ cups all purpose flour
- 1 teaspoon baking powder
- Dash salt
- 1½ cups (3 sticks) butter or margarine
- 1 cup sugar
- 1 egg
- 2 tablespoons thawed frozen concentrated pineapple-orange juice
- Silver decorating candies
- Red and green decorating sugars

1. Sift flour, baking powder and salt onto wax paper.
2. Beat butter or margarine with sugar until fluffy in large bowl with electric mixer at high speed; beat in egg and pineapple-orange juice until well blended.
3. Stir in flour mixture, a quarter at a time, blending well to make a stiff dough.
4. Fit rosette, tree, or animal plate or disk onto cookie press; fill with dough. Press out, 1 inch apart, onto ungreased large cookie sheet. Decorate with silver candies or sprinkle with decorating sugars.
5. Bake in moderate oven (375°) 12 minutes, or until firm but not brown. Remove from cookie sheets to wire racks with spatula; cool completely. Store in metal tin.

FROSTED TAFFY STARS

They're like crispy shortbread with the rich flavor of old-fashioned molasses.

Bake at 325° for 15 minutes.
Makes 4 dozen.

- 1 cup (2 sticks) butter or margarine
- ½ cup light molasses
- 2 teaspoons vanilla
- 2 cups all purpose flour
- 1 cup 10X (confectioners' powdered) sugar
- 1 tablespoon water
- Silver candies

1. Beat butter or margarine with molasses in medium-size bowl with electric mixer at medium speed; stir in 1 teaspoon of the vanilla. Gradually blend in flour. Chill overnight.
2. Roll out, a small amount at a time, to ¼-inch thickness on lightly floured pastry cloth or board. Cut out with 2-inch cutter. Place on cookie sheets.
3. Bake in slow oven (325°) 15 minutes, or until firm. Remove from cookie sheets with spatula; cool completely on wire racks.
4. Blend 10X sugar, water, and remaining 1 teaspoon vanilla until smooth in small bowl. Frost cookies; decorate centers with silver candies. Store in tin between wax paper.

VENETIANS

Tiny, layered cake-cookies, striped like Venetian glass.

Bake at 350° for 15 minutes.
Makes 6 dozen.

- 4 eggs, separated
- 1 can (8 ounces) almond paste
- 1½ cups (3 sticks) butter or margarine, softened
- 1 cup sugar
- 1 teaspoon almond extract
- 2 cups all purpose flour
- ¼ teaspoon salt
- 10 drops green food coloring
- 8 drops red food coloring
- 1 jar (12 ounces) apricot preserves
- 2 squares semisweet chocolate

1. Grease three 13x9x2-inch pans; line with wax paper; grease again.
2. Beat egg whites with electric mixer until stiff peaks form in small bowl.
3. Break up almond paste in a large bowl with a fork. Add butter, sugar, egg yolks and almond extract. Beat with electric mixer at high speed, until fluffy. Blend in flour and salt.
4. Fold beaten egg whites into almond mixture with wire whip.
5. Remove 1 ½ cups batter; spread evenly into a prepared pan. Remove another 1 ½ cups batter and add the green food coloring; spread evenly into second prepared pan. Add red food coloring to remaining 1 ½ cups batter and spread into the last prepared pan.
6. Bake in a moderate oven (350°) 15 minutes, or just until edges are golden brown. (Note: Layers will be thin, only ¼-inch thick.)
7. Remove layers from pans immediately onto large wire racks. Cool thoroughly.
8. Place green layer on jelly roll pan. Heat apricot preserves; strain. Spread ½ of the warm preserves over green layer to edges; slide yellow layer on top; spread with remaining apricot preserves; slide pink layer, right-side up, onto yellow layer.
9. Cover with plastic wrap; weight down with a large wooden cutting board or heavy plate. Place in refrigerator overnight.
10. Melt chocolate over hot water in a small metal cup. Spread to edges of cake; let dry 30 minutes. Trim edges off cake. Cut into 1-inch squares.

MOLASSES COOKIES

Cheryl Kline won a blue ribbon at the N.Y. State Fair for her version of this favorite.

Bake at 350° for 8 minutes.
Makes 9 dozen.

- 4½ cups all purpose flour
- 2 teaspoons baking soda
- 1½ teaspons ground ginger
- ½ teaspoon ground cinnamon
- ⅛ teaspoon salt
- ⅓ cup water
- ½ cup vegetable shortening
- ¼ cup (½ stick) butter or margarine
- 1½ cups light molasses

1. Sift flour, baking soda, ginger, cinnamon and salt onto wax paper.
2. Combine water, shortening and butter or margarine in a medium-size saucepan. Heat just until fats melt; pour into a large bowl. Stir in molasses.
3. Add flour mixture, a third at a time, blending well to make a stiff dough. Cover bowl; chill several hours, or until firm enough to roll.
4. Roll out dough, a quarter at a time, about ⅛-inch thick, on a lightly floured pastry cloth or board. Cut out with a floured 2-inch cookie cutter. Place, 1 inch apart, on lightly greased cookie sheets. Reroll and cut out trimmings. Sprinkle with sugar.
5. Bake in moderate oven (350°) 8 minutes, or until firm. Remove from cookie sheets with spatula; cool completely on wire racks. Store in airtight metal container.

ALMOND PASTRY CRESCENTS

From Morocco come these melt-in-your-mouth morsels, where they are called "Kab el Ghzai" (Gazelle Horns).

Bake at 400° for 12 minutes.
Makes 4 dozen.

- 2¼ cups all purpose flour
- ½ teaspoon salt
- 1 cup (2 sticks) butter or margarine
- 4 tablespoons ice water
- 1 can (8 ounces) almond paste
- 1 egg
- 2 tablespoons granulated sugar
- ⅓ cup ground almonds (see page 60)
- ⅔ cup 10X (confectioners' powdered) sugar

1. Combine flour and salt in a medium-size bowl. Cut in butter or margarine with a pastry blender until mixture is crumbly. Add ice water, a tablespoon at a time; combine with a fork until mixture is moistened.
2. Shape pastry into a ball; wrap in wax paper. Refrigerate 1 hour.
3. Place almond paste in a small bowl; break up with a fork. Beat in egg, the 2 tablespoons of granulated sugar and ground almonds until mixture is thoroughly combined. (Mixture will be sticky.)
4. Turn almond mixture out onto a lightly floured pastry cloth or board. Shape into a ball with floured hands. Divide into thirds. Shape each third into a rope ½-inch thick and 16-inches long. (If mixture sticks, flour hands and surface lightly.) Cut each rope into 16 one-inch pieces; reserve.
5. Roll out pastry, a third at a time, to a 12-inch square on a lightly floured pastry cloth or board. Cut into 16 three-inch squares carefully with pastry wheel.
6. Place one piece of almond paste diagonally across one corner of each pastry square. Lift the point over the paste and roll, jelly roll fashion. Pinch the ends enclosing the almond filling. Curve the pastry into a crescent.
7. Place, 1 inch apart, on ungreased cookie sheet.
8. Bake in hot oven (400°) 12 minutes, or until edges of cookies just begin to brown.
9. Place 10X sugar in a pie plate or on large sheet of wax paper. Place warm cookies, upside down, a few at a time, into sugar and coat, turning once or twice.
10. Place cookies on wire racks to cool completely. Store in wax-paper-separated layers in an airtight tin. Sprinkle with additional 10X sugar before serving.

RASPBERRY SANDWICHES

These tiny cookies are sandwiched with tart preserves and brightly decorated.

Bake at 350° for 10 minutes.
Makes 3 dozen.

- 1 cup (2 sticks) butter or margarine
- ½ cup 10X(confectioners' powdered) sugar
- 1½ cups all purpose flour
- 1 teaspoon vanilla
- ½ cup walnuts or almonds, ground (see page 60)
- 1 cup red raspberry preserves

1. Beat butter or margarine and 10X sugar until well blended in a large bowl with electric mixer at high speed; stir in flour, vanilla and nuts.
2. Roll dough, a level teaspoonful at a time, into balls between palms of hands. Place, 2 inches apart, on a cookie sheet. Grease the bottom of a glass and dip in 10X sugar; press over each ball to make a 1-inch round.
3. Bake in moderate oven (350°) 10 minutes, or until golden around edges. Remove to wire racks; cool.
4. Spread bottoms of half of the cookies with raspberry preserves; top, sandwich-style, with remaining cookies, flat-side down. Sprinkle with 10X sugar just before serving.

MERRY CUTOUTS

Here's baking magic: Cut the same design in the center of each two cookies, then switch the centers for a treat with a difference.

Bake at 350° for 10 minutes.
Makes 4 dozen.

- 3½ cups all purpose flour
- 1 teaspoon baking powder
- ½ teaspoon salt
- 1 cup (2 sticks) butter or margarine
- 1½ cups sugar
- 2 eggs
- 1½ teaspoons vanilla
- ¼ teaspoon lemon extract
  Yellow, green, and red food colorings
- ¼ teaspoon almond extract
  Few drops peppermint extract
- ¼ teaspoon orange extract

1. Measure flour, baking powder and salt into sifter.
2. Beat butter or margarine with sugar until fluffy in large bowl with an electric mixer at high speed; beat in eggs and vanilla.
3. Sift in flour mixture, a third at a time, blending well to make a stiff dough. Divide into quarters and place in separate bowls.
4. Stir lemon extract and a few drops yellow food coloring into dough in one bowl; stir almond extract and a few drops green food coloring into second bowl; stir peppermint extract and a few drops red food coloring into third bowl; stir orange extract into fourth bowl.
5. Wrap each dough in wax paper or plastic wrap; chill several hours, or until firm enough to roll. (Overnight is best.)
6. Roll out half each of the yellow and green doughs, ¼-inch thick, on a lightly floured pastry cloth or board; cut out each with a 2½-inch round or fluted cutter, then cut a fancy shape from center of each with a 1-inch truffle cutter.
7. Place large cookies, 1 inch apart, on cookie sheets. Fit small yellow cutouts in centers of green cookies and small green cutouts in centers of yellow cookies. Repeat with remaining doughs.
8. Bake in moderate oven (350°) 10 minutes, or until firm. Remove from cookie sheets with spatula; cool on wire racks. Store in metal tin.

CHOCOLATE SNOWBALLS

Chocolate wrapped in a snowy coating.

Bake at 350° for 8 minutes.
Makes 5 dozen.

- 2 cups all purpose flour
- 1 teaspoon baking powder
- ½ teaspoon salt
- ¼ teaspoon baking soda
- ¾ cup (1½ sticks) butter or margarine
- ¾ cup firmly packed brown sugar
- 2 squares unsweetened chocolate, melted
- 1 egg
- 1 teaspoon vanilla
- ¼ cup milk
  10X sugar

1. Measure flour, baking powder, salt and baking soda into sifter.
2. Beat butter or margarine with brown sugar until fluffy in medium-size bowl with an electric mixer at high speed; beat in melted chocolate, egg, vanilla and milk. Sift in dry ingredients, a little at a time, blending to make a stiff dough. Chill overnight, or until firm enough to handle.
3. Roll dough, a teaspoonful at a time, into marble-size balls between palms of hands; place, about 2 inches apart, on cookie sheets.
4. Bake in moderate oven (350°) 8 minutes, or until tops are crackled. Remove carefully from cookie sheets; roll in 10X sugar while still hot. Cool on wire racks, then roll again in 10X sugar, coating generously.

MEDALLIONS

One batch of dough makes enough for the base cookies, plus fancy colored toppers.

Bake at 375° for 10 to 15 minutes.
Makes 5 dozen.

- 4¼ cups all purpose flour
- ½ teaspoon salt
- 1½ cups (3 sticks) butter or margarine
- 1 cup sugar
- 1 egg
- 1 teaspoon vanilla
- ½ teaspoon almond extract
  Red and green food colorings
  Almond Frosting (recipe follows)

1. Sift 4 cups of the flour and salt onto wax paper.
2. Beat butter or margarine with sugar until fluffy in large bowl with an electric mixer at high speed; beat in egg and vanilla. Stir in flour mixture, a third at a time, blending well to make a soft dough.
3. Divide dough in half; stir remaining ¼ cup flour into one half for making rounds for base; reserve. Divide remaining half in two equal parts; place each in a small bowl.
4. Blend ¼ teaspoon of the almond extract and enough red food coloring into dough in one bowl to tint a delicate pink, and remaining ¼ teaspoon almond extract and enough green food coloring into dough in second bowl to tint light green. Chill tinted doughs 30 minutes.
5. Roll out plain dough, ⅛-inch thick, on a lightly floured pastry cloth or board; cut into rounds with a floured 2½-inch plain or fluted cutter. Place, 1 inch apart, on cookie sheets.
6. Fit star plate or disk on cookie press; fill with pink dough; press out onto ungreased cookie sheets. Fit press with sunburst plate or disk; repeat with green dough.
7. Bake in moderate oven (375°) 10 minutes for plain cookies and 15 minutes for tinted ones, or until firm. Remove carefully from cookie sheets with spatula; cool completely on wire racks.
8. Place about ¼ teaspoonful ALMOND FROSTING in the center of each plain cookie; top with a tinted one to make a sandwich. Let stand until frosting sets.

ALMOND FROSTING: Makes about ½ cup. Mix ¾ cup 10X (confectioners' powdered) sugar with 2 teaspoons water, 1 teaspoon vanilla, and ¼ teaspoon almond extract until smooth in a small bowl with wire whip.

BASIC BAKING EQUIPMENT

1. Look for heavy-gauge metal round, square and spring form baking and pie pans.
2. An electric hand mixer with powerful motor is essential for good beating.
3. A selection of ceramic and metal bowls will make beating and mixing jobs go more easily. A nest of dry measuring cups also make good tiny pans for melting a bit of butter or chocolate in a skillet over simmering water.
4. Cookie cutters come in a variety of sizes and shapes. Become a collector of special designs and unusual shapes.

RAGGEDY TOP BARS

Cornflakes, peanuts and butterscotch pieces make a great-tasting cookie that's high in nutrition, as well.

Bake at 350° for 30 minutes.
Makes 6 dozen.

  1 cup (2 sticks) butter or margarine
  1 cup firmly packed brown sugar
  1 egg
  2 teaspoons vanilla
1¾ cups all purpose flour
  ½ teaspoon salt
  1 package (6 ounces)
     butterscotch-flavored pieces
  ⅓ cup light corn syrup
  2 tablespoons butter or margarine
  1 cup chopped peanuts
  ½ cup cornflakes

1. Beat the 1 cup butter or margarine and brown sugar until fluffy in a large bowl with electric mixer at medium speed; beat in egg and 1 teaspoon of the vanilla.
2. Turn mixer speed to low and blend in flour and salt. Spread evenly in a 15x10x1-inch jelly roll pan with a spatula.
3. Bake in moderate oven (350°) 25 minutes, or until golden.
4. While cookie base bakes, combine butterscotch pieces, corn syrup, the 2 tablespoons butter or margarine and remaining 1 teaspoon vanilla in the top of a double boiler; heat, stirring several times, until butterscotch pieces melt and mixture is smooth; stir in peanuts and cereal.
5. Spread mixture over cookie base. Bake 5 minutes longer, or until topping is set. Remove pan to wire rack and cool 15 minutes. Cut into 72 bars. Cool completely before removing. Store in metal tin.

WINE COOKIES

These won a blue ribbon for Mrs. Frances Morgenstern at the N.Y. State Fair.

Bake at 400° for 8 minutes
Makes 5 dozen.

2½ cups all purpose flour
  1 teaspoon baking powder
  1 teaspoon salt
  ½ cup (1 stick) butter or margarine
  1 cup sugar
  2 eggs
  2 tablespoons cream sherry
    Granulated sugar
    Sherry Frosting (recipe follows)

1. Sift flour, baking powder and salt onto wax paper.
2. Beat butter or margarine, sugar and eggs in large bowl with an electric mixer at high speed 3 minutes, or until

fluffy; blend in sherry.

3. Stir in flour mixture to make a stiff dough; wrap in wax paper; chill 3 hours, or until firm enough to roll.

4. Roll dough, half at a time, to a 1/8-inch thickness on a lightly floured pastry cloth or board. Cut into rounds with a 3-inch cutter.

5. Place, 1 inch apart, on ungreased cookie sheets; sprinkle with granulated sugar.

6. Bake in hot oven (400°) 8 minutes, or until cookies are lightly browned around edges.

7. Remove to wire racks with spatula; cool. Frost with SHERRY FROSTING.
BAKER'S TIP: For extra wine flavor, layer unfrosted cookies in a metal box; top with wax paper; moisten a paper towel with sherry and place on top of cookies, then cover tightly. Let cookies remain overnight in tin.

SHERRY FROSTING

Makes about 1 1/2 cups.

- 1/2 cup (1 stick) butter or margarine OR: 1/2 cup shortening
- 2 cups sifted 10X (confectioners' powdered) sugar
- 2 tablespoons cream sherry
- Yellow food coloring

Combine butter or margarine or shortening, 10X sugar and sherry in a medium-size bowl; beat with electric mixer at high speed until light and smooth. Tint a pale yellow with a few drops yellow food coloring.

HOLIDAY BONBONS

One of the easiest cookies to make: The cookie press does all the fanciful shaping.

Bake at 375° for 8 minutes.
Makes 10 dozen.

- 1 1/2 cups (3 sticks) butter or margarine
- 1 cup sugar
- 3 egg yolks
- 1 teaspoon vanilla
- 1 teaspoon lemon extract
- 1/4 teaspoon salt
- 3 1/2 cups all purpose flour
  Red and green food colorings
  Colored sugars
  Cinnamon red-hot candies
- 1/2 cup semi-sweet chocolate pieces
- 1 teaspoon vegetable shortening
- 1/4 cup chopped walnuts
  Ornamental Frosting (recipe, page 48)

1. Beat butter or margarine, sugar and egg yolks in large bowl with electric mixer at high speed 3 minutes, or until fluffy. Blend in vanilla, lemon extract and salt. Stir in flour gradually to make a soft dough.

2. Divide dough into 3 parts; tint one part pink with red food coloring and another with green food coloring.

3. Fit your favorite plate or disk onto cookie press; fill press with one color dough. Press dough out onto ungreased cookie sheets. (Rinse out cookie press before filling with another color dough.) Decorate some cookies with colored sugars or cinnamon red-hots before baking.

4. Bake in moderate oven (375°) 8 minutes, or until firm; remove from cookie steets to wire racks with spatula; cool completely.

5. Melt chocolate and shortening in top of a double boiler over hot water; spread on top of some of the cookies and sprinkle with chopped walnuts. Decorate other cookies with OR-NAMENTAL FROSTING, colored sugars and cinnamon red-hots. Store between wax paper layers in metal tin.

HEART COOKIES

A charming Valentine's Day surprise, decorated with your own special message.

Bake at 350° for 10 minutes.
Makes 1 dozen large hearts.

- 3/4 cup honey
- 1/4 cup (1/2 stick) butter or margarine
- 4 1/2 cups all purpose flour
- 1 teaspoon baking soda
- 1 teaspoon salt
- 1/2 teaspoon ground nutmeg
- 2 eggs
- 3/4 cup sugar
- 1/2 cup ground almonds (see page 60)
- 1/3 cup finely chopped candied citron
- 1 tablespoon grated lemon rind
  Simple Sugar Glaze (recipe follows)
  Red food coloring
  Ornamental Frosting (recipe, page 48)

1. Heat honey and butter or margarine in small saucepan just until mixture comes to boiling; cool.

2. Sift flour, baking soda, salt and nutmeg onto wax paper.

3. Beat eggs until fluffy in large bowl with electric mixer at high speed; gradually beat in sugar; continue to beat until very light. Slowly stir in warm honey mixture. Stir in almonds, citron and lemon rind. Gradually stir in flour mixture to make a very stiff dough. Wrap in wax paper; chill overnight.

4. Roll out dough, a quarter at a time, on lightly floured pastry cloth or board to a 1/4-inch thickness; cut into heart shapes with 5-inch cookie cutter. Place, 1 inch apart, on lightly greased cookie sheets.

5. Bake in moderate oven (350°) 10 minutes, or until light brown. Remove from cookie sheets to wire racks; cool completely. Store in airtight container until ready to glaze and decorate.

6. Make SIMPLE SUGAR GLAZE. Color pink or red. Place cookies in a single layer on a wire rack set over wax paper to catch drippings. Spoon glaze over each cookie to cover top and edges completely. Let stand until glaze hardens, about 1 hour.

7. Make ORNAMENTAL FROSTING, then pipe through the #3 writing tip of a cake decorator onto cookies, making your own design and special message. Let decorations dry completely, then wrap in clear plastic.

SIMPLE SUGAR GLAZE

Makes enough to frost 1 dozen large heart cookies.

- 2 cups 10X (confectioners' powdered) sugar
- 1/4 cup milk
- 1 teaspoon vegetable shortening

Combine sugar and milk in a medium-size bowl; stir with a rubber spatula until smooth; stir in shortening until completely blended. Keep bowl covered with damp paper towel to keep glaze from drying. (This glaze tastes great on a variety of cookies.)

DESSERTS IN A HURRY (CHAPTER 4)

ORANGE SNOWBALLS

They're like a snowfall in an orange grove.

Makes 3 1/2 dozen.

- 1 package (10 ounces) shortbread cookies, crushed
- 1 cup flaked coconut
- 2/3 cup 10X (confectioners' powdered) sugar
- 1/2 cup thawed frozen concentrate for orange juice
  10X sugar

1. Mix cookie crumbs, coconut, and the 2/3 cup 10X sugar in a medium-size bowl.

2. Stir in orange juice until well blended.

3. Roll mixture, a teaspoonful at a time, into balls between palms of hands; roll each in 10X sugar in a pie plate to coat generously. Chill at least 2 hours to blend flavors.

CARAWAY CAKES

A box of pancake mix can be the start of quick and easy cookies.

Bake at 350° for 6 minutes.
Makes 6 dozen.

1½ cups pancake mix
½ cup sugar
1 tablespoon caraway seeds
1 egg
½ cup canned applesauce
2 tablespoons melted butter or margarine
¼ cup sugar
1 teaspoon grated lemon rind

1. Combine pancake mix, the ½ cup sugar and caraway seeds in medium-size bowl.
2. Beat egg slightly in small bowl with a fork; blend in applesauce and melted butter or margarine; stir into dry ingredients; mix well.
3. Drop by half teaspoonfuls, 1 inch apart, on greased cookie sheets; sprinkle mixture of ¼ cup sugar and lemon rind on top.
4. Bake in moderate oven (350°) 6 minutes, or until edges are slightly browned; cool cookies 1 minute, then remove with spatula and cool completely on wire racks. Store in metal tin with tight cover.

CAREFREE DROP COOKIES

With a package of cake mix on the pantry shelf, you can have a batch in the oven in minutes. Photo is on pages 1, 2 and 84.

Bake at 375° for 10 minutes.
Makes 6 dozen.

1 package (about 18 ounces) yellow cake mix
1 cup peanut butter
2 eggs
¼ cup (½ stick) butter or margarine, softened
⅓ cup water
2 cups ready-to-eat rice cereal
1 cup raisins

1. Combine half the package of cake mix with peanut butter, eggs, butter or margarine and water in large bowl of electric mixer.
2. Beat with mixer at high speed for 2 minutes. Stir in remaining cake mix, rice cereal and raisins with a wooden spoon until well blended and smooth. Drop by teaspoonfuls, 2 inches apart, onto cookie sheets.
3. Bake in moderate oven (375°) 10 minutes, or until golden. Remove carefully to wire racks with spatula. Cool completely.
Suggested Variation: CAREFREE BARS —Substitute 1 package (about 18

ounces) white cake mix for yellow. Spread dough in a greased 15x10x1-inch jelly roll pan. Bake at 375° for 20 minutes, or until golden. Cool in pan on wire rack 15 minutes. Cut into 40 bars. Cool completely.

SPANGLES

Applesauce and spice give old-time flavor to this time-saving recipe.

Bake at 350° for 6 minutes.
Makes 4 dozen.

1½ cups buttermilk pancake mix
½ cup sugar
¼ teaspoon ground nutmeg
¼ teaspoon ground cinnamon
1 egg
½ cup canned applesauce
2 tablespoons melted butter or margarine
Multicolored sprinkles

1. Combine pancake mix, sugar, nutmeg and cinnamon in a medium-size bowl.
2. Beat egg slightly in small bowl; blend in applesauce and melted butter or margarine; stir into dry ingredients; mix well.
3. Drop by teaspoonfuls, 1 inch apart, on greased cookie sheets; decorate tops with multicolored sprinkles.
4. Bake in moderate oven (350°) 6 minutes, or until edges are slightly browned; cool cookies 1 minute, then remove with spatula and cool on wire racks. Store in a metal tin.

MACE-NUT DROPS

Surprise Dad and the kids with this brown-bag cookie special.

Bake at 375° for 8 minutes.
Makes 5 dozen.

2 cups biscuit mix
1 cup firmly packed brown sugar
1 teaspoon ground mace
¼ cup vegetable shortening
1 egg
⅓ cup milk
1 cup peanuts, chopped

1. Combine biscuit mix, sugar and mace in medium-size bowl; cut in shortening with pastry blender.
2. Blend in egg and milk; sprinkle peanuts on dough and partly fold in. (If peanuts are very salty, rub between paper towels before chopping.)
3. Drop by teaspoonfuls, 1 inch apart, onto greased cookie sheets.
4. Bake in moderate oven (375°) 8 minutes, or until golden brown; remove with spatula and cool completely on wire racks.

COCONUT TRINKETS

Part candy and part cookie, they go together and bake fast. Recipe makes lots, too.

Bake at 350° for 15 minutes.
Makes 5 dozen.

2 packages (4 ounces each) sweet cooking chocolate
1 cup chopped walnuts
1 egg
½ cup sugar
1 can (3½ ounces) flaked coconut
8 candied red cherries

1. Heat chocolate in a 9x9x2-inch baking pan, while oven heats, 5 minutes, or just until soft. Spread in an even layer; sprinkle walnuts on top, pressing in lightly.
2. Beat egg until foamy in small bowl with electric mixer at low speed; beat in sugar until well blended; mix in coconut. Spread evenly on top of chocolate-walnut layer.
3. Cut candied cherries into eighths; place in even rows on top.
4. Bake in moderate oven (350°) 15 minutes, or just until topping is set.
5. Cool in pan on a wire rack; cut into 1-inch squares, but leave in pan. Chill until ready to serve, then cut again into bars and remove. Return remaining bars to refrigerator.

PEANUT CRESCENT BARS

Mrs. Millie Snow of Bloomfield Hills, Michigan won a trip to the Pillsbury Bake-Off® in Boston with this recipe. The photograph is on pages 1 and 84.

Bake at 375° for 25 minutes.
Makes 40 bars.

1 can (8 ounces) refrigerated crescent dinner rolls
1 package (3 ounces) cream cheese
⅔ cup peanut butter
2½ cups 10X (confectioners' powdered) sugar
½ teaspoon vanilla
1 cup coarsely chopped salted peanuts
1 package (6 ounces) semi-sweet chocolate pieces

1. Separate crescent rolls into 2 large pieces. Press into the bottom of a 15x10x1-inch jelly roll pan, sealing perforations while pressing out.
2. Combine cream cheese and peanut butter in a large bowl until smooth with a wooden spoon. Stir 10X sugar and vanilla into mixture until smooth. Spread over dough; sprinkle with nuts.
3. Bake in moderate oven (375°) 25 minutes, or until golden brown;

sprinkle chocolate pieces over; stir lightly to spread melting chocolate. Cool in pan on wire rack 15 minutes; cut into 5 strips, lengthwise, and 8 strips, crosswise, to make 40 bars. Cool completely.

WALNUT STICKS

A delicious, crunchy cookie made from piecrust mix and topped with nuts and spices. Perfect for the picnic basket or a child's lunchbox.

Bake at 425° for 7 minutes.
Makes 5 dozen.

- 1 package piecrust mix
- ¼ cup apricot nectar
- ⅓ cup very finely chopped walnuts
- 3 tablespoons sugar
- ¾ teaspoon ground cinnamon

1. Prepare piecrust mix with apricot nectar instead of water, following label directions; divide in half. Roll out, half at a time, on a lightly floured pastry cloth or board to a 12x7-inch rectangle.
2. Mix walnuts, sugar and cinnamon in a small bowl; sprinkle half over each pastry rectangle; press in firmly with rolling pin. Cut each rectangle lengthwise into 1-inch-wide strips, then crosswise into quarters. Place on cookie sheets.
3. Bake in hot oven (425°) 7 minutes, or until golden. Remove carefully from cookie sheets to wire racks with spatula; cool completely. Store between layers of wax paper in a metal container with a tight-fitting lid.

TOASTY MACAROONS

Would you believe, a cookie without any flour? These are made with coconut, instead.

Bake at 325° for 15 minutes.
Makes 3 dozen.

- 2 cups flaked coconut
- ⅔ cup sweetened condensed milk (not evaporated)
- 1 teaspoon rum extract
- ¼ teaspoon ground ginger
  Red and green candied cherries, sliced

1. Combine coconut, sweetened condensed milk, rum extract and ginger in a medium-size bowl. Stir mixture until well blended.
2. Drop by teaspoonfuls onto foil-lined large cookie sheet. Garnish each cookie with a slice of candied cherry.
3. Bake in slow oven (325°) 15 minutes, or until macaroons are firm. Remove from cookie sheet to wire racks with spatula; cool completely.

SWEETHEART TEACAKES

Just two bites—and these jam-filled dainties are gone! Perfect for a dinner party, or anytime you want a special dessert.

Bake at 350° for 20 minutes.
Makes 4 dozen.

- 1 package (about 18 ounces) yellow cake mix
- 1 package (about 7 ounces) vanilla-flavored creamy frosting mix
- 1 cup apricot jam
  Red cinnamon candies

1. Grease a 15x10x1-inch jelly roll pan; line with greased wax paper.
2. Prepare cake mix, following label directions; spread batter evenly into prepared pan.
3. Bake in moderate oven (350°) 20 minutes, or until center springs back when lightly pressed with fingertip. Cool slightly on wire rack; remove from pan; peel off paper; cool.
4. Set cake flat on cutting board or counter top; cut out 48 tiny rounds with a 1½-inch cutter. Split each round and put together with jam. (Use cake trimmings for family nibbles.)
5. Prepare frosting mix, following label directions; spread on tops of cakes; decorate each with a red cinnamon candy.

HIMBEER BISCUIT SANDWICHES

Raspberry and chocolate team up to create a fancy-looking cookie from pantry-shelf ingredients.

Makes about 2½ dozen.

- 1 package (11 ounces) plain tea biscuits
- ¼ cup seedless raspberry jam
- 1 teaspoon sweet sherry
- 2 teaspoons instant coffee
- ¼ cup boiling water
- 2 packages (4 ounces each) German sweet chocolate, broken into pieces
- 1 tablespoon vegetable shortening

1. Place half of the biscuits, bottom-side up, on wire racks.
2. Melt preserves in a small saucepan over low heat, stirring constantly; add sherry and blend well.
3. Spread ¼ teaspoon jam over each biscuit on wire rack; cover with remaining biscuits.
4. Dissolve instant coffee in boiling water in a small saucepan; add German chocolate and vegetable shortening; place over low heat, stirring often, until chocolate is melted and mixture is creamy; keep warm.
5. Dip ends of biscuit sandwiches,

one at a time, into chocolate mixture; place on wire racks. Allow chocolate to become firm before serving.
BAKER'S TIP: These cookies soften on standing, so make them just before serving time.

RUM-WALNUT COOKIES

A cross between cookie and confection; great with milk, tea or coffee.

Makes 20 cookies.

- 20 packaged shortbread cookies
- 1 package (6 ¾ ounces) caramels
- 1 tablespoon butter or margarine
- 1 tablespoon rum
- 1 package (6 ounces) semi-sweet chocolate pieces
- 1 tablespoon vegetable shortening
- 2 tablespoons hot water or coffee
  Walnut halves

1. Place cookies, right-side up, on wire rack.
2. Combine caramels and butter or margarine in small saucepan; heat slowly, stirring constantly, until caramels melt; stir in rum.
3. Spoon warm caramel over cookies; allow to set 10 minutes.
4. Combine chocolate pieces, vegetable shortening and hot water or coffee in small saucepan; heat, stirring often, until chocolate melts and mixture is creamy.
5. Drop a dab of chocolate mixture over caramel on cookies; press in walnut halves; cool completely on wire rack before placing in metal tin with tight-fitting lid.

PEANUT-CHOCOLATE DROPS

These no-bake cookes can be mixed together in about 10 minutes.

Makes 5 dozen.

- 1 package (12 ounces) semi-sweet chocolate pieces
- 1 can (14 ounces) sweetened condensed milk (not evaporated)
- 2 cups oven-toasted rice cereal (see Cook's Guide)
- 1 cup salted peanuts

1. Melt chocolate pieces over hot water in the top of a double boiler; stir in condensed milk; remove double boiler from water.
2. Stir in rice cereal and peanuts until well blended. Drop by teaspoonfuls onto wax-paper-lined cookie sheets. Chill at least 2 hours, or until firm.
3. Remove with spatula from wax paper; store between layers of wax paper in a loosely covered bowl at room temperature.

COFFEE CRISPS

Piecrust mix and instant coffee make these sugar-topped wafers.

Bake at 400° for 8 minutes.
Makes 4 dozen.

- 1 **package piecrust mix**
- ¾ **cup sugar**
- 2 **tablespoons instant coffee powder**
- 1 **teaspoon baking powder**
- 1 **egg**
- 1 **teaspoon vanilla**
- 1 **tablespoon instant coffee powder**
- 1 **tablespoon sugar**

1. Combine piecrust mix, the ¾ cup sugar, 2 tablespoons instant coffee powder and baking powder in medium-size bowl; stir in egg and vanilla, mixing well to form a very stiff dough. (If dough seems dry and crumbly, knead a few times until smooth.)
2. Shape into a roll about 9-inches long on wax paper; wrap and chill until very firm.
3. Unwrap roll; slice into thin rounds with sharp knife. Place, 1 inch apart, on cookie sheets.
4. Mix the 1 tablespoon instant coffee powder and sugar in cup; sprinkle evenly over cookies.
5. Bake in hot oven (400°) 8 minutes, or until very lightly browned around edge. Remove from cookie sheets with spatula; cool on wire racks.

BAKING BASICS

MELTING TIPS

- If you don't have a double boiler, place small saucepan in a skillet of simmering, not boiling, water.
- Use a double boiler when melting chocolate, making SEVEN-MINUTE FROSTING, or dissolving gelatin in a small amount of liquid.
- Chocolate squares and pieces, shortening and butter may be melted over very low heat in a small heavy saucepan; stir constantly to prevent scorching.
- You can also melt chocolate squares, still individually wrapped, in top of double boiler; carefully lift and scrape out chocolate. Leaving them wrapped cuts down on pot washing time.
- Cool melted ingredients before adding to other mixtures, unless recipe states otherwise.

POPCORN SQUARES

Here's a no-bake cookie that all the family is sure to love.

Makes 48 bars.

- 1 **package (12 ounces) semi-sweet chocolate pieces**
- 1 **jar (7 ounces) marshmallow cream (see Cook's Guide)**
- ¼ **cup light corn syrup**
- 6 **cups unsalted popcorn**

1. Combine chocolate pieces, marshmallow cream and corn syrup in a large saucepan. Heat slowly, stirring constantly, until chocolate melts; add popcorn and toss with wooden spoon until well blended.
2. Pack into a buttered 9x9x2-inch pan. Allow to stand at room temperature for 2 hours. Cut into 48 bars.

COCONUT-LEMON SQUARES

"Sweet and sour" describes these treats perfectly. They're great with a cup of hot tea or coffee. The photograph appears on pages 1 and 84.

Bake at 350° for 15 minutes,
then at 350° for 30 minutes.
Makes 16 bars.

- 1 **cup biscuit mix**
- ¼ **cup sugar**
- ⅓ **cup butter or margarine, softened**
- 2 **eggs**
- 1 **cup firmly packed brown sugar**
- 1 **cup flaked coconut**
- ½ **cup chopped pecans**
- 1 **teaspoon grated lemon rind**
- 1 **tablespoon lemon juice**
  Lemon Glaze (recipe follows)

1. Combine biscuit mix and sugar in a medium-size bowl; cut butter or margarine into mixture with a pastry blender until crumbly. Press into an 8x8x2-inch baking pan.
2. Bake in moderate oven (350°) 15 minutes, or until golden.
3. Beat eggs lightly in a medium-size bowl with a wire whip; beat in sugar until well blended; stir in coconut, pecans, lemon rind and lemon juice until smooth. Pour over baked layer in pan.
4. Bake 30 minutes longer, or until top is golden. Remove pan to wire rack; spread with LEMON GLAZE while still hot, to coat completely. Cool 15 minutes; cut into 2-inch squares. Store in metal container.

LEMON GLAZE: Makes about ¼ cup. Stir 1 teaspoon lemon rind and 1 teaspoon lemon juice into ⅔ cup 10X (confectioners' powdered) sugar in a small bowl until smooth.

VIENNESE SNACKS

Rich morsels of pound cake with apricot glaze and luscious frosting.

Makes 1½ dozen.

- ½ **cup apricot preserves**
- ¼ **cup granulated sugar**
- 7 **tablespoons water**
- 1 **package (10 ounces), frozen pound cake, thawed**
- ¼ **cup cocoa powder (not a mix)**
- 2 **tablespoons dark corn syrup**
- 2 **tablespoons butter or margarine**
- 2 **cups 10X (confectioners' powdered) sugar**

1. Combine apricot preserves, granulated sugar and 4 tablespoons water in a small saucepan; heat until mixture is bubbling, then cook 2 minutes; press through a sieve.
2. Cut cake in thirds both crosswise and lengthwise to make nine pieces, then cut each piece in half to make 18 little bar-shaped cakes. Place on racks over wax paper. Spoon apricot glaze over tops.
3. Combine cocoa, remaining 3 tablespoons water, corn syrup, and butter or margarine in a small saucepan; heat slowly, stirring constantly, until butter is melted. Remove from heat; beat in 10X sugar. Spoon over cakes several times. Sprinkle tops with sliced almonds, if you wish. Store between layers of wax paper in metal tin.

BOURBON BALLS

No baking, no bother, for these deep, dark chocolate confections made merry with a touch of mellow bourbon.

Makes 3 dozen.

- 1 **package (6 ounces) semi-sweet chocolate pieces**
- 3 **tablespoons light corn syrup**
- ¼ **cup bourbon or orange juice**
- ½ **cup sugar**
- 1¼ **cups crushed vanilla wafer cookies (about 36)**
- 1 **cup finely chopped pecans or walnuts**
- 1 **container (4 ounces) chocolate decorating sprinkles**

1. Melt chocolate pieces in top of a double boiler over simmering water; remove from heat. Blend in corn syrup and bourbon or orange juice; stir in sugar, vanilla wafer cookies and pecans until well combined.
2. Roll mixture, a rounded teaspoonful at a time, into balls between palms of hands, Roll balls in chocolate sprinkles to coat generously, pressing firmly as you roll. Place in a jelly roll pan; cover; chill several hours.

ORANGE GUMDROPS

*Mix gumdrops with cake mix and presto—
you have colorful drop cookies.*

Bake at 350° for 10 minutes.
Makes 5 dozen.

½ cup (1 stick) butter or margarine
2 eggs
1 package (about 18 ounces) yellow
cake mix
1 tablespoon grated orange rind
½ cup orange juice
2 cups gumdrops, cut in small
pieces

1. Beat butter or margarine until soft
in large bowl of electric mixer at high
speed; beat in eggs until well blended.
2. Lower speed and blend in cake
mix, orange rind and orange juice
until smooth. Stir in gumdrops with
a wooden spoon.
3. Drop by teaspoonfuls, 2 inches
apart, on cookie sheets.
4. Bake in moderate oven (350°) 10
minutes, or until golden. Remove to
wire racks with spatula to cool. Store
in metal tin with tight lid.
BAKER'S TIP: For greater juice
yield, roll orange on counter before
squeezing.

MARSHMALLOW-PECAN BARS

*Bring a pan of these delectable bars to your
next church bake-sale. They'll go fast!*

Bake at 350° for 45 minutes.
Makes 24 bars.

3 cups biscuit mix
1 cup sugar
2 eggs
½ cup (1 stick) butter or margarine,
softened
1 cup milk
1 tablespoon vanilla
2 envelopes (1 ounce each) liquid
unsweetened chocolate
1 package (about 1 pound)
chocolate frosting mix
¼ cup lukewarm water
1 cup pecan halves
1 cup tiny marshmallows

1. Combine biscuit mix, sugar, eggs,
¼ cup of the butter or margarine,
milk and vanilla in a large bowl. Beat
at low speed with electric mixer until
well blended, then beat at medium
speed for 4 minutes, scraping bowl
several times.
2. Spread half the batter in a greased-
and-floured 13x9x2-inch baking pan.
3. Stir chocolate into remaining batter in bowl; drop by spoonfuls onto
batter in pan; draw a knife through
batters several times to marble.
4. Bake in moderate oven (350°) 45

minutes, or until top springs back
when lightly pressed with fingertip.
Cool in pan on a wire rack.
5. Combine frosting mix, lukewarm
water and remaining ¼ cup butter or
margarine in a medium-size bowl;
beat, following label directions. Fold
in pecans and marshmallows; spread
over top. Let stand until frosting is
firm. Cut into 24 bars. (Bar cookies
store well in pan in which they are
baked, with plastic wrap, then
aluminum foil, covering them.)

FROSTED PEANUT BUTTER
CRISPIES

*These cookie-candies are made with rice
cereal and need no baking.*

Makes 36 bars.

5 cups chocolate-flavored crisp
rice cereal (see Cook's Guide)
⅓ cup peanut butter
18 large marshmallows
2 tablespoons butter or margarine
5 bars (1 ounce each) milk
chocolate

1. Pour chocolate cereal into a large
bowl.
2. Melt peanut butter, marshmallows
and butter or margarine in top of
double boiler over simmering water,
stirring often.
3. Pour peanut butter mixture over
cereal and blend in with well buttered
hands until well blended. Pack into
a buttered 9x9x2-inch pan.
4. Lay candy bars in a single layer
over cereal layer. Heat in a warm oven
2 minutes, or just until candy melts;
spread over with a spatula. Chill until
chocolate firms. Cut into 36
bars.Store in baking pan or between
layers of wax paper in metal tin.

GREEK BUTTER COOKIES

*Three ingredients go into this recipe and it
only takes seven minutes to make! The
cookies improve on standing.*

Makes 20 cookies.

20 packaged shortbread cookies
2 tablespoons brandy
¼ cup 10X (confectioners'
powdered) sugar

1. Place wire rack over wax paper or
cookie sheet; arrange cookies on rack.
2. Sprinkle brandy over cookies, using small spoon; allow to soak in for
5 minutes.
3. Sift 10X sugar over brandy-soaked
cookies, coating well, and store in
metal container.

NO-BAKE CHOCOLATE
TRUFFLES

*Call them cookies or candies, everyone just
wants more of these tasty chocolate treats.
You can make a batch in minutes.*

Makes 6 dozen.

1 package (6 ounces) semi-sweet
chocolate pieces
½ cup orange juice
3 tablespoons light rum
1 package (8½ ounces) chocolate
wafer cookies, crushed
2 cups 10X (confectioners'
powdered) sugar
1 cup very finely chopped walnuts
Chocolate decorating sprinkles
Red candied cherries

1. Melt chocolate pieces in top of a
double boiler over simmering water;
remove from heat. Blend in orange
juice and rum; stir in chocolate cookie
crumbs, 10X sugar, and nuts until well
mixed. Cover; chill in refrigerator
about 2 hours, or until mixture is stiff
enough to handle.
2. Roll dough, a rounded teaspoonful
at a time, into balls between palms of
hands. Roll balls in chocolate sprinkles to coat generously, pressing firmly as you roll. Place on a tray; cover
with aluminum foil; chill several
hours or overnight. Store between
layers of wax paper in metal tin with
a tight-fitting lid.

MOCHA ICEBOX ROLL

*This quickie has been the hostess' festive,
yet simple, dessert since the 1930's. It
doesn't require baking.*

Makes 6 servings.

1 cup heavy cream
2 tablespoons cocoa powder (not a
mix)
2 tablespoons sugar
1½ teaspoons instant coffee powder
1 package (8½ ounces) thin
chocolate cookies
1 square unsweetened chocolate,
grated

1. Combine cream, cocoa, sugar and
coffee in small bowl of electric mixer;
beat with mixer at medium speed until
mixture mounds softly.
2. Put chocolate cookies together
with half the cream mixture in stacks
of 4 or 5 cookies. Arrange stacks on
edge on serving plate to make one
long roll. Frost outside with remaining whipped cream. Garnish roll with
grated chocolate.
3. Refrigerate several hours or overnight. To serve, cut roll diagonally
into slices.

EUROPE'S CLASSICS (CHAPTER 5)

KRAEMMERHUSE

When served in Denmark, these crisp cookie cones are usually heaped with cream and topped with strawberry preserves.

Bake at 425° for 3 minutes.
Makes 18 cones.

  2 egg whites
¼ cup (½ stick) butter or margarine
¼ cup sugar
½ cup all purpose flour
  Snowy Vanilla Cream (recipe follows)
  Strawberry preserves

1. Beat egg whites until they stand in firm peaks in a small bowl with electric mixer at high speed.
2. Beat butter or margarine with sugar until fluffy in a medium-size bowl. Stir in flour, then fold in beaten egg whites, a third at a time, until no streaks of white or yellow remain. (Be sure to fold in egg whites slowly so they'll stay fluffy.)
3. Drop batter, a rounded teaspoonful for each cone, on a well buttered cookie sheet; spread into a 5-inch circle. (Make only two at a time, leaving about 2 inches between edges, as wafers must be rolled while hot.)
4. Bake in hot oven (425°) 3 minutes, or just until golden brown at edges of wafers.
5. Loosen each from cookie sheet with a spatula, but do not remove; pick up at edge with fingers, then roll quickly into a cone. (Hold one end loosely for top, twisting the other end to make a point.) Place, pointed end down in a bottle with a neck about 1-inch wide. (A baby bottle, spice or salad-dressing bottle is just the right size.) Let stand 1 to 2 minutes, or until cool enough to hold its shape, then cool completely on a wire rack. Repeat to make 18 cones.
6. To serve: Place cones on a serving plate; spoon SNOWY VANILLA CREAM into a bowl and strawberry preserves into a second bowl. Let each guest fill a cone, first with cream and then with preserves, in true Danish style.
BAKER'S TIP: Cones keep perfectly for a week or more if packed carefully and stored in a container with a tight-fitting lid.

SNOWY VANILLA CREAM: Makes 2 cups. Beat 1 cup heavy cream with 2 tablespoons 10X (confectioners' powdered) sugar and ½ teaspoon vanilla until stiff in a medium-size bowl with electric mixer at low.

ALMOND SPRITZ COOKIES

Use your cookie press to make six different varieties with just one basic recipe. Your family will love them all.

Bake at 350° for 12 minutes.
Makes 7 dozen.

  1 cup (2 sticks) butter or margarine
¾ cup sugar
  2 eggs
  1 teaspoon vanilla
  1 teaspoon almond extract
  1 cup blanched almonds, ground (see page 60)
2½ cups all purpose flour
  Ornamental Frosting (recipe, page 48)

1. Beat butter or margarine with sugar until fluffy in large bowl with electric mixer at high speed; beat in eggs, vanilla, and almond extract. Stir in ground almonds; gradually sift in flour, blending well to make a soft dough.
2. Divide evenly into 6 parts. Flavor, shape, and decorate each variety, following individual recipes.
3. Bake in moderate oven (350°) 12 minutes, or until firm. Remove from cookie sheets with spatula; cool completely on wire racks, then decorate according to following directions.

FROSTED SNOWFLAKES: Fit snowflake or star plate or disk on cookie press. Fill with one part of dough and press out on ungreased cookie sheets. Bake and cool, following general directions. Decorate centers of cookies with a swirl of plain ORNAMENTAL FROSTING; sprinkle tops lightly with dry cocoa powder.

CHRISTMAS CANES: Fit star plate or disk on cookie press. Fill with second part of dough and press out into 5-inch lengths on ungreased cookie sheets; turn one end of the dough to form a crook for the cane. Bake and cool, following general directions. Tint a small amount ORNAMENTAL FROSTING pale green with a few drops green food coloring. Decorate canes with frosting stripes; top with multicolor sprinkles.

BROWN-EYED SUSANS: Fit sunburst or star plate or disk on cookie press. Fill with third part of dough and press out on ungreased cookie sheets. Bake and cool, following general directions. Tint a small amount ORNAMENTAL FROSTING yellow with a few drops yellow food coloring. Decorate centers of cookies with a tiny swirl of frosting; top with semisweet chocolate pieces.

PARTY WREATHS: Fit star plate or disk on cookie press. Fill with fourth part of dough and press out into 3-inch lengths on ungreased cookie sheets; join ends together to form a circle. Bake and cool, following general directions. Tint a small amount ORNAMENTAL FROSTING pale green with a few drops green food coloring. Decorate wreaths with a frosting swirl; sprinkle the tops of each with red decorating sugar.

GREEN TREES and HOLIDAY DAISIES: Combine remaining dough in a bowl; tint green with a few drops green food coloring. For GREEN TREES, fit tree plate or disk on cookie press. Fill with half the dough and press out on ungreased cookie sheets. Sprinkle with red decorating sugar; top each with a silver candy. For HOLIDAY DAISIES, fit sunburst or star plate or disk on cookie press. Fill with remaining dough and press out on ungreased cookie sheets. Bake and cool both, following general directions. To decorate HOLIDAY DAISIES, tint a small amount ORNAMENTAL FROSTING pink with a few drops red food coloring; flavor, if you wish, with a drop or two of peppermint extract. Swirl in centers of cookies.

SCOTCH SHORTBREAD

Make ahead because the cookies taste even richer if mellowed a few weeks.

Bake at 300° for 45 minutes.
Makes about 4 dozen.

1½ cups all purpose flour
1½ cups sifted 10X (confectioners' powdered) sugar
  1 cup (2 sticks) butter or margarine

1. Sift flour and 10X sugar into medium-size bowl; cut in butter or margarine with pastry blender until mixture is crumbly. Work dough into a ball with hands and knead about 10 minutes, or until very smooth.
2. Pat dough into a 14x12-inch rectangle, ¼-inch thick, on large cookie sheet; cut into 2-inch diamonds or squares with sharp knife, but do not separate cookies.
3. Bake in slow oven (300°) 45 minutes, or until firm and delicately golden.
4. Recut cookies at marks and separate very carefully; remove from cookie sheets with pancake turner. Cool on wire racks. These cookies are very delicate, so handle carefully. Store between layers of wax paper in airtight container.

MADELEINES

The French novelist Marcel Proust made them famous. You'll need special little molds to bake them in; many department stores stock them, or see Buyer's Guide on page 126. The photo is on page 93.

Bake at 350° for 20 minutes.
Makes 2 dozen.

- 1 **cup (2 sticks) butter or margarine**
- 3 **eggs**
- 1 **cup granulated sugar**
- 1 **teaspoon grated lemon rind**
- 1 **teaspoon vanilla**
- 1½ **cups cake flour**

1. Butter madeleine molds well; dust with flour, tapping out any excess.
2. Melt butter or margarine over low heat in a small saucepan; remove from heat. Pour into a 1-cup measure; let stand until solids settle to bottom.
3. Beat eggs with granulated sugar and lemon rind in the top of a large double boiler; place over simmering water. (Do not let water boil or touch bottom of pan.) Beat mixture with an electric mixer at high speed until thick and light, about 6 minutes; remove from water. Pour into a large bowl; stir in vanilla.
4. Measure ¾ cup of the clear liquid butter or margarine into another 1-cup measure; discard solids.
5. Fold flour into egg mixture, then fold in the liquid butter or margarine. Spoon into prepared molds, filling each half full. (Cover remaining batter and let stand at room temperature while baking first batch.)
6. Bake in moderate oven (350°) 20 minutes, or until tops spring back when lightly pressed with fingertip. Cool 5 minutes in molds on wire racks. Loosen around edges with the tip of a small knife; turn out onto racks, tapping gently, if needed, to loosen from bottom. Cool completely. Repeat to make 24 MADELEINES in all. Store in a covered container. Dust each cookie with a bit of 10X sugar before serving.

SWEDISH LACIES

In Sweden, these cookies were once hung over clean broomstick handles to give them their curved shape.

Bake at 375° for 5 minutes.
Makes 18 cookies.

- ⅔ **cup whole blanched almonds**
- ½ **cup sugar**
- ¼ **cup all purpose flour**
- ¼ **teaspoon salt**
- ½ **cup (1 stick) butter or margarine**
- 2 **tablespoons light cream**

1. Chop almonds until very fine on a wooden board with a sharp French knife.
2. Combine nuts with sugar, flour, salt, butter or margarine and cream in a medium-size saucepan.
3. Heat slowly, stirring constantly with a wooden spoon, until mixture bubbles, about 5 minutes; remove from heat; beat with spoon 15 times.
4. Drop by teaspoonfuls, only a few at a time, 4 inches apart, on a well greased cookie sheet.
5. Bake in moderate oven (375°) 5 minutes, or until lacy-looking and just turning brown. Cool in pan on wire rack 2 minutes. Remove with a sharp knife and hang each cookie over a rolling pin, just until cool and holds shape.
BAKER'S TIP: Should cookies become too hard to remove from cookie sheet, return pan to oven for a minute or two to soften them slightly.

FLORENTINES

Fragile and fruit-filled, they may be frosted singly or put together in pairs.

Bake at 325° for 12 minutes.
Makes 2 dozen.

- ⅓ **cup butter or margarine**
- ⅓ **cup honey**
- ¼ **cup sugar**
- 2 **tablespoons milk**
- ⅔ **cup all purpose flour**
- 1 **cup (8 ounces) mixed candied fruits**
- 1 **can (3½ ounces) sliced almonds**
- 3 **squares semisweet chocolate**
- 1 **tablespoon butter or margarine**

1. Melt the ⅓ cup butter or margarine in a medium-size saucepan; remove from heat; stir in honey, sugar and milk.
2. Add flour, candied fruits and almonds; stir until well blended.
3. Return saucepan to very low heat. Cook, stirring contantly, until mixture begins to thicken. (This will only take 2 minutes.) Remove saucepan from heat.
4. Drop mixture by teaspoonfuls, 2 inches apart, onto well greased cookie sheets.
5. Bake in slow oven (325°) 12 minutes, or until golden brown around edges. Cool slightly on cookie sheets, then remove carefully with a pancake turner to wire racks; cool completely.
6. Melt chocolate squares and 1 tablespoon butter or margarine in a metal cup over simmering water. Spread the bottom of half the cookies with chocolate and top each with a second cookie. Allow chocolate to become firm before storing between layers of wax paper or transparent wrap in metal container.

MUFFIN TINS AND SIFTERS

Muffin tins come in assorted sizes from large to tiny. Some have white, black or brown non-stick coatings. Use large sifters to mix dry ingredients together; shake out 10X sugar with small ones.

PARISIENNES

Grated chocolate and ground almonds make these meringue cookies something special.

Bake at 275° for 20 minutes.
Makes 10 dozen.

- 3 egg whites
- ½ teaspoon salt
- ¼ teaspoon cream of tartar
- 1 cup superfine granulated sugar
- 4 squares semisweet chocolate, grated
- 1 cup blanched almonds ground (recipe, this page)
- 1 package (6 ounces) semi-sweet chocolate pieces
- 1 tablespoon vegetable shortening
- ⅓ cup finely chopped pistachio nuts

1. Beat egg whites with salt and cream of tartar in a small deep bowl with electric mixer at high speed, until foamy-white and double in volume; add sugar, 1 tablespoon at a time, beating until meringue stands in firm peaks. Gently fold in grated chocolate and almonds with a wire whip.
2. Fit a pastry bag with a #22 star tip and fill with meringue mixture. Press out into small kisses, 1 inch apart, on lightly greased cookie sheets, or drop meringue mixture by half-teaspoonfuls onto cookie sheets.
3. Bake in very slow oven (275°) 20 minutes, or just until set. Remove carefully from cookie sheets with spatula; cool on wire racks.
4. Melt semi-sweet chocolate pieces with shortening in top of double boiler over hot water. Dip cookies first into chocolate, then into nuts. Allow chocolate to set before storing in a metal tin with a tight-fitting lid between layers of wax paper.

PERSIAN CRACKERS

Chopped almonds and sesame seeds top this Middle Eastern sweet.

Bake at 350° for 10 minutes.
Makes 6 dozen.

- ½ cup firmly packed brown sugar
- ⅓ cup vegetable oil
- ⅔ cup water
- 1 cup blanched almonds, ground (recipe, this page)
- 1½ cups whole wheat flour
- 1½ cups quick-cooking rolled oats
- 1 teaspoon salt
- ½ cup chopped unblanched almonds
- ¼ cup sesame seeds

1. Combine brown sugar, oil and water in a large bowl with a wooden spoon. Stir in ground almonds, then the whole wheat flour, oats and salt

until well blended and smooth.
2. Turn out onto a lightly floured pastry cloth or board; knead 5 minutes, adding only enough extra flour to keep dough from sticking.
3. Roll out to an 18x16-inch rectangle; sprinkle chopped almonds and sesame seeds over dough; roll into dough lightly; cut into 2-inch squares. Place on cookie sheets.
4. Bake in moderate oven (350°) 10 minutes, or until cookies are golden; remove to wire racks with a spatula; cool completely. Store in containers with tight-fitting lids.

PFEFFERNUSS DROPS

These cardamom cookies have all the spicy flavor of the old-fashioned German kind.

Bake at 350° for 8 minutes.
Makes 6 dozen.

- 1¾ cups all purpose flour
- 1 teaspoon ground cinnamon
- ¼ teaspoon baking soda
- ¼ teaspoon salt
- ¼ teaspoon ground nutmeg
- ⅛ teaspoon ground cloves
- ⅛ teaspoon pepper
- ½ teaspoon anise seeds, crushed
- ½ teaspoon ground cardamom
- ¼ cup candied citron, finely chopped
- ¼ cup candied orange rind, finely chopped
- 2 tablespoons butter or margarine
- 1¼ cups sifted 10X (confectioners' powdered) sugar
- 1 egg
  Red and green candied cherries
- 1 teaspoon milk

1. Sift flour, cinnamon, baking soda, salt, nutmeg, cloves and pepper into a medium-size bowl; stir in anise seeds, cardamom, citron and orange rind until well mixed.
2. Beat butter or margarine and 1 cup of the 10X sugar until well mixed in medium-size bowl with electric mixer at medium speed. Beat in egg, then flour mixture, just until blended. Chill overnight, or until firm enough to handle.
3. Roll dough, about 1 teaspoonful at a time, into small balls; place, 2 inches apart, on cookie sheets. Top each with a piece of candied cherry.
4. Stir milk into remaining ¼ cup 10X sugar until smooth in small cup. Drizzle very lightly over top of each cookie.
5. Bake in moderate oven (350°) 8 minutes, or until very lightly browned. Remove from cookie sheets at once with spatula; cool completely on wire racks.

PETITS PAINS AUX AMANDES

These Belgian delicacies contain a generous splash of brandy.

Bake at 350° for 10 minutes.
Makes 5 dozen.

- 4 cups all purpose flour
- 1 teaspoon baking powder
- 1 teaspoon cinnamon
- 1½ cups ground almonds*
- 1 cup firmly packed brown sugar
- ¾ cup (1½ sticks) butter or margarine, melted
- ½ cup milk
- ¼ cup brandy

1. Sift flour, baking powder and cinnamon into a large bowl; stir in almonds and sugar until well blended with a wooden spoon.
2. Combine butter or margarine, milk and brandy in a 2-cup measure; pour into bowl; stir until well blended. Divide dough in half; shape each into a 10-inch roll on wax paper; roll up in wax paper and twist ends to seal. Chill overnight, or until ready to slice and bake.
3. Cut each roll into ¼-inch slices on a wooden board with a sharp French knife; arrange in rows on cookie sheets.
4. Bake in moderate oven (350°) 10 minutes, or until golden; remove from pan with spatula; cool on wire racks; store in metal tins.
*BAKERS'S TIP: To grind almonds: Place almonds, ½ cup at a time, in the container of an electric blender; cover. Process at high speed 30 seconds, or until very finely ground; turn onto wax paper. Continue until all almonds are ground.

JAN HAGELS

Here is a diamond-shaped Scandinavian cookie with a cinnamon-nut glaze baked right on top. Just right with good hot coffee.

Bake at 350° for 25 minutes.
Makes 6 dozen.

- 1 cup (2 sticks) butter or margarine, softened
- 1 cup sugar
- 1 egg, separated
- 1 teaspoon almond extract
- 2 cups all purpose flour
- ½ cup blanched sliced almonds
- 1 tablespoon sugar
- ¼ teaspoon ground cinnamon

1. Beat butter and the 1 cup sugar until fluffy in a large bowl with electric mixer at high speed. Add egg yolk and almond extract, blending thoroughly. Stir in flour.

2. Turn dough into an ungreased 15x10x1-inch jelly roll pan. Spread evenly to edges with a spatula.

3. Beat egg white until foamy-white; spread evenly over dough; spread nuts on top. Combine the 1 tablespoon sugar with cinnamon; sprinkle over.

4. Bake in a moderate oven (350°) 25 minutes, or until lightly browned. Remove from oven; let cool in pan on wire rack, 10 minutes. Cut into 8 lengthwise strips, then into 12 diagonal cuts to form diamond shapes. Cool thoroughly in pan; remove carefully with a spatula.

TOASTED ANISE BARS

Serve these twice-baked cookies with a cup of espresso or cappuccino.

Bake at 350° for 20 minutes,
then at 350° for 10 minutes.
Makes 5 dozen.

    6 eggs, separated
    ¾ teaspoon cream of tartar
    ¾ cup granulated sugar
    ¾ cup firmly packed brown sugar
    1½ cups all purpose flour
    1 teaspoon baking powder
    1 teaspoon salt
    2 tablespoons anise seeds

1. Beat egg whites until foamy in large bowl of electric mixer at high speed; add cream of tartar; beat until double in volume; add granulated sugar, 1 tablespoon at a time, until meringue forms stiff peaks.

2. Beat egg yolks and brown sugar until thick and light in small bowl of mixer at high speed. Fold egg yolk mixture into meringue with a wire whip until well blended.

3. Sift flour, baking powder and salt into egg mixture; add anise seeds; fold into mixture with wire whip until well blended.

4. Grease and flour a 15x10x1-inch jelly roll pan; tap out excess flour; spread batter in prepared pan.

5. Bake in moderate oven (350°) 20 minutes, or until center springs back when lightly touched with fingertip. Cool in pan on wire rack for 5 minutes.

6. Cut layer in half and remove; split each half crosswise with a serrated knife, then cut into 2½x1-inch bars, to make 60 pieces.

7. Arrange bars, cut-side up, in a single layer on a large cookie sheet and in jelly roll pan.

8. Bake in moderate (350°) 10 minutes, or until lightly toasted. Remove from pan to wire racks with spatula; cool completely. Store in container with a tight-fitting lid.

SWEDISH SAND TARTS

Bake these almond morsels in tiny molds, then dust with sugar and top with jelly.

Bake at 325° for 10 minutes.
Makes 6 dozen.

    1 cup (2 sticks) butter or margarine
    1 cup sugar
    1 egg
    ½ teaspoon almond extract
    2 cups all purpose flour
    ¼ teaspoon salt
       10X sugar
       Red currant jelly

1. Beat butter or margarine with sugar until light in medium-size bowl with electric mixer at high speed; beat in egg and almond extract. Gradually sift in flour and salt, blending well. Chill dough overnight, or until firm enough to handle.

2. Pinch off about a half teaspoonful at a time and press into ungreased individual sand tart tins, or miniature fluted tart pans. (Shop for them where fancy imported housewares are sold.) Place on cookie sheet.

3. Bake in slow oven (325°) 10 minutes, or until lightly golden. Cool in tins until easy to handle, then remove and invert onto wire racks.

4. When ready to serve, dust cookies lightly with 10X sugar; top with a dot of currant jelly or frosting from a 4-ounce tube.

SPRINGERLE

"Springerle" is both the name of the cookie and the special rolling pin that presses the pretty patterns into the dough.

Bake at 325° for 25 minutes.
Makes 6 dozen.

    4 eggs
    2 cups sugar
    1 teaspoon anise extract
    4¼ cups all purpose flour
    1 teaspoon baking soda
       Anise seeds

1. Beat eggs in the large bowl of an electric mixer at high speed about 5 minutes, or until very thick; add sugar, 1 tablespoon at a time, beating well after each addition. Beat in anise extract.

2. Sift in flour and baking soda, stirring to make a stiff dough.

3. Roll out dough a quarter at a time, on a lightly floured pastry cloth or board, to ½-inch thickness. Then, using springerle rolling pin (see page 32), roll over dough only once, pressing designs into dough to a ¼-inch thickness. Cut cookies apart on dividing lines with sharp knife.

4. Grease cookie sheets; sprinkle lightly with anise seeds. Carefully place cookies, 1 inch apart, on anise seeds. Let stand 24 hours, uncovered, in cool place (not refrigerator). (Cookies will appear to have white frosting.)

5. Bake in slow oven (325°) 25 minutes, or until cookies are set, but not brown.

6. Remove cookies to wire racks with spatula; cool completely. Store in tightly covered container about 2 weeks to season.

NÜRNBERGERS

Chewy, honey-spice cookies from the famous city of toys—Nuremberg, Germany.

Bake at 400° for 8 minutes.
Makes 5 dozen.

    3½ cups all purpose flour
    ½ teaspoon baking soda
    ½ teaspoon ground cinnamon
    ¼ teaspoon ground cloves
    ¼ teaspoon ground cardamom
    ¼ teaspoon ground ginger
    1 cup honey
    ¾ cup firmly packed brown sugar
    1 egg
    2 tablespoons orange juice
    1 container (4 ounces) candied
       orange rind, finely chopped
    ⅓ cup finely chopped almonds
       Sugar Glaze (recipe, page 63)
       Candied red and green cherries

1. Sift flour, baking soda, cinnamon, cloves, cardamom and ginger onto wax paper.

2. Beat honey, brown sugar, egg and orange juice in a large bowl with electric mixer at medium speed, until creamy and smooth.

3. Blend in flour mixture with wooden spoon until thoroughly combined. Add orange peel and almonds. (Dough will be stiff and sticky.) Wrap dough in wax paper; chill overnight.

4. Roll out dough, a quarter at a time, to a ⅛-inch thickness, on a well floured pastry cloth or board with a well floured rolling pin. Cut into 2½-inch rounds with a cookie cutter. Place, 1 inch apart, on greased large cookie sheets.

5. Bake in a hot oven (400°) 8 minutes, or until firm. Remove to wire racks with spatula.

6. While cookies are hot, brush with hot SUGAR GLAZE. Decorate with candied cherry halves and pieces of cherries, if you wish, while glaze is warm. Store cookies for two or three weeks to mellow between layers of wax paper in an airtight tin.

SWEDISH SLICE-OFFS

Keep the cookie dough in the refrigerator, then just slice and bake at company time.

Bake at 350° for 10 minutes.
Makes 3 dozen.

- ½ cup blanched whole or slivered almonds, ground
- ½ cup (1 stick) butter or margarine, softened
- ½ cup sugar
- 2 tablespoons light molasses
- 1 cup all purpose flour
- ½ teaspoon baking soda
- ¼ teaspoon salt

1. Grind almonds: Place in container of electric blender, ¼ cup at a time; cover; process on high 30 seconds, or until very fine. (Or you can chop them with a French knife until fine.)
2. Beat butter or margarine with sugar until fluffy in large bowl with an electric mixer at medium speed; beat in almonds and molasses. Turn speed to low; blend in flour, baking soda and salt to make a soft dough.
3. Shape dough into a roll, 1¼ inches in diameter, on a sheet of wax paper; roll up and twist ends to seal. Chill at least 4 hours, or until ready to bake.
4. Place roll on a wooden board and cut into ¼-inch slices with a French knife. Place in rows on cookie sheets. (You can return uncut portion of roll to the refrigerator. It will keep up to 2 weeks, if tightly sealed.)
5. Bake in moderate oven (350°) 10 minutes, or until slices are firm when touched lightly with fingertip. Remove from sheet with spatula; cool on wire racks. Store in metal tin.

CAPPUCCINO CRISPS

Like their beverage namesake, these cookies are topped with cinnamon, but they have an added flavor, chocolate.

Bake at 350° for 12 minutes.
Makes 3 dozen.

- ¾ cup all purpose flour
- ¼ teaspoon salt
- ½ cup vegetable shortening
- ⅔ cup sugar
- 2 tablespoons instant coffee
- 1 tablespoon cocoa powder (not a mix)
- 1 teaspoon ground cinnamon
- 1 egg
- ½ teaspoon vanilla
  Cinnamon Frosting (recipe follows)
  Chocolate sprinkles

1. Sift flour and salt onto wax paper and reserve.
2. Beat vegetable shortening and sugar until very fluffy in medium-size bowl with electric mixer at medium speed; add coffee, cocoa and cinnamon; beat until smooth.
3. Beat in egg until well blended; beat in vanilla.
4. Add sifted dry ingredients, a third at a time, beating just until blended. Drop by rounded teaspoonfuls, 2 inches apart, onto greased cookie sheets.
5. Bake in moderate oven (350°) 12 minutes, or until edges are firm and tops dry; carefully remove from cookie sheets with spatula to wire racks; cool completely.
6. Frost with CINNAMON FROSTING; top with chocolate sprinkles before frosting sets. Store in metal tin.

CINNAMON FROSTING: Makes about ¼ cup. Beat 2 teaspoons water and ¼ teaspoon ground cinnamon into 1 cup 10X (confectioners' powdered) sugar until smooth in small bowl with wire whip.

KRUMKAKE

A crisp, delicate cookie made in a special iron available in large department stores. It's a Christmas favorite in Scandinavia.

Makes 3 dozen.

- 2 eggs
- ¾ cup sugar
- 1¼ cups all purpose flour
- ½ teaspoon ground cardamom
- ¾ cup heavy cream

1. Beat eggs with sugar in a medium-size bowl with electric mixer at high speed until very thick and lemon-colored. (Beating will take 5 minutes —don't underbeat.)
2. Sift flour and cardamom onto wax paper.
3. Add flour mixture, alternately with cream, to bowl.
4. Heat krumkake iron in its holder, to moderately hot on top of range (a few drops of water will dance about). Do not allow to become too hot.
5. Drop about a tablespoon of batter on hot iron; bring cover down; do not press hard. Cook, over moderate heat, 30 seconds on each side of iron; peel cookie carefully from iron with a spatula; quickly roll around handle of a wooden spoon or form (which may come with your krumkake iron). Cookie will stiffen at once. Remove from spoon handle or form. Continue with remaining batter.
6. Store cookies in an airtight container (they keep very well). They can be served as is, or filled with flavored whipped cream and a few fresh berries just before serving.

PEPPARKAKOR

A German Christmas wouldn't be official without this spicy cutout cookie.

Bake at 350° for 7 minutes.
Makes 6 dozen.

- 1⅔ cups all purpose flour
- ½ teaspoon baking soda
- ½ teaspoon salt
- ¾ teaspoon ground ginger
- ½ teaspoon ground cinnamon
- ¼ teaspoon ground cloves
- ¼ teaspoon ground cardamom
- ⅓ cup butter or margarine
- ⅓ cup sugar
- ¼ cup light molasses
- 1 teaspoon grated orange rind
- ¼ cup finely chopped toasted almonds
  Ornamental Frosting (recipe, page 48)

1. Sift flour, soda, salt, ginger, cinnamom, cloves and cardamom onto wax paper.
2. Beat butter or margarine with sugar until fluffy in a large bowl with electric mixer at high speed; beat in molasses, orange rind and almonds. Stir in flour mixture, a third at a time, blending well to make a stiff dough. Chill several hours, or overnight.
3. Roll out dough, a third at a time, to a ⅛-inch thickness, on a lightly floured pastry cloth or board; cut into fancy shapes with floured 2-inch cookie cutters. Place, 1 inch apart, on lightly greased cookie sheets.
4. Bake in moderate oven (350°) 7 minutes, or until firm. Remove from cookie sheets to wire racks with spatula; cool completely.
5. Make ORNAMENTAL FROSTING. Fit a #2 writing tip onto a cake-decorating set; fill with frosting. Press out onto cookies in designs of your choice; let stand until frosting is firm. Store in metal tin.

ITALIAN ANISE COOKIES

Two bakings make this sliced cookie toasty and delicious.

Bake at 350° for 20 minutes.
Broil for 5 minutes.
Makes 4 dozen.

- 1 cup chopped almonds
- 3 cups all purpose flour
- 1 cup sugar
- 1 tablespoon baking powder
- 1¾ teaspoons salt
- 2 teaspoons grated lemon rind
- 2 teaspoons anise seed, crushed
- 4 eggs, well beaten
- 2 tablespoons light cream

1. Sprinkle chopped almonds in a 15x10x1-inch jelly roll pan. Toast in

oven while oven preheats, 10 minutes, or until golden; remove; cool.

2. Sift flour, sugar, baking powder and salt into a large bowl; stir in lemon rind, anise seeds, eggs and cream with a wooden spoon until mixture makes a soft dough.

3. Roll out half the dough to a 10x8-inch rectangle on a lightly floured pastry cloth or board; sprinkle with half the toasted almonds; roll up, jelly roll fashion, starting from the 10-inch side. Place, seam-side down, in jelly roll pan. Repeat with remaining dough and nuts to make a second roll; flatten each roll to a 1-inch height.

4. Bake in moderate oven (350°) 20 minutes, or until rolls are lightly browned. Cool in pan on wire rack 15 minutes. Remove rolls to wooden board with a long spatula; cut into ½-inch slices and place, cut-side down, in a single row in jelly roll pan. (You might have to make more than one panful.)

5. Broil 4 inches from heat for 5 minutes, or until toasted. Cool on wire racks; store in a metal tin.

ISCHL TARTLETS

This is our own special version of a cookie that's very popular in Viennese pastry shops.

Bake at 350° for 8 minutes.
Makes 3 ½ dozen.

2 ¾ cups all purpose flour
½ teaspoon baking powder
1 cup (2 sticks) butter or margarine, softened
1 package (3 ounces) cream cheese, softened
1 cup sugar
1 egg
½ cup blanched almonds, ground (see page 60)
1 tablespoon grated lemon rind
1 jar (12 ounces) raspberry preserves
10X (confectioners' powdered) sugar

1. Sift flour and baking powder onto wax paper.

2. Beat butter, cream cheese, sugar and egg until fluffy in a large bowl with an electric mixer at high speed.

3. Stir in flour mixture, blending thoroughly. Stir in ground almonds and lemon rind. Turn dough out onto wax paper (mixture will be sticky). Shape into a ball. Chill several hours, or overnight.

4. Roll out dough, half at a time, to a ⅛-inch thickness, on a lightly floured pastry cloth or board with a lightly floured rolling pin. Cut into rounds with a 3-inch cookie cutter.

Place on cookie sheets; cut out a ½-inch circle from half the rounds with a thimble. Repeat with rest of dough.

5. Bake in moderate oven (350°) 8 minutes, or until edges of cookies are lightly browned. Remove cookie sheets from oven; let stand 1 minute. Remove cookies with a wide spatula to wire racks; cool completely.

6. Heat raspberry preserves in a small saucepan. Spread solid cookies with a thin layer of hot preserves. Top each with cutout cookie; press together gently to make a "sandwich." Place on wire rack. Sprinkle tops of tartlets with confectioners' sugar. Spoon a dab of preserves into the opening of each tart; let preserves set slightly. Store between layers of wax paper in an airtight tin.

LEBKUCHEN

Honey and citron are essential ingredients in this classic German cookie.

Bake at 350° for 10 minutes.
Makes 5 dozen.

¾ cup honey
¾ cup firmly packed brown sugar
1 egg
2 teaspoons grated lemon rind
3 tablespoons lemon juice
3½ cups all purpose flour
1 teaspoon salt
1 teaspoon ground cinnamon
1 teaspoon ground nutmeg
½ teaspoon ground allspice
½ teaspoon ground ginger
¼ teaspoon ground cloves
½ teaspoon baking soda
1 container (8 ounces) candied citron, finely chopped
1 cup chopped unblanched almonds
Sugar Glaze (recipe follows)

1. Heat honey to boiling in a small saucepan; pour into a large bowl; cool about 30 minutes.

2. Stir in brown sugar, egg, lemon rind and lemon juice, blending well.

3. Sift flour, salt, cinnamon, nutmeg, allspice, ginger, cloves and baking soda onto wax paper.

4. Stir flour mixture into honey mixture, a third at a time. Stir in citron and almonds. Dough will be stiff, but sticky. Wrap in wax paper; chill several hours, or until firm.

5. Roll out dough, an eighth at a time, on lightly floured pastry cloth or board, to a 6x5-inch rectangle. Cut into 8 rectangles, 2½ x 1½ inches each. Place, 1 inch apart, on greased cookie sheets.

6. Bake in moderate oven (350°) 10 minutes, or until firm. Remove to wire

racks with spatula.

7. While cookies are hot, brush with hot SUGAR GLAZE, then press on a Christmas cutout, if you wish. Cool cookies completely before storing. Store in a tightly covered container at least 2 weeks to mellow.

SUGAR GLAZE: Makes 2 cups. Combine 1 ½ cups granulated sugar and ¾ cup water in a medium-size saucepan. Bring to boiling; reduce heat; simmer 3 minutes. Remove from heat; stir in ½ cup 10X (confectioners' powdered) sugar.

BAKING WITH KIDS (CHAPTER 6)

PEANUT BUTTER BARS

These moist, chewy bar cookies drizzled with sugar glaze and chocolate will be a favorite with the kids.

Bake at 350° for 35 minutes.
Makes 36 bars.

1 cup crunchy peanut butter
½ cup (1 stick) butter or margarine, softened
1 teaspoon vanilla
2 cups firmly packed brown sugar
3 eggs
1 cup all purpose flour
½ teaspoon salt
¼ cup 10X (confectioners' powdered) sugar
2 teaspoons water
¼ cup semi-sweet chocolate pieces
1 teaspoon vegetable shortening

1. Beat peanut butter, butter or margarine and vanilla until well blended in a large bowl with an electric mixer at high speed; beat in sugar until fluffy; beat in eggs, one at a time.

2. Stir in flour and salt just until well blended; spread batter in a greased 13x9x2-inch baking pan.

3. Bake in moderate oven (350°) 35 minutes, or until center springs back when lightly touched with fingertip. Remove pan from oven to wire rack; cool slightly.

4. Combine 10X sugar with water in a small bowl; stir until smooth; drizzle from a spoon over still-warm cookies in pan; swirl with bowl of spoon to make a random pattern.

5. Melt chocolate with shortening over simmering water in top of double boiler. Drizzle over the white glaze for a black-and-white pattern. When cool, cut into 36 rectangles with a sharp knife. Carefully lift out of pan with spatula.

Kids' cookies continued on page 109.

The art of decorating cakes was once a secret guarded by famous chefs who excelled in creating elaborate, sumptuous fare for their clients. It's not hard to see why, for the visual beauty of attractively prepared food has always been a source of great pride in cooking—and pleasure in eating. But now,

ENHANCE
CAKES WITH

CUSTOM FINISHES

anyone can make a cake worthy of admiration. In fact, with a little practice and our step-by-step instructions, you'll soon be finishing cakes that a professional baker would charge a handsome sum for! Begin with the frosting techniques on the next page. Then go on to pages 66 & 67 and learn how to make the fancier trims for our festive cakes in Chapter 3. If you've never done this before, you might try making a batch of Decorator's Frosting (page 73) and practicing on the backs of pans or on cookie sheets until you gain confidence. Once you do, you're on your way to memorable cakes.

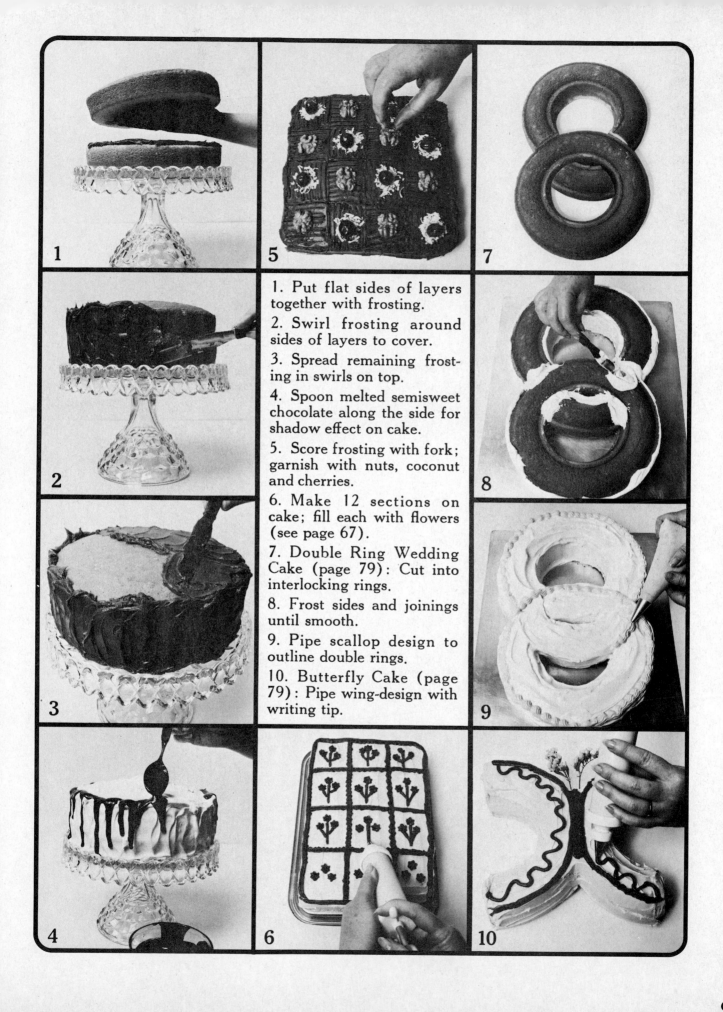

1. Put flat sides of layers together with frosting.

2. Swirl frosting around sides of layers to cover.

3. Spread remaining frosting in swirls on top.

4. Spoon melted semisweet chocolate along the side for shadow effect on cake.

5. Score frosting with fork; garnish with nuts, coconut and cherries.

6. Make 12 sections on cake; fill each with flowers (see page 67).

7. Double Ring Wedding Cake (page 79): Cut into interlocking rings.

8. Frost sides and joinings until smooth.

9. Pipe scallop design to outline double rings.

10. Butterfly Cake (page 79): Pipe wing-design with writing tip.

USE THESE FLOWERS AND TRIMS FOR ALL FESTIVE DESSERTS

HOW TO MAKE FULL ROSES

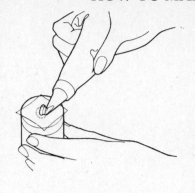

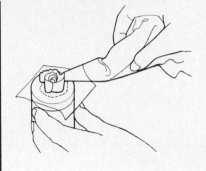

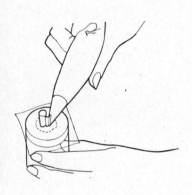

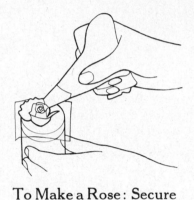

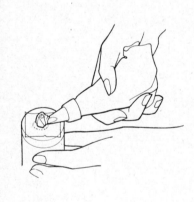

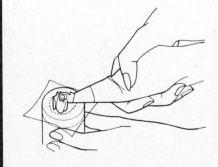

DECORATIVE EDGES

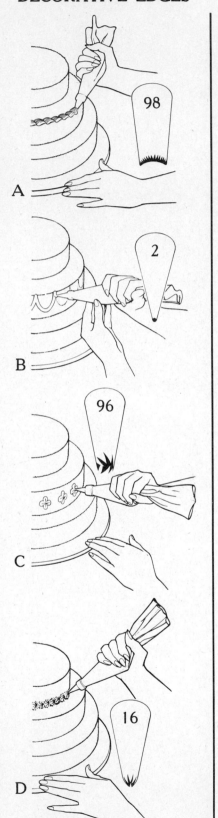

To Make a Rose: Secure wax paper square to top of small jar. Using #127 tip on pastry bag, press out frosting, while turning jar, to form cone; tilt tip slightly and overlap three tight petals around cone; tilt tip more and shape larger overlapping petals out and around to form full rose. Allow to dry 3 hours or overnight.

A. To Make Shell: Use #98 tip and press around.

B. To Make Scallop: Outline pattern on side with wooden pick; use #2 tip to fill.

C. To Make Drop Flowers: Use #96 tip and squeeze, turning bag as far from left to right as possible; pull away.

D. To Make Star Edge: Use #16 tip; press out frosting; pull away.

HOW TO DECORATE ANY SPECIAL CAKE LIKE A PASTRY CHEF

PRACTICE WRITING

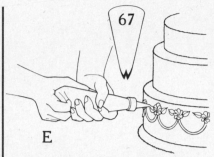

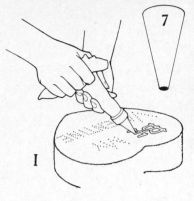

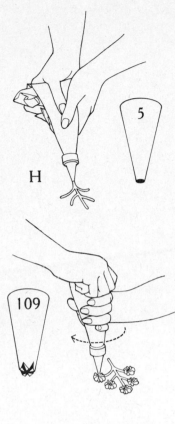

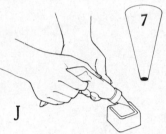

E. Combine Scallop edge with Drop Flowers and finish the design with #67 leaf tip.

F. Make Fleur-de-Lis with #16 tip. Begin with curve at top left; drawer down; continue to make 6 curves.

G. To Make Star Rope: Make lines between Fleur-de-Lis with #2 tip; use #14 tip for string of star flowers.

SIMPLE SIDE TRIMS

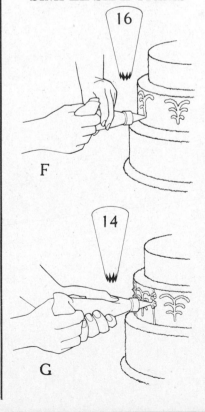

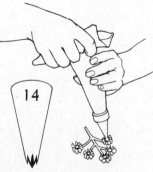

H. To Make Flower Spray: Use #5 tip to make stems of bouquet. Place #109 tip on pastry bag. Hold bag upright, with hand as far to left as possible; squeeze, turning hand as far to right as possible; relax pressure. Use #14 tip and contrasting frosting to make flower centers. Finish bouquet with touches from #67 leaf tip.

I. Printing with Frosting: Use #7 tip and begin by practicing with horizontal and vertical lines. Outline message on cake with wooden pick; then print, just touching tube to surface and using steady pressure on pastry bag.

J. Outlining Petit Fours: Use #7 tip and use a contrasting frosting to make simple boarder.

K. Writing with Frosting: Use #5, 6 or 7 tip and work with sweeping movements of both arms; follow the outlined message on cake.

The baking of extra-special cakes has long been associated with important holidays and events, for it's a thoughtful gift of one's time that lends a personal, as well as symbolic, touch to an occasion. How can we ever forget the cakes that were made to honor our own birthdays and graduations, and the heart-shaped cakes we received on Valentine's Day in the past? Or the rich fruit and spice cakes our

Chapter 3
ELEGANT CAKES FOR
SPECIAL OCCASIONS

grandmothers baked for dinner at Thanksgiving and Christmastime? We wouldn't want to. This chapter offers a fine selection of just such cakes (and cookies, too) to make any occasion more festive. Our queenly Rose Pink Wedding Cake (opposite) and the attractive cakes on the following pages are just a few of the ones you'll want to try, now that you've mastered our decorating techniques. Recipe for our Scandinavian "cookie" cake, Kransekage, is on page 48; other recipes start on page 73.

A BRIDE is special. And this regal Rose Pink Wedding Cake is a special way to tell her so.

ROMANTIC...
a Sweetheart Cake
made with your own
hands. Perfect for Valen-
tine's Day, birthdays
and graduations.

CHRISTMAS
is the time for
Bûche de Noël,
a symbolic yule
log filled with
coffee cream.

"WREATH CAKE," or Kransekage, is the party cookie-cake of Norway. Splendid for an anniversary celebration.

YOUR ANNIVERSARY

May sweet and happy memories
Bless this day for you
And every day of the future years
Bring gladness just as true

ROSE PINK WEDDING CAKE

You can be the proud creator of this memorable cake. Just follow the directions below. If you haven't had too much experience with decorating cakes, practice well ahead of time, following directions on pages 66 and 67. The photograph is on page 69. Makes one 3-tier cake plus decorative top that serves 100, or 75, if the top tier is kept for first anniversary.

POUND CAKE TIERS

Bake at 325° from 1 hour to 1 hour, 30 minutes.
Makes three tiers—8, 10 and 12 inches.

- **6 packages (about 1 pound each) pound cake mix**
- **12 eggs**
  Liquid as label directs
- **3 tablespoons apricot brandy**
  Apricot Glaze (recipe follows)
  Wedding Cake Frosting (recipe follows)
  Decorator's Frosting (recipe follows)

1. Grease and line tiered cake pans with wax paper; grease paper and then dust with flour, tapping out excess.
2. Prepare 2 packages pound cake mix with 4 eggs, liquid called for on label, and 1 tablespoon apricot brandy, following label directions.
3. Pour batter into 10-inch pan to fill half the pan. If there is additional batter, pour into largest pan.
4. Repeat twice. Pour batter into 12-inch pan to fill half the pan, then fill half the 8-inch pan. Bake remaining batter in one or more greased 10-ounce custard cups.
5. Arrange one oven rack in top third of oven and the second rack in the bottom third of the oven. Place 12-inch pan on bottom rack in center of oven. Place 10-inch pan at back left of top rack and 8-inch pan at front right of top rack. (Be sure pans do not touch each other, door, sides, or back of oven.)
6. Bake in slow oven (325°) 1 hour. Then begin to test layers. The cakes are done when a cake tester or long wooden skewer inserted into the center of each cake layer comes out clean. (Baking times will vary with the width and depth of individual cake pans and also the size and shape of your oven.) All layers should be baked by 1 hour, 30 minutes. If the layers on the top rack are getting too brown but do not test done, cover layers lightly with a piece of aluminum foil for the last part of baking. Bake custard-size cakes 30 minutes, or until they test done.
7. Remove layers from oven and cool on wire racks for 20 minutes. Then line wire racks with towels. Loosen each cake around edge with a sharp knife. Turn cake pan on side and shake layer gently to be sure cake has loosened from pan. Turn out layer onto towel-lined wire rack and peel off wax paper. Cool cake completely. (Towel-lined wire racks make it much easier to handle the larger cakes.)
8. Brush tops and sides of layers with APRICOT GLAZE.

APRICOT GLAZE

Makes 1¼ cups.

- **1 jar (12 ounces) apricot preserves**
- **¼ cup apricot brandy**

Heat apricot preserves until very warm in a small saucepan. Stir in apricot brandy. Strain. (The glaze adds flavor and helps retain moisture.)

WEDDING CAKE FROSTING

Makes enough to frost ROSE PINK WEDDING CAKE.

- **1 cup (2 sticks) butter or margarine**
- **¾ cup vegetable shortening**
- **3 packages (1 pound each) 10X (confectioners' powdered) sugar, sifted**
- **½ teaspoon salt**
- **¼ cup milk**
- **3 tablespoons apricot brandy**
- **3 tablespoons light corn syrup**
- **1 tablespoon vanilla**

1. Beat butter or margarine and shortening until soft in large bowl of electric mixer at medium speed. Beat in 10X sugar and salt until mixture is crumbly and all of the sugar has been added.
2. Add milk, brandy, corn syrup and vanilla. Beat until mixture is smooth and spreadable. (Keep every bowl of frosting covered with a dampened paper towel while frosting cake.)

DECORATOR'S FROSTING

Makes enough to decorate ROSE PINK WEDDING CAKE.

- **½ cup (1 stick) butter or margarine**
- **½ cup vegetable shortening**
- **2 packages (1 pound each) 10X (confectioners' powdered) sugar, sifted**
- **¼ teaspoon salt**
- **3 tablespoons milk**
- **2 tablespoons apricot brandy**
- **2 tablespoons light corn syrup**
- **1 teaspoon vanilla**
  Red and green food coloring

1. Beat butter or margarine and shortening until soft in large bowl of electric mixer at high speed. Beat in 10X sugar and salt until mixture is crumbly and all sugar has been added.
2. Add milk, brandy, corn syrup and vanilla to bowl. Beat until mixture is very thick and smooth. (Cover bowl with dampened paper towel; cover with plastic wrap to keep frosting from hardening.)

To Assemble Wedding Cake:

1. Place 13-inch cardboard round on turntable. (Cardboard between each layer makes cutting easier.) Center 12-inch POUND CAKE TIER on cardboard. Frost top and side thinly with WEDDING CAKE FROSTING.
2. Center 10-inch cardboard round on cake layer and top with 10-inch cake layer; frost. Center 8-inch cardboard round on cake and top with 8-inch cake layer; frost. Center 10-ounce custard layer on top; frost. (This thin basic coat of frosting keeps any stray crumbs in place, and provides a smooth base for final frosting. Allow frosting to dry 1 hour.)
3. Frost cake all over with a smooth, thick layer of the WEDDING CAKE FROSTING.
4. Follow designs for cake as we decorated it, or work out your own pattern. To make different designs, follow directions on pages 66 and 67.
5. Put a small amount of DECORATOR'S FROSTING in each of two small bowls; tint one a pale pink and the other a pale green with red and green food colorings. Reserve.
6. Tint remaining frosting medium pink and make 25 roses, following directions on page 66. Allow to dry at least 3 hours. (For a two-tone rose effect, tint part of the DECORATOR'S FROSTING a deeper pink.)
7. Fit #98 shell tip on pastry bag; press out frosting in overlapping shell design around entire bottom of 12-inch tier, making sure to cover all cardboard completely.
8. Fit the #2 writing tip onto pastry bag. Press out frosting, following scallop directions on page 66, all the way around.
9. Fit the #96 drop flower tip onto pastry bag. Press out flowers, following drop flower directions on page 66.
10. Fit #16 star tip on pastry bag; press out *Fleur-de-Lis*, following directions on page 67.
11. Fit #2 writing tip and then #16 star tip onto pastry bag and make star rope, following directions on page 67.
12. With #16 star tip on pastry bag, press out frosting in overlapping design around bottom of 8-inch tier.
13. Fit #109 drop flower tip on pastry bag. Press out flowers, following flower directions on page 67.
14. Fit #16 star tip on pastry bag; press out frosting in overlapping

sign around custard cup layer.

15. Fit #98 shell tip on pastry bag. Pipe a large mound of frosting onto the center of top tier of cake. Peel roses off wax paper and arrange, alternating shades of pink, onto frosting mound.

16. Fit #2 writing tip onto clean pastry bag; fill bag with green frosting. Make stems for flower sprays, following directions on page 67.

17. Fit the #67 leaf tip onto pastry bag; fill bag with green frosting. Pipe leaves onto cake, following our picture on page 69.

BAKER'S TIPS:

Special Items You Will Need:
- 1 three-tier cake pan set (8-, 10-, 12-inch)*
- 1 ten-ounce custard cup
- Cake decorating set with 2 pastry bags, coupling, 8 tips (# 109, 98, 2, 96, 18, 16, 67)*
- 1 plastic 12-inch turntable*
- 3 rounds heavy cardboard (13-, 10-, 8-inch)

*See Buyer's Guide, page 126.

Work Schedule:
Your cake may be made in two days, following our plan. If you wish to bake, decorate, and freeze the cake two or three weeks before the wedding, be sure to measure your freezer space first. The cake is 14 inches wide, 15 inches tall.

1st day: Bake POUND CAKE LAYERS; brush all cakes with APRICOT GLAZE; make roses.

2nd day: Assemble cake.

Handy Notes for Baking Cakes:
- Different sets of cake pans will vary in volume. In the set we used, measuring to the brim, the 12-inch pan holds 22 cups, the 10-inch holds 14 cups, and the 8-inch holds 8 cups. Measure your pans with water to determine the volume of each.
- Each package of pound cake mix makes about 3½ cups of batter.
- Each pan should be filled half full with batter.

Making the Decorations for the Cake:
If this is to be your first experience with a cake decorating set, it would be wise to prepare half the recipe for DECORATOR'S FROSTING and practice the designs on pages 66 and 67, before you start your cake. A little practice and you suddenly become a pro.

Freezing Tips:
- If you are not assembling POUND CAKE LAYERS at once, you may wrap cooled, unfrosted layers in aluminum foil and freeze. They may be frozen for up to three months.
- If decorated cake is to be frozen, place in freezer as is; freeze until

frosting is very firm, then cover all over with aluminum foil. Remove the day before the wedding.

BÛCHE DE NOËL

The Yule log of Christmas past is recreated with a chocolate jelly roll coated with a rich frosting to resemble the tree's bark. MUSHROOM MERINGUES are the classic garnish. Photo is on page 71.

Bake at 375° for 12 minutes.
Makes 12 servings.

    1 cup cake flour
    ¼ cup cocoa powder (not a mix)
    1 teaspoon baking powder
    ¼ teaspoon salt
    3 eggs
    1 cup granulated sugar
    ⅓ cup water
    1 teaspoon vanilla
       10X sugar
       Coffee Cream Filling (recipe follows)
       Chocolate Butter Frosting (recipe follows)
       Mushroom Meringues (recipe, page 46)

1. Grease a 15x10x1-inch jelly roll pan; line with wax paper; grease.

2. Sift flour, cocoa, baking powder and salt onto wax paper.

3. Beat eggs until thick and creamy in small bowl of electric mixer at high speed; beat in granulated sugar, 1 tablespoon at a time, beating all the time until mixture is very thick. Stir in water and vanilla; fold in flour mixture. Spread batter evenly in pan.

4. Bake in moderate oven (375°) 12 minutes, or until center springs back when lightly pressed with fingertip.

5. Loosen around edges of pan with a sharp knife; invert pan onto a clean towel dusted with 10X sugar; peel off wax paper. Starting at a long side, roll up cake, jelly roll fashion; wrap in towel; cool completely.

6. Unroll cake carefully; spread with COFFEE CREAM FILLING; reroll.

7. Cut a ½-inch-thick slice from one end of cake roll; remove inner coil and reshape tightly to form a "knot" on a log; frost with a bit of CHOCOLATE BUTTER FROSTING. Frost cake roll with remaining frosting; draw the tines of a fork, lengthwise, through frosting to resemble "bark"; press "knot" onto side. Sprinkle ends of roll with chopped pistachio nuts as photographed on page 71; chill until serving time. Decorate plate with MUSHROOM MERINGUES. Cut crosswise into slices.

COFFEE CREAM FILLING: Makes 2 cups. Combine 1 cup heavy cream, 1 tablespoon instant coffee powder

and ½ cup 10X (confectioners' powdered) sugar in a medium-size bowl; beat until stiff with mixer at medium.

CHOCOLATE BUTTER FROSTING: Makes enough to frost jelly roll. Melt ¼ cup (½ stick) butter or margarine and 2 squares unsweetened chocolate in small saucepan; cool slightly. Add 2 cups 10X (confectioners' powdered) sugar, ¼ cup milk, and ½ teaspoon vanilla; beat with wire whip until frosting is smooth.

TOASTED ALMOND TORTE

Chocolate cones crown a coffee-flavored frosting. Perfect for Dad's birthday.

Bake at 350° for 30 minutes.
Makes two 9-inch layers.

    ½   cup semi-sweet chocolate pieces
    1   package (about 18 ounces) yellow cake mix
    2   eggs
        Water
    1   package (6 ounces) sliced almonds
    1   package (15 ounces) creamy fudge frosting mix
    ½   cup (1 stick) butter or margarine
    1   tablespoon instant coffee
    1   package (15 ounces) creamy vanilla frosting mix
    1½ cups 10X (confectioners' powdered) sugar

1. Cut six 3-inch rounds from wax paper; shape each into a cone; fasten with cellophane tape.

2. Melt chocolate pieces in the top of a double boiler over simmering water; cool, then spread thinly inside paper cones to cover completely. Stand each upright in a small bottle; chill.

3. Prepare cake mix with eggs and water, following label directions. Divide batter between two greased 9-inch layer cake pans.

4. Bake in moderate oven (350°) 30 minutes; or until layers spring back when lightly touched with fingertip. Cool in pans on wire racks 10 minutes; loosen around edges with narrow spatula; cool completely on racks.

5. While cakes bake, spread almonds in a shallow pan; heat in same oven 10 minutes, or until lightly toasted.

6. Prepare fudge frosting mix with ¼ cup of butter or margarine and warm water, following label directions.

7. Dissolve instant coffee in ¼ cup warm water in a medium-size bowl; add vanilla frosting mix and remaining ¼ cup butter or margarine; prepare, following label directions; stir in 10X sugar until smooth. Measure out

1 cup and set aside. Put cake layers together with remaining coffee frosting. Place on a serving plate. Spread chocolate frosting on side and top of cake; sprinkle with toasted almonds.
8. Fit a # 27 star tip tube onto a cake-decorating set; fill with saved 1 cup coffee frosting; press into chocolate cones to fill. Carefully peel paper from cones; arrange on top of cake. Press remaining coffee frosting in rosettes around bottom of cake. Chill until serving time.

CHERRY PIE-CAKE

Here's the perfect choice of dessert for Washington's Birthday.

Bake at 375° for 20 minutes.
Makes one 9-inch cake

⅔ cup all purpose flour
½ teaspoon baking powder
2 eggs
1 teaspoon salt
⅓ cup sugar
⅓ cup light corn syrup
½ teaspoon vanilla
   Cherry Filling (recipe follows)
½ cup heavy cream, whipped

1. Sift flour and baking powder onto wax paper.
2. Beat eggs and salt in small bowl of electric mixer at high speed; beat in sugar, then corn syrup, until mixture becomes thick and lemon-colored. Stir in flour mixture and vanilla, blending well.
3. Turn into a greased and floured 9-inch layer cake pan.
4. Bake in moderate oven (375°) 20 minutes, or until cake springs back when lightly touched with fingertip. Cool in pan 10 minutes. Remove with small spatula and cool completely on wire rack. Place on serving plate.
5. Fill a pastry bag with whipped cream and pipe around edge. Fill center with CHERRY FILLING; chill.

CHERRY FILLING

Makes 2 cups.
1 can (16 ounces) water-pack tart red cherries
½ cup sugar
3 tablespoons cornstarch
½ teaspoon salt

1. Drain cherry juice into a 1-cup measure; add enough water to make 1 cup.
2. Combine sugar, cornstarch and salt in a medium-size saucepan; stir in cherry liquid. Cook, stirring constantly, until sauce thickens and bubbles 1 minute; remove from heat; stir in cherries; cool completely.

MRS. STEIDEL'S LINZER TORTE

A tradition in Mrs. Elizabeth Steidel's home at Christmas. You will have two generous cakes with this recipe—one to serve and one to give a friend.

Bake at 350° for 1 hour, 10 minutes.
Makes two 10-inch cakes.

3 cups unbleached all purpose flour
1⅔ cups sugar
2 tablespoons unsweetened cocoa powder (not a mix)
2 teaspoons baking powder
1½ teaspoons ground cinnamon
1 teaspoon salt
½ teaspoon ground cloves
1 cup (2 sticks) sweet butter or margarine
2 eggs, beaten
1 package (6 ounces) almonds, ground (see page 60)
¼ cup Kirsch or cherry brandy
   Rind and juice of 1 lemon
1 jar (12 ounces) red raspberry preserves
1 jar (12 ounces) red currant jelly
2 tablespoons Kirsch or lemon juice
1 egg yolk
10X sugar

1. Sift flour, sugar, cocoa, baking powder, cinnamon, salt and cloves into a large bowl. Cut in butter or margarine with a pastry blender or two knives until mixture is mealy.
2. Stir in eggs, almonds, ¼ cup Kirsch, lemon rind and juice into mixture until mixture is well blended. Cover dough with plastic wrap and chill 1 hour, or until dough is firm.
3. Grease two 10-inch springform pans, or two 9x9x2-inch baking pans. Dust lightly with flour; tap out any excess.
4. Heat raspberry preserves, currant jelly and 2 tablespoons Kirsch or lemon juice until melted in a medium-size saucepan; cool to room temperature.
5. Divide dough into quarters. Roll out a quarter on a lightly floured pastry cloth or board to fit pan; place in pan.
6. Spread a third of preserves mixture on dough in pan. Roll out a second quarter of dough into finger-thick strips on pastry board or cloth. Arrange strips to make an edge around pan, then a lattice over preserves. Press the tines of a fork around edge of dough to make a pretty pattern. Repeat with remaining pastry and another third of preserves mixture to make a second cake. Beat egg yolk with 1 teaspoon water in a cup and brush over pastry.
7. Bake in moderate oven (350°) 1

hour, 10 minutes, or until pastry is golden. Cool in pans on wire racks. Remove cakes from pans and fill lattice spaces with remaining preserves mixture. Sprinkle with 10X sugar and serve.
BAKER'S TIP: A LINZER TORTE is even more delicious if allowed to mellow a week or so before serving. Wrap in heavy-duty aluminum foil and store at room temperature a week, or label, date and freeze up to four months.

PASSOVER NUT CAKE

A fine choice of dessert for the family seder.

Bake at 325° for 40 minutes.
Makes one 9-inch square.

5 eggs, separated
⅔ cup sugar
2 tablespoons vegetable oil
5 tablespoons matzo meal
2 tablespoons grated lemon rind
1 cup walnuts, finely chopped
   Lemon-Wine Sauce (recipe follows)

1. Grease bottom of a 9x9x2-inch square baking pan; line with wax paper; grease paper.
2. Beat egg whites in large bowl of electric mixer at high speed until stiff.
3. Beat egg yolks in small bowl of electric mixer at high speed until thick and lemon-colored. Add sugar and continue beating until thick and creamy, about 2 minutes. Stir in oil, matzo meal and lemon rind.
4. Fold egg yolk mixture into egg whites with wire whip until well blended; fold in nuts; pour into pan.
5. Bake in slow oven (325°) 40 minutes, or until cake tester inserted in center of cake comes out clean.
6. Cool in pan 10 minutes; loosen around edges with a knife; turn out onto wire rack; remove wax paper; cool completely. Sprinkle with 10X sugar; serve with LEMON-WINE SAUCE.

LEMON-WINE SAUCE

Makes 2½ cups.
¾ cup sugar
1 tablespoon cornstarch
2 egg yolks
1 whole egg
1½ cups Sauternes wine
¾ cup water
1 teaspoon grated lemon rind

Combine sugar and cornstarch in a small saucepan; beat in egg yolks and whole egg; stir in wine and water. Bring slowly to boiling, stirring constantly; remove from heat immediately; stir in lemon rind. Serve warm.

MEGEVE CAKE

Fauchon's, that famous gourmet shop on Rue Madeleine in Paris, reveals its recipes for this rich pâtisserie. It will make your reputation as a pastry chef.

Bake at 300° for 30 minutes.
Makes 10 servings.

Meringue
- 3 egg whites
- 1 cup superfine sugar

Filling
- ⅔ cup heavy cream
- 7 squares semisweet chocolate
- 3½ squares unsweetened chocolate
- ¼ cup (½ stick) butter or margarine
- 4 egg whites
- 1 cup superfine sugar
- Chocolate Curls (recipe follows)
- 10X sugar

1. Make meringue: Grease 1 large and 1 small cookie sheet; dust with flour, tapping off excess. Using an 8-inch layer cake pan as a guide, draw two 8-inch circles on large cookie sheet and one on small one.
2. Beat the 3 egg whites until foamy-white and double in volume in large bowl of electric mixer at high speed. Sprinkle in sugar, 1 tablespoon at a time, beating all the time, until sugar dissolves completely and meringue stands in firm peaks. Divide mixture in the 3 circles; spread out to edge.
3. Bake in slow oven (300°) 30 minutes, or until layers are firm and golden. Cool 5 minutes on cookie sheets on wire racks, then loosen meringue layers carefully with a wide spatula and slide onto racks; cool.
4. Make filling: Heat cream in top of double boiler over simmering, not boiling, water; add semisweet and unsweetened chocolates. Stir often with a wooden spoon until chocolate melts. Stir in butter or margarine.
5. Beat egg whites until foamy-white in large bowl of mixer; gradually add sugar, beating well after each addition; continue beating until meringue is glossy and stands in firm peaks.
6. Fill bottom of double boiler partly with ice and water; set top of boiler with chocolate mixture in ice water. Beat chocolate mixture with mixer at high speed until light and fluffy and almost double in volume; scrape down side of double boiler often. Fold chocolate into meringue with a wire whip until no streaks of white or brown remain.
7. Place 1 meringue layer on serving plate; spread with about 1½ cups chocolate filling; repeat with another layer and 1½ cups filling. Place third layer on top. Frost side and top with remaining filling. Place CHOCOLATE CURLS on side and pile high on top of cake; chill. Thirty minutes before serving, remove cake from refrigerator for ease in slicing; sprinkle with 10X sugar. Cut in wedges with sharp serrated knife. Return any unused cake to refrigerator.

CHOCOLATE CURLS: Using long strokes with a vegetable parer, shave 3 squares semisweet chocolate into long curls and onto wax paper. Freeze until ready to use.
BAKER'S TIP: Chocolate will curl more easily if squares are warm.

DUBLIN HOLLY CAKE

A festive dark fruitcake is wrapped in marzipan and frosted with butter cream in the traditional Irish manner.

Bake at 325° for 1 hour, 30 minutes.
Makes one 10-inch angel tube cake.

- 1 jar (1 pound) candied mixed fruits
- 1 package (11 ounces) currants
- 1½ cups chopped walnuts
- 2 tablespoons grated orange rind
- 4 cups all purpose flour
- 2 teaspoons apple pie spice
- 1 teaspoon baking soda
- 1 teaspoon salt
- 1 cup (2 sticks) butter or margarine
- 1⅓ cups firmly packed brown sugar
- 3 eggs
- 1 cup stout or dark ale
- Christmas Marzipan (recipe follows)
- Butter Cream Frosting (recipe, page 10)

1. Grease a 10-inch angel cake tube pan; dust with flour; tap out excess.
2. Combine candied fruits, currants, chopped walnuts and orange rind in a very large bowl.
3. Sift flour, apple pie spice, baking soda and salt onto wax paper. Sprinkle 1 cup of mixture over fruits and nuts and toss to coat.
4. Beat butter or margarine, brown sugar and eggs in large bowl of electric mixer at high speed 3 minutes, or until fluffy.
5. Stir in remaining flour mixture, alternately with stout or ale, beating after each addition for smooth batter.
6. Pour batter over prepared fruit and nuts and fold just until well blended. Spoon batter into prepared pan.
7. Bake in slow oven (325°) 1 hour, 30 minutes, or until center springs back when lightly pressed with fingertip. Cool in pan on wire rack 15 minutes; loosen around edge and tube with a knife; turn out onto wire rack; cool completely.
8. To decorate: Prepare CHRISTMAS MARZIPAN. Roll out ⅓ of mixture to an 8½-inch round, using the bottom of baking pan as a guide; cut out center circle of tube.
9. Place marzipan round on top of inverted cake on serving plate. Roll out remaining marzipan to a strip, 27-inches long and 3-inches wide (you can do this in sections, then press together); wrap around side of cake.
10. Frost cake with BUTTER CREAM FROSTING and garnish top with candied cherries and walnuts.

CHRISTMAS MARZIPAN

Makes about 1½ cups.
- 1 can (8 ounces) almond paste
- 1 cup 10X (confectioners' powdered) sugar
- 3 tablespoons light corn syrup

Break up almond paste into tiny pieces in a small bowl; blend in 10X sugar and corn syrup until mixture forms a stiff dough. Roll out to shape on a pastry cloth or board lightly coated with 10X sugar.

GROOM'S CAKE

The top tier of our ROSE PINK WEDDING CAKE can be made of fruit cake batter. This is the cake layer that traditionally is saved for the first anniversary.

Bake at 275° 2 hours, 15 minutes to 2 hours, 45 minutes.
Makes one 8x2-inch layer and two 9x5x3-inch loaves.

- 2 jars (1 pound each) mixed candied fruits
- 1 package (15 ounces) golden raisins
- 1 can (7 ounces) flaked coconut
- 2 cups chopped walnuts
- 2 packages (about 1 pound each) pound cake mix
- 4 eggs
- 1 cup liquid
- 2 tablespoons apricot brandy
- Apricot Glaze (recipe, page 73)

1. Grease and flour an 8x2-inch layer cake pan. Grease and line two 9x5x3-inch loaf pans with wax paper; grease paper.
2. Combine mixed fruits, raisins, coconut and chopped nuts in a very large bowl or kettle. Add 1½ cups dry pound cake mix and toss to coat fruits and nuts evenly with mix.
3. Prepare pound cake mix with eggs, liquid called for on label and apricot brandy, following label directions.
4. Pour batter over prepared fruits and nuts and stir until evenly mixed.
5. Divide batter among prepared layer and loaf pans. Place one oven rack in center of oven and arrange all three pans on same oven rack.

6. Bake in very slow oven (275°) 2 hours, then begin to test cakes. The cakes are done when a cake tester or long wooden skewer is inserted into center of cake and comes out clean. (The cake may be done in another 15 minutes or may take up to 45 minutes longer. The time varies with the brand of cake mix you use and the size and shape of your oven.)

7. Remove layers from oven and cool on wire racks 30 minutes. Loosen cakes around edges with a thin-bladed knife and turn out onto racks; remove wax paper; cool cakes completely. Brush with APRICOT GLAZE.

BAKER'S TIP: If not assembling cake at once, you may wrap cooled cakes in aluminum foil or plastic wrap; refrigerate or freeze. The cake will stay fresh and moist for one month in the refrigerator and up to three months in the freezer.

KING'S CAKE

At Mardi Gras time in New Orleans, the person who gets the bean in his or her portion becomes king or queen for a day or a week.

Bake at 375° for 30 minutes.
Makes 1 twelve-inch ring cake.

½ cup (1 stick) butter or margarine
1 small can evaporated milk (⅔ cup)
½ cup granulated sugar
2 teaspoons salt
5 eggs
2 envelopes active dry yeast
⅓ cup very warm water
1 tablespoon grated lemon rind
1 tablespoon grated orange rind
5 ½ cups all purpose flour
1 dry bean
1 cup 10X (confectioners' powdered) sugar
2 tablespoons water
Candied citron slices
Tiny candy decorettes
Gold and silver dragees

1. Combine butter or margarine, evaporated milk, granulated sugar, and salt in a small saucepan. Heat slowly until butter or margarine is melted. Cool until lukewarm.
2. Beat 4 of the eggs in a large bowl with a wire whip; stir in milk mixture.
3. Sprinkle yeast and 1 teaspoon sugar into very warm water in a cup. ("Very warm" water should feel comfortably warm when dropped on wrist.) Stir until yeast dissolves; allow to stand until mixture bubbles, about 10 minutes. Add to egg mixture, blending well. Add lemon rind and orange rind.
4. Beat in flour with a wooden spoon, about 1 cup at a time, to make a stiff dough. Turn out onto a lightly floured pastry cloth or board; knead until smooth and elastic, about 10 minutes, adding only enough extra flour to keep dough from sticking.
5. Place in a greased large bowl; turn dough to coat all over with shortening; cover with a towel. Let rise in a warm place, away from draft 1 hour, or until double in bulk.
6. Punch dough down; knead a few times; divide in half. Using palms of hands, roll half to a rope about 20-inches long; lift ends and twisting loosely one or two times, place on a greased large cookie sheet in half circle; repeat with second half of dough, pinching ends of ropes together to form a large ring. Lift ring slightly at one side and push the bean about 1 inch into the dough from the bottom. Cover with towel; let rise again in warm place, away from draft, 45 minutes, or until double in bulk.
7. While dough rises, beat remaining egg in a small bowl with a wire whip. Brush over dough.
8. Bake in moderate oven (375°) 30 minutes, or until deep golden brown and ring gives a hollow sound when tapped. Slide carefully from sheet to wire rack. Cool.
9. Before serving, mix 10X sugar with water in a cup until smooth. Drizzle over ring, then decorate with candied citron, decorettes, and dragees.
10. On serving, cut cake into same number of wedges as there are persons to be served.

SWEETHEART CAKE

The perfect way to celebrate Valentine's Day. The same cake, with an appropriate message, is lovely for a young lady's birthday or graduation, or an engagement party. The picture is on page 70.

Bake at 350° for 35 minutes.
Makes two 9-inch heart-shaped layers.

2¼ cups cake flour
1½ cups sugar
1 tablespoon baking powder
1 teaspoon salt
2 eggs, separated
⅓ cup vegetable oil
1 cup milk
1 teaspoon vanilla
1 teaspoon almond extract
Sweetheart Frosting (recipe follows)
Red and green food coloring

1. Grease bottoms of two heart-shaped layer cake pans or two 9-inch layer cake pans; line with wax paper and grease paper.
2. Sift cake flour, 1 cup of the sugar, baking powder and salt into large bowl of electric mixer.
3. Beat egg whites until foamy-white and double in volume in small bowl of mixer at high speed. Sprinkle in remaining ½ cup sugar, 1 tablespoon at a time, beating all the time, until meringue forms soft peaks.
4. Blend vegetable oil and ½ cup of the milk into flour mixture, then beat 2 minutes with mixer at medium speed. Stir in egg yolks, remaining ½ cup milk, vanilla, and almond extract; beat 1 minute at medium speed.
5. Fold in meringue with wire whip until no streaks of white remain. Pour into prepared pans.
6. Bake in moderate oven (350°) 35 minutes, or until tops spring back when lightly pressed with fingertip.
7. Cool in pans on wire racks 5 minutes. Loosen around edges with knife and turn out onto racks; peel off paper; cool completely.
8. Make SWEETHEART FROSTING. Measure ½ cup frosting into a small bowl; tint pale green with green food coloring. Reserve another ½ cup frosting. Tint remaining frosting pale pink with red food coloring.
9. Put layers together with pink SWEETHEART FROSTING. Frost sides and top of cake, spreading frosting with spatula as smoothly as possible. (Dip spatula into a cup of hot water often while frosting cake.)
10. Reserve ¼ cup pink frosting. Tint remaining pink frosting a deeper pink with more red food coloring. Fit #21 star tip onto pastry bag; press out frosting in overlapping design around entire bottom of cake.
11. Fit #7 writing tip onto second pastry bag; fill with reserved white SWEETHEART FROSTING; print "Be My Valentine" on top of cake, following directions on page 67.
12. Fit #96 drop flower tip onto pastry bag with deep pink frosting; make drop flowers on cake, as photographed on page 70, following directions on page 66.
13. Fit #14 star tip onto pastry bag with white frosting; press a tiny center into each drop flower. Then make white flowers, as photographed on page 70. Clean #14 tip and place on pastry bag filled with remaining pink frosting. Press tiny centers into white flowers.
14. Fit #7 writing tip onto bag filled with green frosting. Make scroll as pictured on page 70. Then make stems for flower spray, following directions on page 67.
15. Fit the #67 leaf tip onto pastry bag; pipe leaves, following picture.

SWEETHEART FROSTING

Makes enough to fill, frost and decorate heart-shaped cake.

- ¾ cup (1½ sticks) butter or margarine
- 6 cups 10X (confectioners' powdered) sugar, sifted
  Dash salt
- 3 tablespoons cream
- 2 tablespoons light corn syrup
- 1 teaspoon vanilla
- ½ teaspoon almond extract

Beat butter or margarine until soft in large bowl of electric mixer at medium speed. Beat in 10X sugar and salt until mixture is crumbly and all of the sugar has been added. Add cream, corn syrup, vanilla and almond extract. Beat until mixture is smooth.

GREEK CHRISTMAS BREAD

Crunchy walnuts and sesame seeds combine with honey for a luscious filling in this festive holiday treat.

Bake at 350° for 45 minutes.
Makes 1 large loaf.

- ½ cup (1 stick) butter or margarine
- ⅓ cup sugar
- ¼ cup milk
- ½ teaspoon crushed anise seeds
- 1 teaspoon salt
- 1 envelope active dry yeast
- ¼ cup very warm water
- 2 eggs
- 3½ cups all purpose flour
  Walnut Filling (recipe follows)
  Candied red cherries
  Sesame seeds
  Candied yellow and green pineapple slices

1. Combine butter, sugar, milk, anise seed and salt in a small saucepan; heat the mixture slowly, stirring often, until the butter melts; then cool to lukewarm.
2. Dissolve yeast and 1 teaspoon sugar in very warm water in a large bowl. ("Very warm" water should feel comfortably warm when dropped on wrist.) Stir until well blended and allow to stand 10 minutes, or until mixture begins to bubble.
3. Beat eggs in a cup until well blended; add all but 2 tablespoons of beaten egg to yeast; reserve remaining egg for Step 6. Strain cooled butter mixture into bowl. Beat in enough flour with wooden spoon to make a soft dough; turn out onto a lightly floured surface. Knead until smooth and elastic, about 5 minutes, using

enough of remaining flour to keep dough from sticking.
4. Place dough in a buttered bowl; turn to bring buttered side up. Cover with a clean towel or plastic wrap. Let rise in a warm place, away from draft, 1½ hours, or until double in bulk.
5. Punch dough down; turn out onto lightly floured surface; knead a few times; pat out to an 8-inch round and cut off a 1½-inch piece; reserve. Pat out remaining dough to a 12-inch round; spread with WALNUT FILLING; draw edges towards center to cover filling and press together to seal.
6. Place dough, seam-side down, on a lightly greased cookie sheet; pat with hands into an 8-inch round. Brush with part of the reserved beaten egg. Cut reserved dough in half; roll out one piece to a 10-inch rope and place down center of bread; roll remaining dough into an 8-inch rope and lay over first rope to form a cross; brush well with beaten egg. Make small cuts into ropes and insert red cherries.
7. Cover; let rise in a warm place, 45 minutes, or until almost double in bulk; brush with remaining beaten egg; sprinkle with sesame seeds.
8. Bake in moderate oven (350°) 45 minutes, or until bread gives a hollow sound when tapped. Cool on wire rack; garnish with slivers of candied yellow and green pineapple slices to add additional "jewels" to the cross.

WALNUT FILLING

Makes enough to fill 1 loaf.

- ½ cup chopped walnuts
- ¼ cup sesame seeds
- 3 tablespoons honey

Combine walnuts, sesame seeds and honey in a small bowl to blend well.

STRAWBERRY CAKE

Celebrate the Fourth of July in fine all-American style: Bake this delicate layer cake and top it with luscious fresh berries.

Bake at 350° for 30 minutes.
Makes two 9-inch layers.

- 2⅔ cups cake flour
- 1½ cups sugar
- 2 teaspoons baking powder
- ¼ teaspoon salt
- 1⅓ cups heavy cream
- 4 eggs
- 1½ teaspoons vanilla
  Strawberry Butter Cream (recipe, page 10)

1. Grease two 9-inch layer cake pans; dust with flour; tap out any excess.
2. Measure flour, sugar, baking

powder and salt into a sifter.
3. Beat cream in large bowl until stiff with electric mixer at high speed.
4. Beat eggs in a small bowl until very thick and light with mixer at high speed; beat in vanilla; fold into whipped cream. Sift dry ingredients over cream mixture; gently fold in with wire whip until batter is smooth; pour batter into prepared pans.
5. Bake in moderate oven (350°) 35 minutes, or until centers spring back when lightly pressed with fingertip.
6. Cool layers in pans on wire racks 10 minutes; loosen around edges with a knife; turn out onto wire racks; cool.
7. Put layers together with STRAW-BERRY BUTTER CREAM; frost side and top with remaining frosting; garnish with strawberries, if you wish.

OLD WORLD EASTER BREAD

Original recipes for this sweet bread come from Russia, where it is called "Kulich."

Bake at 350° for 40 minutes.
Makes 1 loaf.

- ⅓ cup milk
- ¼ cup sugar
- ½ teaspoon salt
- ¼ cup (½ stick) butter or margarine
- 1 envelope active dry yeast
- ¼ cup very warm water
- 1 egg, beaten
- 2 cups all purpose flour
- ¼ cup candied orange peel
- ¼ cup golden raisins
- ¼ teaspoon ground nutmeg
- 2 tablespoons fine dry bread crumbs
- ½ cup 10X (confectioners' powdered) sugar
- 1 tablespoon water
  Yellow food coloring

1. Heat milk with sugar, salt and butter or margarine in small saucepan; cool just until warm.
2. Sprinkle yeast and 1 teaspoon sugar into very warm water in medium-size bowl. ("Very warm" water should feel comfortably warm when dropped on wrist.) Stir until yeast dissolves; allow to stand until mixture bubbles, about 10 minutes; then stir in cooled milk mixture and egg.
3. Beat in 1 cup of the flour until smooth with a large wooden spoon; stir in orange peel, raisins and nutmeg; beat in remaining 1 cup flour to make a soft dough. Beat 100 times with either a wooden spoon or dough hook of electric mixer.
4. Coat top of dough lightly with butter or margarine, cover with clean towel. Let rise in warm place, away from draft, 1 hour, or until doubled.

5. Brush a 6-cup tall mold or 6-cup deep bowl with oil; sprinkle with bread crumbs. Punch dough down; beat 100 times with either a wooden spoon or dough hook of electric mixer. Spoon into mold.

6. Cover with clean towel; let rise in warm place, away from draft, 45 minutes, or until double in bulk.

7. Bake in moderate oven (350°) 40 minutes, or until loaf gives a hollow sound when tapped. Cool 5 minutes on wire rack; remove from mold.

8. Mix 10X sugar and water in a cup to make a thin frosting; drizzle half over loaf, letting it run down side. Blend a drop or two of yellow food coloring into remaining frosting to tint yellow; drizzle over. Decorate top with a few slivered almonds.

SPRINGTIME CROWN

Golden roses cascade down a regal cake.

Bake at 325° for 50 minutes.
Makes one 10-inch angel tube cake.

1 package (14½ ounces) angel food
    cake mix
    Water
2 packages (7 ounces each) fluffy
    white frosting mix
1 pound 10X (confectioners'
    powdered) sugar, sifted
    Green, red, and yellow food
    colorings

1. Prepare cake mix with water, following label directions. Spoon into a 10-inch angel cake tube pan.

2. Bake in slow oven (325°) 50 minutes, or until cake begins to pull from side of pan.

3. Invert pan onto a large bottle; cool 1 hour; loosen around edge and tube; remove from pan.

4. Prepare 1 package of the frosting mix with boiling water, following label directions; stir in 10X sugar, 1 cup at a time, just until frosting is stiff enough to hold its shape. Spoon a third into a small bowl; tint green with a few drops food coloring. Stir a few drops each red and yellow food colorings into remaining to tint light orange; measure out ¼ cup; reserve.

5. Make 15 roses, following directions on page 66; let dry until firm.

6. Prepare remaining package of frosting mix with boiling water, following label directions; tint pale yellow with food coloring; frost cake. Peel roses from wax paper; arrange on cake.

7. Fill pastry bag with green frosting; change to #67 leaf tip; press out leaves around roses.

PARTY RING CAKE

With this basic recipe you can make a BUTTERFLY CAKE for a springtime birthday or double the recipe and make a DOUBLE-RING WEDDING CAKE. The photos of both cakes are on page 65.

Bake at 350° for 35 minutes.
Makes one 12-inch ring cake.

3 cups cake flour
2 teaspoons baking powder
½ teaspoon salt
1 cup (2 sticks) butter or margarine
2 cups sugar
4 eggs
1 teaspoon vanilla
1 cup milk

1. Grease and flour one 12-inch ring cake pan; tap out excess.

2. Sift flour, baking powder and salt onto wax paper.

3. Beat butter or margarine, sugar, eggs and vanilla in large bowl of mixer at high speed 3 minutes.

4. Beat in flour mixture, alternately with milk, with mixer at low speed. Scrape side of bowl with rubber scraper after each addition. Pour batter into prepared pan.

5. Bake in moderate oven (350°) 35 minutes, or until center springs back when lightly pressed with fingertip.

6. Cool in pan on wire rack 10 minutes; loosen around edges with a knife; turn out onto wire racks and cool completely. Spread with favorite frosting, or use to make one of the party cakes below.

BUTTERFLY CAKE: Bake and cool PARTY RING CAKE. Cut cake in half, lengthwise; place half-circles, rounded sides together, on serving plate; cut a ½-inch slice from each cake half; remove and press cake pieces together to give shape of butterfly. (See shape on page 65.) Make LEMON BUTTER CREAM (recipe, page 10); remove 1 cup of frosting; tint remaining a rich yellow with yellow food coloring. Frost entire cake with frosting. Stir 1 square unsweetened chocolate, melted, into reserved frosting. Fit a decorating set with a #16 star tip; fill with chocolate frosting. Make a double ruffle row in center of cake joinings to form "body" and pipe a ruffle around inner half-circles to make "wings." Fit a #5 writing tip in decorating set; pipe a scallop pattern on wings. Insert two tiny flowers for the "antennae."

DOUBLE-RING WEDDING CAKE: Make two batches of PARTY RING CAKE; cool completely. Holding one ring over the second ring, overlap cake so that a small space shows in center. Mark overlapped area on lower cake with a knife; cut section out between marks and reserve. Place rings side-by-side on serving tray; cut a piece from reserved cake to fit inside uncut ring to complete interlocking double-ring effect. (See illustration #7 on page 65.) Make SEVEN-MINUTE FROSTING (recipe, page 6). Frost all surfaces of cake, frosting inside of rings first, then outside. (See illustration #8 on page 65.) Swirl frosting in wide sweeps over rings with spatula. Tint remaining frosting pale pink with red food coloring. Fit a pastry bag with #16 star tip. Pipe a ruffle boarder to outline double rings. Garnish top of cake with the bride's favorite fresh flowers, if you wish.

BAKING BASICS

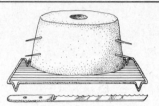

THE PERFECT CUT

• To split a sponge tube cake, insert wooden picks evenly all around cake; use picks as guide for knife, always cutting toward center of cake with long, thin serrated knife; cut across and through.

• When slicing a sponge, angel or chiffon cake, use serrated knife or special cake breaker.

• For fruit cakes and heavy cakes, use sharp French knife.

• Dip knife in hot water and wipe with damp cloth or paper towel before slicing to prevent frosting from sticking to knife. Also helpful in cutting cheesecakes.

• Some cakes, such as tea breads and pound cakes, slice better the day after they're baked.

• Here's the number of servings you can expect to get from a cake:

9x5x3-inch loaf	8
8-inch square	8 or 9
9-inch square	9
8-inch double layer	10-12
9-inch double layer	12-16
13x9x2-inch	12-16
10-inch fluted or tube	10-12
10-inch jelly roll	10

• To keep a square double-layer cake from collapsing when you cut it, slice a quarter at a time.

Chapter 3 continued on page 118.

Delicious cakes and cookies don't have to be time-consuming to prepare. In this chapter there are dozens of effortless desserts to make when you're in a rush. Our Strawberry Basket (on page 82-83) is a perfect example of a cake that's not only easily made, but good to look at and eat as well. It's made from a mix, and our photos on page 83 show you how to put it together fast. The Neapolitan Ribbon at right is a streamlined version of a classic French 7-layer cake, and it never tasted better.

Chapter 4
GREAT-
TASTING

DESSERTS
IN A HURRY

The Coconut-Lemon Squares, Carefree Drop Cookies and Peanut Crescent Bars at the left, top and middle of page 84 are made from items on hand; recipes are on pages 54 & 56. Also featured in this section: Desserts that don't require baking (including a marvelous cheesecake) and even a Sachertorte to make in 10 minutes! They'll bring you applause as well as save you time.

NEAPOLITAN RIBBON:
1. Pour tinted cake batter into baking pans for layers.
2. Make cake ribbons by spooning melted jelly over each thin layer.

STRAWBERRY BASKET: 1. Cut a cone-shaped piece from center of cake and lift off.
2. Arrange almond slices in three rows around jelly-glazed side.
3. Beat strawberry-gelatin mixture into whipped cream in electric mixer.

83

PEANUT CRESCENT BARS (right): 1. Press refrigerated crescent rolls into bottom of jelly roll pan, sealing perforations.

2. Spread over a mixture of peanut butter, cream cheese and 10X sugar to coat the crust evenly. Sprinkle with chopped nuts.

PECAN-DATE RING

Brown sugar syrup gives a homemade touch to a popular date-bread mix.

Bake at 350° for 40 minutes.
Makes one 8-inch ring.

- ½ cup (1 stick) butter or margarine
- ½ cup firmly packed brown sugar
- ½ teaspoon vanilla
- ½ cup chopped pecans
- 1 package (15 ounces) date-bread mix
  Egg
  Water

1. Melt butter or margarine in a small saucepan; remove from heat. Stir in brown sugar and vanilla.
2. Sprinkle pecans into a greased 7-cup ring mold; pour sugar syrup over.
3. Prepare date-bread mix with egg and water, following label directions; spoon over pecan mixture in mold.
4. Bake in moderate oven (350°) 40 minutes, or until a wooden pick inserted near center comes out clean. Let stand 10 minutes in mold on a wire rack; invert onto a serving plate.

MICHIGAN CHERRY SQUARES

Bright red cherries are crowned with a super creamy topping for a rich dessert.

Bake at 450° for 8 minutes,
then at 350° for 45 minutes.
Makes 2 dozen.

- 1 package piecrust mix
- 1 can (21 ounces) cherry pie filling
- 1 can (about 14 ounces) sweetened condensed milk (not evaporated)
- 1 can (3½ ounces) flaked coconut
- 1 cup chopped pecans
- ¼ cup all purpose flour
- ¼ cup firmly packed brown sugar
- 2 tablespoons butter or margarine, melted

1. Prepare piecrust mix, following label directions. (Or use your favorite 2-crust pie recipe.) Pat dough into the bottom of a 13x9x2-inch baking pan.
2. Bake in very hot oven (450°) 8 minutes, or until lightly browned. Remove to wire rack. Lower oven temperature to moderate (350°).
3. Spoon canned cherries over pastry; spread condensed milk over cherries. Combine coconut, pecans, flour, brown sugar and melted butter or margarine in a small bowl until crumbly with a pastry blender. Sprinkle over condensed milk.
4. Bake in moderate oven (350°) 45 minutes, or until crumbs are golden. Cool in pan on wire rack. Cut into 24 bars. Keep in refrigerator.

STRAWBERRY BASKET

Party-perfect yet it's really simple to make. Just follow the step-by-step photos on page 83.

Bake at 325° for 50 minutes.
Makes one 10-inch angel tube cake.

- 1 package (14½ ounces) angel food cake mix
  Water
- 1 envelope unflavored gelatin
- 2 cups spirited strawberry-flavored beverage (see Cook's Guide)
- ½ cup apple jelly
  Toasted sliced almonds
- 1 can (about 1 pound) chocolate frosting
- 1 cup heavy cream
- 2 tablespoons sugar
- 1 pint strawberries, washed, hulled and sliced

1. Prepare cake mix with water, following label directions. Pour into an ungreased 10-inch angel tube pan.
2. Bake in slow oven (325°) 50 minutes, or until top springs back when lightly touched with fingertip. Invert pan onto a one-quart bottle. Allow to hang until cake cools.
3. While cake cools, soften gelatin in ½ cup strawberry beverage in a small saucepan. Heat slowly, stirring constantly, until gelatin dissolves; pour into a small bowl with remaining 1½ cups strawberry beverage; stir to blend; chill 40 minutes, or until thick as unbeaten egg.
4. Invert cake onto pastry board; starting ½ inch in from outer edge, cut a cone-shape piece from center, using a serrated knife and a sawing motion; lift out.
5. Melt apple jelly in a small saucepan and brush all over cake; arrange almonds in three rows around cake. Fit a decorating set with a #98 shell tip; fill with chocolate frosting. Pipe lines, at 45° angles around cake, between almond rows to indicate basket, as shown in picture on page 82.
6. Place cake on serving plate; pipe frosting around bottom edge.
7. Beat cream with sugar in small bowl of electric mixer at medium speed; gradually add strawberry mixture and beat until creamy and smooth. Fold in sliced strawberries. (If mixture does not mound, place bowl into a second bowl of ice and water and fold gently a few minutes, until mixture begins to mound.
8. Spoon strawberry mixture into angel cake, mounding on top. Chill until serving time.
BAKER'S TIP: The center part of angel cake and remaining chocolate frosting make a delicious dessert, too.

TEN-MINUTE SACHERTORTE

Four dark layers with a double filling and chocolate frosting make this beauty.

Makes 1 loaf.

- 1 package (10 ounces) frozen chocolate pound cake, thawed
- 1 jar (12 ounces) apricot preserves
- 1 can (1 pound) chocolate frosting
- 3 tablespoons brandy

1. Cut chocolate pound cake into 4 slices, lengthwise, with a long knife.
2. Heat apricot preserves slowly in a small saucepan, stirring constantly, just until hot; press through a sieve into a small bowl; cool.
3. Spread each of 3 cake layers with ⅓ cup of the chocolate frosting, then ⅓ cup of the apricot preserves; stack back together on a serving plate. Top with plain layer; sprinkle whole loaf with brandy.
4. Frost sides and top of torte thinly with remaining chocolate frosting; chill. Cut in thin wedges to serve, for it is very rich.

SHADOW CREAM CAKE

Four thin cream-filled layers are topped with vanilla frosting and trimmed with chocolate.

Bake at 350° for 30 minutes.
Makes two 9-inch layers.

- 1 package (about 18 ounces) yellow cake mix
- 1 package (about 4 ounces) vanilla-flavored pudding mix
- 1 package (6 ounces) semi-sweet chocolate pieces
- 1 package (about 1 pound) vanilla frosting mix
- 1 tablespoon vegetable shortening

1. Prepare and bake cake mix in two 9-inch layer cake pans, then cool, following label directions. Remove from pans.
2. Prepare pudding mix, following label directions; remove from heat. Stir in ½ cup of the semi-sweet chocolate pieces until melted; chill.
3. Prepare frosting mix, following label directions.
4. Split each cake layer to make 4 thin layers. Put together with pudding filling between each; place on serving plate. Spread prepared frosting on top and side of cake.
5. Melt remaining ½ cup semi-sweet chocolate pieces with shortening in small saucepan over hot water; drizzle from tip of teaspoon around edge of cake, letting it drip down side to make a ring of chocolate on frosting. (See photograph on page 65.)

DOUBLE-BERRY CREAM CAKE

A gourmet dessert can be ready in less than 15 minutes, and be greeted with cheers.

Makes 6 servings.

1 pint raspberries
1 pint blueberries
¼ cup sugar
3 tablespoons sweet white wine
2 packaged sponge cake layers
1 pint vanilla ice cream

1. Wash raspberries and blueberries; stem; drain well. Mash ½ cup of the raspberries in a medium-size bowl; stir in sugar and wine. Let stand 15 minutes; stir in remaining berries.
2. Place 1 sponge layer on a serving plate; cover with about a third of the ice cream and half of the berry mixture. Top with remaining cake layer, ice cream and berries. Serve with whipped cream, if you wish.

NEAPOLITAN RIBBON

Colorful layers of thin pound cake are joined with tangy apple jelly and lavishly coated with chocolate. Photo is on page 81.

Bake at 350° for 15 minutes.
Makes 1 cake.

1 package (about 1 pound) pound cake mix
2 eggs
   Liquid as label directs
   Yellow, red and green food coloring
½ cup apple jelly
¼ cup crème de cocoa
2 tablespoons butter or margarine
3 tablespoons light corn syrup
¼ cup water
1 package (6 ounces) semi-sweet chocolate pieces
   Chopped pistachio nuts

1. Prepare pound cake mix with eggs and liquid, following label directions.
2. Measure 1 cupful of batter in a small bowl; tint a bright yellow with a few drops yellow food coloring. Repeat with remaining batter, tinting pink and green with food coloring; pour into three greased 9x9x2-inch baking pans. (Or bake one layer; wash pan; repeat twice.)
   3. Bake layers in moderate oven (350°) 15 minutes, or until cake springs back when lightly pressed with fingertip. Cool in pans 10 minutes. Loosen layers around edges with sharp knife and turn out onto wire racks; cool completely.
4. Trim cake layers to square off edges. Cut each layer into 2 even strips, about 4-inches wide.
5. Combine apple jelly and crème de cocoa in a small saucepan. Heat slowly until jelly melts.
6. To make cake: Place 1 green strip on cookie sheet. Spoon apple syrup over cake. Top with a yellow strip; spoon apple syrup over; then top with pink strip and more apple syrup. Repeat with 3 more strips of cake. Brush sides with syrup.
7. Combine butter or margarine, corn syrup and water in a small saucepan. Bring to boiling. Remove from heat. Stir in chocolate pieces until melted. Beat mixture for about 3 minutes, or until stiff enough to spread on cakes.
8. Frost cake with chocolate and sprinkle with chopped pistachio nuts.

BAKING BASICS

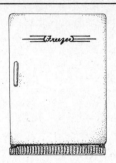

FREEZING CAKES AND COOKIES

Freezing Cakes:
• Unfrosted cakes freeze best—up to 4 months. Wrap in aluminum foil, plastic wrap, or large plastic bags; thaw at room temperature 1 hour.
• Frosted cakes should be frozen on piece of cardboard or a cookie sheet until firm, then wrapped in aluminum foil, plastic wrap or very large plastic bags; freeze up to 3 months and thaw at room temperature 2 hours.
Freezing cookies:
• Both dough and baked cookies can be frozen and stored for 9-12 months.
• Baked cookies should be frozen in strong box lined with plastic wrap or foil; separate each layer with more wrap or foil; thaw cookies at room temperature 10 minutes.
• Cookie dough may be frozen in foil or plastic wrap.
• Drop cookie dough should be thawed until just soft enough to use.
• Refrigerator cookie rolls should be thawed just enough to slice.
• Rolled cookies can be frozen already shaped; place, still frozen, onto cookie sheets.
• Freeze bar cookie dough in pan in which it is to be baked; cover with plastic wrap, then foil.

SANDWICH CAKES

Pound cake slices are your starter for this extra-quick dessert.

Bake at 450° for 10 minutes.
Makes 4 servings.

4 slices frozen pound cake, cut ½-inch thick
½ cup canned crushed pineapple, well drained
2 tablespoons butter or margarine
4 tablespoons brown sugar

1. Place pound cake slices on a cookie sheet; spread with pineapple.
2. Blend butter or margarine and brown sugar with a fork in measuring cup; sprinkle over pineapple.
3. Bake in very hot oven (450°) 10 minutes, or until topping is bubbly.
4. Serve warm, plain or with whipped cream, if you wish. (Peach slices can be substituted for pineapple.)

COCONUT ICE CREAM CAKE

This cream-frosted dessert gives you cake and ice cream all in one. It's a perfect make-ahead, too.

Bake at 325° for 50 minutes.
Makes one 10-inch angel tube cake.

1 package (14½ ounces) angel food cake mix
2 pints strawberry ice cream
1 cup heavy cream
2 tablespoons 10X (confectioner's powdered) sugar
1 teaspoon vanilla
   Few drops red food coloring
¾ cup flaked coconut

1. Prepare and bake cake mix in a 10-inch angel cake tube pan, then cool, following label directions. Remove cake from pan; wash pan.
2. Slice cake crosswise into 3 even layers; return top layer to pan. (Set middle layer aside for another dessert or a snack time treat.)
3. Spoon ice cream in an even layer over cake in pan; top with remaining cake layer. Cover pan with aluminum foil; freeze 24 hours, or until very firm.
4. About 2 hours before serving, beat cream, 10X sugar and vanilla until stiff in small bowl of electric mixer at high speed; fold in a few drops red food coloring to tint delicate pink.
5. Unmold cake onto chilled serving plate. Frost with whipped cream; sprinkle top and side with coconut. Return to freezer until serving time.
6. Slice into wedges with a sharp long-blade knife. Wrap any remaining cake in aluminum foil and store in freezer, up to 3 months.

WHIRLIGIG PEAR CAKE

Plan to serve this dessert at the table so everyone can see how pretty it is.

Makes 4 servings.

- 1 can (about 1 pound) pear halves
- 2 tablespoons lemon juice
- 2 tablespoons brown sugar
- 1 tablespoon cornstarch
- 1 packaged sponge cake layer

1. Drain and measure syrup from pears into a 1-cup measure; add water to make ¾ cup. Add lemon juice.
2. Mix brown sugar and cornstarch in small saucepan; stir in syrup mixture. Cook, stirring constantly, until sauce thickens and bubbles 1 minute.
3. Place a sponge cake layer on deep serving plate; arrange drained pears, cut-side down, in wheel design on top. Spoon hot sauce over and let soak into cake. Serve warm.

FEBRUARY SHORTCAKE

With frozen fruits you can have the flavor of summer all winter long.

Bake at 450° for 15 minutes.
Makes two 8-inch layers.

- 2 packages refrigerated buttermilk biscuits
- 1 cup all purpose flour
- ½ cup firmly packed brown sugar
- ½ cup (1 stick) butter or margarine
- 2 packages (10 ounces each) quick-thaw frozen strawberries
- 2 firm ripe bananas
- 1 container (4½ ounces) frozen whipped topping, thawed

1. Separate biscuits, following label directions. Place in a single layer in each of two 8-inch layer cake pans; press together to fill any holes and make an even layer.
2. Mix flour and brown sugar in a small bowl; cut in butter or margarine with pastry blender, until mixture is crumbly. Sprinkle over biscuit layers to coat biscuits completely.
3. Bake in very hot oven (450°) 15 minutes, or until firm and golden. Cool 10 minutes in pans on wire racks. Loosen around edges with a knife; carefully remove from pans.
4. While layers bake, thaw fruits, following label directions. Peel bananas; slice; combine with strawberries, stirring lightly.
5. Stack biscuit layers, shortcake style, on a serving plate with fruit mixture between and on top. Spoon part of the whipped topping in center. Cut shortcake into wedges; serve with remaining whipped topping. Garnish with grated orange rind, if you wish.

RAINBOW ICE CREAM CAKE

Your freezer does all the work and you take all the bows. This party dessert is easy.

Bake at 350° for 30 minutes.
Makes one 9-inch cake.

- 1 package (about 18 ounces) chocolate cake mix
- 2 eggs
   Water
- 1 quart strawberry ice cream, softened
- 1 quart pistachio ice cream, softened
- 2 envelopes (2 ounces each) whipped topping mix
   Milk
   Red food coloring
- 3 tablespoon light rum
   Chopped pistachio nuts

1. Grease 2 nine-inch layer cake pans; dust with flour; tap out any excess.
2. Prepare cake mix with eggs and water, following label directions; pour into prepared pans.
3. Bake in moderate oven (350°) 30 minutes, or until centers spring back when lightly pressed with fingertip. Cool in pans on wire racks 10 minutes. Loosen layers around edges with a knife; turn out onto racks; cool completely. Split each layer, crosswise, using a sawing motion with a knife.
4. While layers bake, cut two 18-inch lengths of plastic wrap and fit into two 8-inch layer cake pans.
5. Spread half the strawberry ice cream evenly in each cake pan. Top with half the pistachio ice cream in each pan. (Or use your favorite flavor combinations.) Cover ice cream with plastic wrap; freeze until ready to use.
6. Place one split cake layer on cookie sheet. Remove one ice cream layer from pan; peel off plastic wrap and place on split layer; repeat with 2 more split layers and second ice cream layer. (The extra split layer will make a nice treat for supper topped with a scoop of coffee ice cream.) Freeze entire cake while making frosting.
7. Beat whipped topping mix with milk, following label directions. Tint a pale pink with red food coloring and flavor with rum.
8. Frost side and top of cake with part of frosting; pile remaining frosting onto center of cake and swirl out with teaspoon; sprinkle with nuts.
9. Freeze until frosting is firm; then cover with plastic wrap.
10. When ready to serve, loosen cake around edge of cookie sheet with a spatula dipped in hot water; transfer to serving plate with spatula and pancake turner. Use a sharp knife for neater, easier slicing.

COTTAGE PUDDING

Stir up a tangy sauce to top a store-bought sponge layer for a quick dessert.

Makes 6 servings.

- ½ cup sugar
- 2 tablespoons cornstarch
- ¼ teaspoon salt
- 1 cup orange juice
- 2 tablespoons butter or margarine
- 1 teaspoon grated lemon rind
   Juice of 1 lemon
- 1 packaged sponge cake layer

1. Combine sugar, cornstarch and salt in a medium-size saucepan. Stir in orange juice.
2. Cook, stirring constantly, until sauce thickens and bubbles 1 minute; remove from heat; stir in butter or margarine, lemon rind and juice.
3. Place sponge cake layer on serving plate; spoon sauce over and serve.

CALIFORNIA SUPPER CAKE

Let the apprentice baker in your family whip up this tangy cake.

Bake at 350° for 30 minutes.
Makes one 9-inch square.

- 2 cups biscuit mix
- ½ cup granulated sugar
- 2 eggs
- 1 tablespoon grated orange rind
- ½ cup orange juice
- ⅓ cup butter or margarine, softened
- 1 teaspoon vanilla
- ⅓ cup firmly packed brown sugar
- ½ cup chopped walnuts
- 1 tablespoon cream

1. Combine biscuit mix, granulated sugar, eggs, orange rind, orange juice, vanilla and 3 tablespoons of the butter or margarine in the large bowl of electric mixer. Beat at low speed ½ minute to blend ingredients. Turn mixer speed to medium; beat 4 minutes. Scrape bowl often with rubber spatula.
2. Turn the batter into a buttered 9x9x2-inch baking pan.
3. Bake in moderate oven (350°) 30 minutes, or until center of cake springs back when lightly pressed with fingertip. Cool cake a few minutes on a wire rack.
4. Combine brown sugar, chopped walnuts, remaining butter and cream in small bowl of mixer; beat at medium speed until well blended. Spread on cake. Broil, with top 3 inches from heat, just until topping is bubbly and lightly browned, about 2 minutes. Cool cake on wire rack. Cut into squares. Serve with cinnamon-flavored tea, if you wish.

MISSISSIPPI SHORTCAKE

Sweetened strawberries and whipped cream layered between crisp biscuit "cookies."

Bake at 450° for 8 minutes.
Makes 6 servings.

- **2 cups biscuit mix**
- **¼ cup sugar**
- **⅔ cup milk**
- **3 tablespoons melted butter or margarine**
- **1 quart strawberries, washed, hulled, sliced and sweetened**
- **1 cup heavy cream, whipped**

1. Combine biscuit mix and 2 tablespoons of the sugar in medium-size bowl. Stir in milk, following label directions for making biscuits.
2. Turn out onto lightly floured pastry cloth or board; knead lightly 10 times. Roll out to ¼-inch thickness on lightly floured pastry cloth or board; cut with floured 2-inch cutter.
3. Place on ungreased cookie sheet; prick all over with fork; brush with melted butter or margarine; sprinkle with remaining 2 tablespoons sugar.
4. Bake in very hot oven (450°) 8 minutes, or until golden.
5. As soon as biscuits are done, put shortcakes together by layering strawberries and whipped cream between hot biscuits in individual deep soup bowls for each serving.

NO-BAKE CHEESECAKE

Your refrigerator "bakes" this creamy-smooth gelatin version of cheesecake.

Makes one 8-inch cake.

- **1 package (6 ounces) lemon-flavored gelatin**
- **2 cups hot water**
- **½ cup cold water**
- **2 eggs, separated**
- **3 cups (1½ pounds) cream-style cottage cheese**
- **1 teaspoon grated lemon rind**
- **Dash salt**
- **¼ cup sugar**
- **1 cup heavy cream**
- **Fresh mint**

1. Dissolve gelatin in hot water in a medium-size saucepan. Pour ½ cup into a 1-cup measure; stir in cold water; set aside at room temperature while preparing custard mixture.
2. Beat egg yolks slightly in a small bowl with a fork; slowly stir in a generous ½ cup of the hot gelatin mixture, then stir back into remaining gelatin mixture in saucepan. Cook, stirring constantly, 3 minutes; remove from heat. Chill 30 minutes, or just until thick as unbeaten egg white.

3. Pour the saved 1 cup gelatin mixture into an 8x8x2-inch pan; chill 15 minutes, or just until sticky-firm.
4. Press cottage cheese through a sieve into a large bowl; stir in thickened gelatin-custard mixture, lemon rind and salt.
5. Beat egg whites until foamy-white and double in volume in the small bowl of electric mixer at high speed; beat in sugar, 1 tablespoon at a time, until meringue forms soft peaks. Beat cream until stiff in a medium-size bowl with mixer at high speed.
6. Fold meringue, then whipped cream into thickened gelatin-cheese mixture until no streaks of white remain; spoon over sticky-firm gelatin layer in pan. Chill at least 6 hours.
7. When ready to serve, run a sharp-tip thin-bladed knife around top of dessert, then dip mold very quickly in and out of a pan of hot water. Cover with a serving plate; turn upside down; gently lift off mold. Garnish with sprigs of fresh mint.

TICKTACKTOE JEWEL CAKE

Surprise—the filling is fruity gelatin.

Makes one 8-inch cake.

- **1 can (about 1 pound) fruit cocktail**
- **1 package (3 ounces) strawberry-flavored gelatin**
- **1 cup boiling water**
- **1 nine-inch packaged sponge cake layer**
- **1 container (9 ounces) frozen whipped topping, thawed**

1. Drain syrup from fruit cocktail into a 1-cup measure.
2. Dissolve gelatin in boiling water in a medium-size bowl; stir in ½ cup of the fruit syrup.
3. Chill gelatin mixture 30 minutes, or until thick as unbeaten egg white; fold in fruit cocktail. Spoon into an 8-inch layer cake pan. Chill several hours, or until firm.
4. Place a piece of plastic wrap or aluminum foil over a large flat plate. Loosen gelatin layer around edge with a knife; dip pan *very* quickly in and out of hot water; turn out onto wrapped plate. Split cake layer; spread each half with ¼ cup of the whipped topping; place half, topping-side down, over gelatin layer. Cover with a serving plate; turn upside down; lift off plate and peel off wrap. Place remaining cake layer, spread-side down, over gelatin.
5. Frost side and top of cake with remaining whipped topping. Chill until serving time.

SAVANNAH CAKE SQUARES

Broiled frosting is rich with peanut butter, coconut and cream.

Bake at 350° for 40 minutes.
Makes one 13x9x2-inch cake.

- **1 package (about 18 ounces) yellow cake mix**
- **½ cup (1 stick) butter or margarine**
- **1 cup flaked coconut**
- **1 cup firmly packed brown sugar**
- **½ cup crunchy peanut butter**
- **⅓ cup light cream**

1. Prepare cake mix and bake in a greased 13x9x2-inch baking pan, following label directions.
2. While cake bakes, melt butter or margarine in a medium-size saucepan; remove from heat. Stir in brown sugar, peanut butter and cream.
3. Remove cake from oven; turn heat to *Broil*. Spread topping evenly over hot cake.
4. Broil, 4 to 6 inches from heat, 1 minute, or just until frosting bubbles; cool. Cut into squares. Garnish with whole peanuts, if you wish.
BAKER'S TIP: Omit peanut butter; add 1 cup chopped walnuts.

CHOCOLATE ANGEL RING

Easy, different way with angel food cake mix: Add cocoa to the batter.

Bake at 350° for 45 minutes.
Makes one 10-inch angel tube cake.

- **1 package (14½ ounces) angel food cake mix**
- **Water**
- **¼ cup cocoa powder (not a mix)**
- **1 tablespoon instant coffee powder**
- **½ cup boiling water**
- **1 package (7 ounces) fluffy white frosting mix**
- **Flaked coconut**

1. Prepare cake mix with water, following label directions. Sprinkle cocoa, alternately with 2 more tablespoons water, over batter and fold in completely; pour batter into a 10-inch angel cake tube pan.
2. Bake in moderate oven (350°) 45 minutes, or until a long skewer inserted near center comes out clean.
3. Hang cake in pan upside down over a quart-size bottle; cool completely. Loosen cake around edge and tube with a long, thin knife; invert onto a large serving plate.
4. Dissolve instant coffee in boiling water in a small deep bowl; add frosting mix. Prepare, following label directions. Spread over side and top of cake. Sprinkle generously with coconut. Cut into wedges.

BLUEBERRY RING

Coffee cake at its easiest blends lemon with muffin mix.

Bake at 375° for 40 minutes.
Makes one 8-inch tube cake.

2 packages (13½ ounces each) blueberry muffin mix
2 teaspoons grated lemon rind
2 eggs
1 cup milk
3 tablespoons light corn syrup
2 tablespoons lemon juice

1. Grease an 8-cup tube mold.
2. Combine muffin mix and lemon rind in a large bowl; stir in eggs and milk, following label directions. Spoon into prepared mold.
3. Bake in moderate oven (375°) 40 minutes, or until a wooden pick inserted near center comes out clean. Cool in mold on a wire rack 10 minutes; loosen around side and tube with a knife; invert onto a plate.
4. Mix corn syrup and lemon juice in a cup; spoon over warm cake to glaze lightly; cool cake completely. Garnish with fresh mint, if you wish. Serve with fruit for a special dessert.

FROSTING-BERRY CAKE

Anytime is Maytime when the centerpiece is a cake topped with strawberries shaped from creamy pink frosting.

Bake at 350° for 50 minutes.
Makes one 8-inch deep cake.

1 package (about 18 ounces) spice cake mix
2 eggs
Water
2 packages (15 ounces each) creamy vanilla frosting mix
½ cup (1 stick) butter or margarine
Green and red food colorings
2 cups 10X (confectioners' powdered) sugar
Red decorating sugar

1. Grease a deep square 10-cup glass-ceramic casserole. Or use a 10-cup deep round casserole; flour lightly.
2. Prepare cake mix with eggs and water, following label directions; pour into prepared casserole.
3. Bake in moderate oven (350°) 50 minutes, or until top springs back when lightly pressed with fingertip. Cool in casserole on a wire rack 10 minutes; turn out onto rack; cool completely.
4. Prepare 1 package of the frosting mix with ¼ cup of the butter or margarine and warm water, following label directions; frost cake.
5. Prepare remaining package of frosting mix with remaining butter or margarine and warm water, following label directions; measure out ½ cup and tint green with food coloring. Fit a #2 writing tip onto a cake-decorating set; fill with green frosting; press out onto sides of cake to form lattice.
6. Stir 10X sugar into remaining frosting until smooth and very stiff. Divide in half; tint one half green and the other pink with food colorings.
7. Pinch off green frosting, ½ teaspoonful at a time, and shape into ovals; flatten each with palm of hand to make leaves; draw on markings with a wooden pick; let firm.
8. Pinch off pink frosting, 1 teaspoonful at a time, and shape into strawberries; roll in red sugar on wax paper to coat well.
9. Arrange strawberries, tips up, on top of cake; tuck leaves between strawberries to cover top and look like a basket of strawberries. Serve with a ginger ale and orange juice punch and strawberries, if you wish.

CHERRY PARTY CAKE

Company coming and you've got little time to bake? Here's a make-ahead that's sure to win raves.

Bake at 350° for 40 minutes.
Makes one 13x9x2-inch cake.

1 package (about 18 ounces) white cake mix
1 package (3 ounces) cherry-flavored gelatin
½ teaspoon ground ginger
1 cup boiling water
1 cup cold water
1 cup heavy cream
2 tablespoons sugar
Toasted almond slices

1. Prepare white cake mix, following package directions. Pour into a greased 13x9x2-inch baking pan.
2. Bake in moderate oven (350°) 40 minutes, or until top springs back when lightly touched with fingertip. Cool in pan on wire rack 15 minutes. Poke with a dinner fork to a depth of ½ inch at ⅛-inch intervals.
3. Dissolve gelatin and ginger in boiling water in a small bowl; stir in cold water. Spoon warm gelatin evenly over cake. Chill 4 hours, or until serving time.
4. Beat cream and sugar together until stiff in small bowl of electric mixer at high speed.
5. Loosen cake around edges with a narrow spatula; invert onto wire rack, then onto rectangular serving board.
6. Frost top of cake with whipped cream and garnish with almonds.

QUICK-AND-EASY POUND CAKE

Just start with a cake mix, then add pudding mix, oil and two extra eggs for a cake too moist and delicious to frost.

Bake at 350° for 50 minutes.
Makes one 10-inch fluted tube cake.

1 package (about 18 ounces) yellow cake mix
1 package (about 4 ounces) lemon-flavored instant pudding mix
½ teaspoon ground mace
4 eggs
¼ cup vegetable oil
1 cup water
10X sugar

1. Combine cake mix, lemon pudding mix, mace, eggs, oil and water in the large bowl of electric mixer.
2. Beat at low speed to blend; increase speed to medium; beat 2 minutes, or until batter is thick and creamy. Pour into a well greased and floured 12-cup fluted tube pan or a greased and floured 9-inch angel cake tube pan.
3. Bake in moderate oven (350°) 50 minutes, or until top springs back when lightly touched with fingertip. Cool in pan on wire rack 15 minutes. Loosen around edge and tube with a narrow spatula. Turn out onto wire rack; cool completely. Sprinkle with 10X sugar just before serving. Top with cherry ice cream, if you wish.

PETALED HONEY RING

Surprise the family with a hot-from-the-oven coffee cake that's ready in minutes.

Bake at 350° for 25 minutes.
Makes one 9-inch ring.

2 packages refrigerated butterflake dinner rolls
3 tablespoons currants
3 teaspoons grated lemon rind
3 tablespoons honey
¼ cup (½ stick) butter or margarine, melted

1. Separate each package of rolls to make 24 even pieces. Place 12 pieces in a well buttered 7-cup ring mold to make an even layer. Sprinkle 1 tablespoon of the currants and 1 teaspoon of the lemon rind over layer, then drizzle 1 tablespoon each of the honey and melted butter or margarine over.
2. Make two more layers the same way; place remaining rolls on top. Drizzle remaining butter over.
3. Bake in moderate oven (350°) 25 minutes, or until firm and golden. Loosen at once around edge with knife; invert onto a serving plate. Let stand 10 minutes. To serve, pull off layers with two forks; serve warm.

DAFFODIL TORTE

This rich four-tier beauty, with its fillings of cream and preserves, hides several secrets for fast fixing.

Bake at 325° for 50 minutes.
Makes one 10-inch angel tube cake.

- 1 package (14½ ounces) angel food cake mix
  Yellow food coloring
- 1 cup (8 ounces) dairy sour cream
- ½ cup finely chopped almonds
- ¾ cup apricot preserves
  10X sugar

1. Prepare angel cake mix, following label directions; spoon half the batter into a second bowl; tint pale yellow with food coloring.
2. Spoon batters, alternating white and yellow, into a 10-inch angel cake tube pan to make a layer. Repeat with remaining batters, alternating colors, to make a second layer. (Do not stir batters in pan.)
3. Bake in slow oven (325°) 50 minutes, or until golden and top springs back when lightly pressed with fingertip.
4. Invert pan, placing tube over a quart-size bottle; cool cake completely in this position.
5. Loosen around edge and tube with a long, thin knife. Turn out onto a wire rack. Split into 4 even layers.
6. Mix sour cream with almonds in a small bowl.
7. Place largest cake layer on a serving plate; spread with a third of the cream-nut mixture, then ¼ cup of the apricot preserves. Repeat with remaining layers and fillings, stacking cake back into shape. Sprinkle 10X sugar over top and side. Chill several hours, or overnight. Garnish with candied mint, if you wish. Slice into wedges with a sharp, thin-bladed knife.

EASY NÖEL FRUITCAKE

When you start with a handy fruit-bread mix, the cake goes together like lightning.

Bake at 350° for 1 hour.
Makes one 6-cup tube cake.

- 1 package (17 ounces) apricot-nut bread mix
- 1 jar (1 pound) mixed candied fruits
- 1 cup chopped pecans
- ½ cup seedless raisins
- ½ cup whole blanched almonds
- ¼ cup light corn syrup
- 2 tablespoons sherry

1. Grease a 6-cup fluted tube pan or 8½x3⅝x2⅝-inch loaf pan; line bottom with wax paper; grease paper. (If tube pan isn't flat on bottom, grease *very well;* dust with flour; tap out.
2. Combine mix with fruit, pecans and raisins in a large bowl; mix, following label directions. Turn into pan. Arrange almonds on batter.
3. Bake in moderate oven (350°) 1 hour, or until center springs back when lightly pressed with fingertip.
4. Cool in pan on wire rack 10 minutes. Turn out of pan; remove wax paper; cool completely.
5. Heat corn syrup and sherry just until bubbly in small pan; brush over cake. Decorate with candied cherries.

COFFEE CROWN CAKE

"Luscious" is the word for this handsome yeast loaf, delicately flavored with orange and spice and topped with raisins.

Bake at 350° for 30 minutes.
Makes one 10-inch fluted tube cake.

- ¾ cup milk
- ⅓ cup sugar
- 2 packages active dry yeast
- ½ cup very warm water
- 2 eggs, beaten
- 4 cups biscuit mix
- 1 teaspoon ground cardamom
- ½ cup candied orange peel
- ½ cup golden raisins
- ½ cup 10X (confectioners' powdered) sugar
- 1 tablespoon water

1. Heat milk in small saucepan; stir in sugar; cool to lukewarm.
2. Dissolve yeast in very warm water in large bowl. ("Very warm" water should feel comfortably warm when dropped on wrist.) Stir in cooled milk mixture and beaten eggs.
3. Beat in 2 cups biscuit mix and cardamom with wooden spoon, until smooth. Stir in orange peel and raisins, saving about 1 tablespoonful of each for decorating top. Beat in remaining biscuit mix to make a soft dough; then beat about 100 strokes.
4. Cover bowl with clean towel; let rise in warm place, away from draft, 1 hour, or until double in bulk.
5. Punch dough down; beat another 100 strokes; pour into well greased 12-cup fluted tube pan or 9-inch angel cake tube pan.
6. Cover with clean towel; let rise again in warm place, away from draft, 1 hour, or until double in bulk.
7. Bake in moderate oven (350°) 30 minutes, or until golden. Cool in pan on wire rack 10 minutes; turn upside down and remove from pan; cool.
8. Blend 10X sugar and water in cup; drizzle over crown; decorate with saved orange peel and raisins.

PINK LEMONADE SQUARES

Here's a real glamour dessert. Made with frozen lemonade mix, it's so simple.

Bake at 325° for 15 minutes.
Makes one 8-inch cake.

- 1 package (about 7 ounces) vanilla wafers
- ½ cup (1 stick) butter or margarine, melted
- 1 can (6 ounces) frozen pink lemonade concentrate
- ¾ cup water
- 48 marshmallows
- 1 cup heavy cream

1. Crush vanilla wafers into crumbs in a plastic bag with a rolling pin. (There should be about 2 cups.)
2. Mix crumbs and melted butter or margarine in a medium-size bowl; measure out ½ cup and reserve. Press remaining crumbs in bottom and up sides of a 8x8x2-inch baking dish.
3. Bake in slow oven (325°) 15 minutes; cool on wire rack.
4. Combine concentrate for lemonade and water in a medium-size saucepan; heat slowly until lemonade thaws and mixture is hot. Add marshmallows; continue heating, stirring constantly, just until marshmallows melt and mixture is smooth. Chill several hours, or until syrupy and thick.
5. Beat cream until stiff in a medium-size bowl with electric mixer at medium speed; fold into marshmallow mixture until no streaks of white remain. Spoon into cooled crust; sprinkle reserved crumbs over top.
6. Freeze several hours, or until firm. Cut into squares; serve plain or top with additional whipped cream and a slice of candied lemon peel.
BAKER'S TIP: Dessert cuts neater if allowed to stand at room temperature 30 minutes before serving.

MERRY-GO-ROUND CAKE

California nectarines and almonds top a festive tube cake. Save this recipe for the July-August nectarine season.

Bake at 350° for 50 minutes.
Makes one 10-inch angel tube cake.

- ½ cup (1 stick) butter or margarine
- ½ cup firmly packed brown sugar
- 4 fresh nectarines, halved and pitted
- ¼ cup sliced almonds
- 1 package (about 18 ounces) yellow cake mix

1. Beat butter or margarine and sugar until smooth in a small bowl with a wooden spoon. Spread over bottom

and side of a 10-inch angel cake tube pan. Arrange nectarine halves, cut-side down, in pan; sprinkle with nuts.

2. Prepare cake mix, following label directions; pour over nectarines.

3. Bake in moderate oven (350°) 50 minutes, or until a long wooden skewer inserted into center comes out clean. Cool in pan on wire rack 10 minutes; loosen cake around edge and tube of pan; invert onto rack; cool. BAKER'S TIP: If top of cake begins to get too brown while baking, lay a piece of aluminum foil on top for the final period of baking.

MACE COFFEE CAKE

A quickie—with hot roll mix.

Bake at 375° for 20 minutes.
Makes 1 large coffee cake.

- ¾ cup warm water
- 1 package hot roll mix
- 1 egg
- 1 tablespoon grated orange rind
- ¼ teaspoon ground mace
- ¼ cup raisins
- ¼ cup coarsely chopped pecans
- 1½ cups 10X (confectioners' powdered) sugar
- 2 tablespoons orange juice
- ½ teaspoon vanilla

1. Place warm water in a large bowl; sprinkle with yeast packet from hot roll mix; stir until dissolved.

2. Beat in egg, flour mixture from hot roll mix, orange rind, mace, raisins and pecans; blend thoroughly.

3. Cover. Let rise in warm place, away from draft, until light and double in bulk, about 45 minutes.

4. Punch dough down; turn out onto a well floured pastry cloth or board; cover with bowl; let rest 10 minutes.

5. Roll dough out to a 14-inch circle. Roll dough over rolling pin for easy lifting and place on large cookie sheet.

6. Place a glass in center. Make 20 equally spaced cuts, up to glass.

7. Take two strips, side by side, and twist together; pinch the ends. Continue around, until you have 10 twists.

8. Remove the glass from the center of the circle. Coil one of the twists and place in spot where the glass had been. Bring the remaining sets up around center coil. When finished, you'll have 9 coils arranged in a circle.

9. Cover; let rise 30 minutes, or until almost double in bulk.

10. Bake in a moderate oven (375°) 20 minutes, or until golden brown. Slide onto a wire rack.

11. Combine 10X sugar, orange juice and vanilla. Drizzle over warm cake. Garnish with whole pecans.

SHORTCAKE SEVILLE

Orange pinwheel biscuits bake in layers to stack warm with sweetened fruit and gobs of whipped cream.

Bake at 425° for 25 minutes.
Makes one 8-inch cake.

- 3 pints strawberries
- ¾ cup sugar
- 4 cups biscuit mix
- 1⅓ cups milk
- 2 tablespoons grated orange rind
- 2 cups heavy cream
- 1 tablespoon vanilla

1. Wash and hull strawberries; slice into a medium-size bowl; sprinkle with ¼ cup of the sugar; toss lightly to mix. Let stand while making cake.

2. Prepare biscuit mix with milk, following label directions for rolled biscuits. Roll out half to a 16x12-inch rectangle on a lightly floured pastry cloth or board.

3. Mix remaining ½ cup sugar and orange rind in a cup; sprinkle half over dough; roll up, jelly roll fashion. Cut into 16 one-inch-thick slices. Place, cut-side down, in a greased 8x8x2-inch baking pan, to make 4 rows of 4 biscuits each. Repeat with remaining dough and sugar mixture; place in second 8x8x2-inch pan.

4. Bake in hot oven (425°) 25 minutes, or until golden.

5. Beat cream and vanilla until stiff in a medium-size bowl with electric mixer at high speed.

6. Remove biscuits from pans by turning upside down on a wire rack so as not to break layers. Place one layer on a flat serving plate; top with half of the berries, then second layer and remaining berries. Spoon part of the whipped cream on top and serve remaining separately. To serve, break apart with two forks, placing two biscuits on each dessert plate.

PEACH MELBA UPSIDE-DOWN CAKE

Peaches and raspberry preserves form the luscious topping; just add ice cream.

Bake at 350° for 55 minutes.
Makes one 9-inch cake.

- ¼ cup (½ stick) butter or margarine
- ½ cup raspberry preserves
- 1 can (1 pound) cling peaches, drained
- 1 package (about 1 pound) pound cake mix
- 2 eggs
  Liquid, as label directs
- ½ teaspoon ground mace

1. Melt butter or margarine in a 9x9x2-inch baking pan in oven while oven preheats.

2. Stir raspberry preserves into melted butter or margarine; arrange peach halves, evenly spaced, in pan.

3. Prepare pound cake mix with eggs, liquid and mace, following label directions; pour over prepared fruit.

4. Bake in moderate oven (350°) 55 minutes, or until center springs back when lightly touched with fingertip.

5. Remove pan from oven and cool on wire rack 5 minutes; loosen cake from sides of pan with a knife; invert pan onto serving plate.

BAKING BASICS

LIQUID INGREDIENTS

• Use a glass measuring cup to measure milk and other liquids. Place on table or counter at eye level and fill to desired line.

• Milk: Unless otherwise stated, all recipes in this book use whole milk.

• Buttermilk: Whole, skim or nonfat milk that's been soured; makes a moist cake; good for gingerbread and other spice cakes.

• Evaporated milk: Whole milk with 60% water removed.

• Heavy cream: Also known as whipping cream; contains 36-40% butterfat. You can whip this cream.

• Light cream: Contains 18-30% butterfat. It will *not* whip.

• Sour cream: Commercial product with 18-20% butterfat; light cream that's been soured.

• Sweetened condensed milk: Whole milk with half the water removed and sugar added; very rich. *Not* the same as evaporated milk.

• When measuring sticky liquids such as honey, corn syrup and molasses, lightly oil cup before filling; liquid will pour out more easily.

• LIQUID MEASUREMENTS:
1 ounce = 2 tablespoons
½ pint = 1 cup (8 ounces)
1 pint = 2 cups (16 ounces)
1 quart = 4 cups (32 ounces)
*In Canada ½ pint = 1¼ cups (10 ounces); 1 pint = 2½ cups (20 ounces); 1 quart = 5 cups (40 ounces).

Chapter 4 continued on page 120

Lush, elegant pastries have always been a tradition in Europe, where famous pastry shops like Demel's in Vienna and Fauchon's in Paris are practically national monuments. But you don't have to journey that far to experience them. You can have the authentic flavor of Europe right in your own home, for this chapter includes both classics by great international chefs, and also cherished recipes passed down through generations of European families. The French Madeleines (recipe, page 59) and Petits Fours at right are just two you'll want to try. The pages following are chock full of delights like Hungarian Doboschtorte, Italian

Chapter 5
THE
FINEST OF

EUROPE'S
CLASSICS

rum cake and Greek Baklava, among other savory confections. And even better, we've streamlined the more complicated recipes so you can enjoy the benefits of great taste without all the unnecessary fuss. Bon appétit!

DELICATELY
sweet are these
beautiful French
pastries: Puffy
Madeleines and
fondant-coated
Petits Fours.

93

INTERNATIONAL
flair: Shown clockwise are
Cassata alla Siciliana, an
Italian cheese-filled rum cake;
Savarin with Rum Sauce from
France; Ceri's Chocolate
Cheesecake, German-
inspired and rich, Presnitz,
a fruity pastry from
Trieste, and one very English
Dundee Cake.

ELEGANT
Gâteau Saint-
Honoré—cream-
laden French cake
named after the
patron of
bakers.

CERI'S CHOCOLATE CHEESECAKE

Inspired by the Viennese Sacher Torte, this cake is rich and should be thinly sliced. Photo is on page 95.

Bake at 325° for 1 hour.
Makes one 9-inch cake.

Crust
- 1½ cups crushed chocolate cookie crumbs (5 ounces)
- ½ cup ground almonds (see page 60)
- ½ cup (1 stick) butter or margarine, melted
- ½ teaspoon ground cinnamon

Filling
- ¾ cup sugar
- 3 packages (8 ounces each) cream cheese, softened
- 3 eggs
- 1 package (8 ounces) semisweet chocolate squares, melted
- 2 tablespoons cocoa powder (not a mix)
- 1 teaspoon vanilla
- 2 tablespoons apricot brandy
- 1 container (16 ounces) sour cream
- ¼ cup all purpose flour

Glaze
- ½ cup apricot preserves
- ¼ cup apricot brandy
- Whole apricots, canned or fresh

1. Make crust: Combine chocolate crumbs, ground almonds, butter or margarine and cinnamon until well blended in a medium-size bowl. Press into side and bottom of a well buttered 9-inch springform pan. Chill.
2. Make filling: Beat sugar and cream cheese until fluffy in large bowl of electric mixer at high speed. Gradually blend in eggs, one at a time. Stir in melted chocolate, cocoa, vanilla and brandy. Beat in sour cream; fold in flour; pour into prepared pan.
3. Bake in moderate oven (325°) 1 hour, or until cake is set at edge but still soft in center. Turn off oven and keep cake in oven, with door closed, 1 hour. Cool in pan on wire rack until at room temperature, then chill overnight, or until firm. Carefully remove side of pan; place cake on wire rack over a sheet of wax paper.
4. Make glaze: Heat apricot preserves in a small saucepan; press through sieve; return to pan and add ¼ cup brandy. Brush onto top of cake. Garnish with whole apricots and rosettes of whipped cream, if you wish. To make rosettes, whip ½ cup heavy cream in tall narrow bowl with electric mixer at high speed until almost stiff; add 2 tablespoons apricot brandy and finish whipping; pipe onto cake with pastry bag fitted with #20 star tip.

BAKER'S TIPS: This cake is excellent when served still chilled. If the glaze should run off top of cake, melt any leftover glaze over low heat in small saucepan and brush onto cake again, just before serving. The cheesecake is also good served ungarnished or doused with unwhipped heavy cream and brandy and topped with sliced almonds.

PETITS FOURS

Some of the most beautiful additions to a pastry tray. Tiny pieces of chiffon cake are coated with fondant and gaily decorated. Picture is on page 93.

Bake at 350° for 30 minutes.
Makes 6 dozen tiny cakes.

- 2¼ cups cake flour
- 1¼ cups sugar
- 1 tablespoon baking powder
- 1 teaspoon salt
- 2 eggs, separated
- ⅓ cup vegetable oil
- 1 cup milk
- 1 teaspoon vanilla
  Apricot Glaze (recipe, page 73)
  Fondant Frosting (recipe follows)
  Vanilla-Almond Cream (recipe, page 37)
  Green, yellow and red food coloring
- ½ square unsweetened chocolate, melted

1. Grease a 15x10x1-inch jelly roll pan; line bottom with wax paper; grease paper.
2. Sift cake flour, 1 cup of the sugar, baking powder and salt into large bowl of electric mixer.
3. Beat egg whites until foamy-white and double in volume in small bowl of mixer at high speed; sprinkle in remaining ¼ cup sugar, 1 tablespoon at a time, beating all the time until meringue forms soft peaks.
4. Blend vegetable oil and ½ cup of the milk into flour mixture, then beat 2 minutes with mixer at medium speed. Stir in egg yolks, remaining ½ cup milk and vanilla; beat 1 minute at medium speed. Fold in meringue with wire whip until no streaks of white remain. Pour into prepared pan.
5. Bake in moderate oven (350°) 30 minutes, or until top of cake springs back when lightly pressed with finger.
6. Cool in pan on wire rack 5 minutes; loosen around edges with a knife; invert onto a large rack or clean towel; peel off wax paper; cool cake completely. Wrap tightly in aluminum foil or plastic wrap and store. (If cutting layer into PETITS FOURS immediately, freeze 30 minutes to set crumbs.)
7. When ready to frost and decorate, unwrap cake and place on a cutting board; trim crusts. Cut cake into 36 diamonds, 10 squares, 20 rectangles, and 12 one-and-a-half-inch rounds, or as you wish.
8. Place cakes, 2 inches apart, on wire racks over aluminum foil. Spoon APRICOT GLAZE over to coat completely. Allow to dry 3 hours, or until sticky and firm.
9. Make FONDANT FROSTING.
10. Replace foil under wire racks. Spoon on the first layer of frosting to cover completely. Scrape any frosting that drips onto foil back into bowl. Let cakes stand 2 hours.
11. When ready to add final coat of frosting, divide remaining frosting into three custard cups; stir almond extract and few drops coloring to tint frosting a pale green into one cup; stir lemon extract and a few drops of food coloring to tint frosting pale yellow into the second cup; stir a few drops of peppermint extract and red food coloring to tint frosting pale pink into the third cup.
12. Working with a third of the frosted cakes, spoon frosting over cakes to cover tops and sides completely. (If frosting gets too thick to spoon, stir in a drop or two of hot water to dilute.)
13. Prepare VANILLA-ALMOND CREAM. Divide among 4 tiny cups. Tint one each with green, yellow and red food colorings. Stir melted chocolate into last cup. Decorate cakes, following picture on page 93 and decorating directions on page 67.

FONDANT FROSTING

Makes enough to frost 6 dozen tiny cakes.

- 3 cups granulated sugar
- ¼ teaspoon cream of tartar
- 1½ cups water
- 1 package (1 pound) 10X (confectioners' powdered) sugar, sifted
- ¼ teaspoon salt
- 1 teaspoon vanilla
- ½ teaspoon almond extract
- ¼ teaspoon lemon extract
  Few drops peppermint extract

1. Combine granulated sugar, cream of tartar and water in a large saucepan; heat slowly, stirring constantly, until sugar dissolves, then cook, without stirring, to 226° on a candy thermometer; remove mixture from heat.
2. Cool to 125°, then gradually beat in 10X sugar, salt and vanilla until smooth and syrupy.

SAVARIN WITH RUM SAUCE

French born Marcelle Krieger's recipe for Savarin is unusual because it has no yeast. You make and bake it in minutes. The photo is on page 95.

Bake at 325° for 30 minutes.
Makes one 6-inch ring.

- 1 cup all purpose flour
- ¼ cup sugar
- 2 eggs
- 3 tablespoons sweet butter or margarine, softened
- 2 tablespoons light cream
- 1 ½ teaspoons baking powder
  Rum Sauce (recipe follows)
  Sliced peaches
  Whipped cream

1. Sift flour and sugar into a medium-size bowl; add eggs, butter or margarine and cream. Beat with a wire whip to blend; stir in baking powder.
2. Butter a 4-cup ring mold; spoon batter evenly into pan.
3. Bake in slow oven (325°) 30 minutes, or until top springs back when lightly touched with fingertip. Pour part of RUM SAUCE over cake while still in mold; cool on wire rack 30 minutes.
4. Remove from mold and place on serving plate; fill center with sliced peaches. Fit a #16 star tip onto pastry bag and fill with whipped cream; pipe around edge of cake. Serve with remaining RUM SAUCE.

RUM SAUCE: Makes about 1 cup. Combine ½ cup granulated sugar and 1 cup water in a medium-size saucepan. Bring to boiling; lower heat slightly; boil 10 minutes; remove from heat; pour in ⅓ cup dark rum. Serve warm.

BAKING BASICS

LEAVENING ACTION

- Baking powder reacts first on contact with liquid, then on contact with heat. (All recipes in this book use the double-action kind.)
- Baking soda—also called "bicarbonate of soda"—helps to neutralize acids, such as brown sugar, coffee and chocolate. (Use only when called for

in recipe. Baking soda is *not* a substitute for baking powder.)
- Cream of tartar helps stabilize foams, such as meringues. (If you don't have cream of tartar on hand, substitute 1 teaspoon lemon juice for each ¼ teaspoon cream of tartar.)
- Be sure to thoroughly mix baking powder and baking soda with other dry ingredients by sifting or stirring with wire whip for uniform leavening and texture.
- Yeast is the microscopic living organism that makes bread and certain cakes rise.
It is available in two forms:
  Fresh—comes in .6-ounce and 2-ounce blocks; it should be kept refrigerated, but not for too long.
  Active dry—comes in ¼-ounce packets. Dated for freshness, it keeps much longer if stored in airtight container in cool, dry place.
- Substitute 1 small block fresh yeast for 1 package active dry yeast.
- In Canada, always dissolve dry yeast in warm water, even if using rapid-mix recipes.
- Brewer's yeast is *not* a substitute for baker's yeast; it is a nutritional supplement.

LILIAN KYRKOS' KARITHOPETA

There are many versions of this Greek walnut cake, but here's the favorite of Family Circle's resident Grecian authority.

Bake at 350° for 35 minutes.
Makes one 8-inch square cake.

- 1 cup all purpose flour
- 1½ teaspoons baking powder
- ½ teaspoon ground cinnamon
- ¼ teaspoon salt
- ⅛ teaspoon ground nutmeg
- ¾ cup (1½ sticks) butter or margarine, softened
- ¾ cup sugar
- 3 eggs
- 2 teaspoons grated orange rind
- ¼ cup milk
- 1½ cups finely chopped walnuts
  Honey Syrup (recipe, page 100)

1. Sift flour, baking powder, cinnamon, salt and nutmeg onto wax paper; reserve.
2. Beat butter or margarine with sugar until fluffy in large bowl of electric mixer at high speed. Add eggs, one at a time, beating well after each addition. Add orange rind.
3. Stir in flour mixture alternately with milk, beating after each addition until batter is smooth. Add nuts. Pour into greased 8x8x2-inch baking pan.
4. Bake in moderate oven (350°) 35 minutes, or until center springs back

when lightly pressed with fingertip.
5. Cool cake in pan on wire rack 10 minutes; gradually pour *cool* syrup over cake, letting syrup soak into cake before adding more. Or cool cake completely, then pour *hot* syrup over.
6. To serve, cut cake into twenty-four 2-inch diamond shapes.

PRESNITZ

A pastry from the Italian seaport of Trieste. Diane Riordam brings this recipe to us from her grandmother, Pina Nicoletti. The cake is pictured on page 94.

Bake at 375° for 1 hour.
Makes 1 large cake.

Filling
- ¼ cup (½ stick) butter or margarine
- 2 tablespoons dry breadcrumbs
- ¾ cup raisins
- 1 package or can (16 ounces) walnuts
- 2 squares semisweet chocolate, broken
- ¼ cup pignoli (pine nuts)
- 1 jar (4 ounces) mixed chopped candied fruits
- 1 large apple, pared and shredded (about 1 cup)
  Rind of ½ orange, grated
  Rind of ½ lemon, grated
- ⅓ cup honey
- ⅓ cup sugar
- 2 teaspoons ground cinnamon
- 2 teaspoons vanilla
Dough
- 2 cups all purpose flour
- 1 teaspoon salt
- 1 teaspoon sugar
- ¼ cup (½ stick) butter or margarine
- 1 egg, separated
- ½ cup lukewarm water

1. Make filling: Melt butter or margarine in a small skillet; add bread crumbs; stir until well blended and brown; remove from heat and reserve.
2. Cover raisins with boiling water in a small bowl; let stand 5 minutes; drain and reserve.
3. Grind walnuts and chocolate into a large bowl; add drained raisins, pignoli, candied fruits, grated apple, orange and lemon rinds, honey, sugar, cinnamon and vanilla. Stir with a wooden spoon until blended.
4. Make dough: Combine flour, salt and sugar in a medium-size bowl; work in butter or margarine, egg yolk and lukewarm water with fingers to make a stiff dough. Turn out onto a wooden board. Bang 12 times onto board from a 2-foot height; cover dough with a heated large pot; let rest 5 minutes.
5. Stretch a clean small sheet or a softly laundered old tablecloth smoothly on kitchen table; sprinkle

with flour. Roll dough on sheet into a 30x12-inch rectangle, using more flour if needed to prevent sticking.

6. Sprinkle butter or margarine and bread crumb mixture over dough. Spread fruit and nut mixture as evenly as possible in a 3-inch-wide strip over one long edge of dough, 1 inch in from edge. Fold short edges of dough over filling to make a neat rectangle.

7. Lift sheet at long side and begin rolling up, using sheet to lift dough, until dough is completely rolled up.

8. Form roll into coil on a greased 15x10x1-inch jelly roll pan. Brush with beaten egg white. Place a pan of hot water in the lower rack of oven. Place jelly roll pan on rack in top third of oven.

9. Bake in moderate oven (375°) 1 hour, or until cake is golden. Cool in pan on wire rack 15 minutes; loosen cake with spatula; lift onto wire rack to cool completely. Cake is even better if left to mellow several days.

Editors' Note: Mrs. Nicoletti's recipe omits the ⅓ cup sugar. If you prefer the European taste of a less sweet cake, try it without the sugar. This is especially delicious with espresso.

CASSATA ALLA SICILIANA

Our version of Italian rum cake begins with a sponge cake that's split and filled with a delectable ricotta cheese-almond mixture. The photo is on pages 94 and 95.

Bake at 325° for 1 hour.
Makes one 9-inch angel tube cake.

- **1 cup cake flour**
- **½ teaspoon salt**
- **6 eggs, separated**
- **1 cup sugar**
- **1 teaspoon vanilla**
- **1 container (1 pound) ricotta cheese**
- **½ cup 10X (confectioners' powdered) sugar**
- **1 square semisweet chocolate, grated**
- **2 tablespoons rum**
- **1 teaspoon vanilla**
- **½ cup candied red cherries, quartered**
- **½ cup toasted slivered almonds**
  Rum Sauce (recipe, page 98)

1. Measure cake flour and salt into a sifter.

2. Beat egg whites until foamy-white and double in volume in large bowl of electric mixer at high speed. Beat in ½ cup of the sugar, 1 tablespoon at a time, until meringue forms soft peaks. (Your test: Peaks will be just stiff enough to bend slightly as the beater is raised.)

3. Beat egg yolks until thick and lemon-colored in small bowl of mixer at high speed, then beat in the remaining ½ cup sugar, 1 tablespoon at a time, until mixture is very thick and fluffy. (Raise the beater again, and the yolk mixture should run off in a very thick stream.) Beat in vanilla.

4. Sift flour mixture into egg yolk mixture all at once, then fold in with wire whip, turning batter over and over gently from bottom of bowl until flour is blended completely. (A light touch keeps the mixture fluffy.)

5. Add egg yolk mixture to meringue, then fold in until no streaks of white or yellow remain. (Batter should be fluffy and light.)

6. Pour batter into an ungreased 9-inch angel cake tube pan. (The ungreased side gives the cake a wall to climb on during baking). Run a small spatula or knife through batter to spread it evenly and bring any large air bubbles to the top. (If the air is left in, the baked cake will have tiny holes or tunnels in it.)

7. Bake cake in slow oven (325°) 1 hour, or until top springs back when lightly pressed with fingertip and cake is richly golden.

8. Turn cake pan upside down and hang the tube over quart-size bottle; let cool completely.

9. To turn out, loosen cake around edge and tube with a knife; invert onto a wire rack, then turn right-side up.

10. Combine ricotta cheese, 10X sugar, grated chocolate, rum and vanilla in a medium-size bowl; beat with wire whip until smooth; add cherries and nuts; stir until blended.

11. Split cake into 4 layers, following directions on page 79. Place bottom layer on cookie sheet; spread with a third of ricotta mixture; repeat with layers and filling to reshape cake; garnish with candied cherries and almonds, if you wish.

12. Spoon RUM SAUCE over cake until absorbed. Chill at least 4 hours, or overnight. Slide onto serving plate with spatula and pancake turner. If there is any leftover cake, cover with plastic wrap and store in refrigerator; serve within a few days.

BAKER'S TIP: The best way to separate eggs is to break them, one at a time, into a custard cup, then place whites in a large bowl and yolks in a small bowl. (The tiniest bit of yolk in the whites will keep them from beating up, and that's why it's good practice to use a custard cup first.) Eggs separate best when cold from refrigerator, but after separating, let them stand at room temperature to warm so they will beat up to their highest volume.

BAKLAVA

To the Greeks we give credit for this nut-filled pastry bathed in a honey syrup.

Bake at 325° for 50 minutes.
Makes 3½ dozen servings.

- **3 cups shelled walnuts (about ¾ pound)**
- **½ cup sugar**
- **1½ teaspoons ground cinnamon**
- **2 packages (8 ounces each) phyllo or strudel pastry leaves**
- **½ cup (1 stick) unsalted butter or margarine, melted**
- **1 tablespoon water**
  Honey Syrup (recipe, next page)

1. Place walnuts on a 15x10x1-inch jelly roll pan; toast in a moderate oven (350°) 10 minutes. Whirl walnuts, while still warm, ½ cup at a time, at high speed, in container of electric blender until finely ground. (You may use a food grinder, if you wish.) Remove ground walnuts to a medium-size bowl. Repeat this procedure until all of the walnuts are ground. Mix in sugar and cinnamon.

2. Brush bottom of a 13x9x2-inch baking pan with melted butter or margarine. Fold two phyllo leaves in half; place on the bottom of pan; brush with butter. Place two more folded leaves in pan; brush with butter. (Keep rest of pastry leaves covered with a clean damp kitchen towel to prevent drying out.)

3. Sprinkle top with ½ cup nut mixture. Add two more folded leaves; brush with butter.

4. Repeat five more times. Stack remaining pastry leaves; brushing every other one. Brush top leaf with remaining butter; sprinkle with the 1 tablespoon water.

5. With a sharp knife, mark off the BAKLAVA. Cut through *only* the top layer of the phyllo, making 5 lengthwise cuts, 1½ inches apart (you will have 6 equal strips). Then cut diagonally again at 1½-inch intervals, making diamonds (9 strips). This is the traditional shape of the BAKLAVA.

6. Bake in a slow oven (325°) 50 minutes, or until top is golden. Remove pan to wire rack. Cut *all the way* through the diamonds; separating slightly. Pour cooled honey syrup over. Cool thoroughly in pan on rack. Cover with foil; let stand overnight for syrup to be absorbed. No refrigeration necessary.

BAKER'S TIP: Phyllo or strudel pastry leaves can be found in specialty food stores that sell Greek and Middle Eastern foods. Look for one in the yellow pages of the phone book.

HONEY SYRUP

Makes 2 cups.

1 small lemon
1 cup sugar
1 cup water
1 two-inch piece stick cinnamon
2 whole cloves
1 cup honey
1 tablespoon brandy

1. Pare rind (thin yellow, no white) from lemon; squeeze out 1½ teaspoons lemon juice into a small cup; set aside.
2. Place lemon rind, sugar, water, cinnamon stick and cloves in a heavy medium-size saucepan. Bring to boiling; lower heat; continue to cook, without stirring, 25 minutes, or until mixture is syrupy (230° on a candy thermometer).
3. Stir in honey; pour through strainer into a 2-cup measure. Stir in reserved lemon juice and brandy; cool to room temperature.

DUNDEE CAKE

A traditional light English fruitcake that's as delicious with a cup of tea in May as in December. The picure is on page 94.

Bake at 325° for 1 hour, 15 minutes.
Makes 2 medium-size fruitcakes.

1 package (15 ounces) raisins
1 package (11 ounces) currants
1 jar (4 ounces) candied mixed fruits
1 lemon
4 cups all purpose flour
2 teaspoons baking powder
1 teaspoon salt
1 teaspoon ground cinnamon
¼ teaspoon ground nutmeg
1½ cups (3 sticks) butter or margarine
1½ cups sugar
6 eggs
½ cup brandy or orange juice
½ cup light corn syrup
¼ cup brandy or orange juice

1. Grease well two 6-cup tube molds; dust with flour; tap out excess. Or use two 9x5x3-inch loaf pans.
2. Combine raisins, currants and mixed fruits in a large bowl. Grate lemon rind and add to fruits; squeeze lemon for juice and reserve.
3. Sift flour, baking powder, salt, cinnamon and nutmeg onto foil. Sprinkle 1 cup over fruits; toss.
4. Beat butter or margarine, sugar and eggs until fluffy in large bowl of electric mixer at high speed for 3 minutes.
5. Stir in remaining flour mixture, alternately with the ½ cup brandy or orange juice and reserved lemon juice, beating well, until batter is smooth.
6. Pour batter over prepared fruit and fold just until well blended. Spoon batter into prepared pans.
7. Bake in slow oven (325°) 1 hour, 15 minutes, or until centers spring back when lightly pressed with fingertip. Cool in pans on wire racks for 15 minutes; loosen around edges with a knife; carefully turn out onto wire racks; cool completely. Wrap cakes in cheese cloth; sprinkle with brandy; wrap in plastic bags. Allow to ripen at least 1 week before slicing.
8. To decorate: Heat corn syrup and ¼ cup brandy or orange juice until bubbly in a saucepan; brush over.
9. Garnish with candied mixed fruits.

DOBOSCHTORTE

What a creation! Six thin cake layers are filled with dark chocolate cream, then topped with a thin layer of golden caramel.

Bake at 350° for 20 minutes.
Makes six 9-inch torte layers.

1½ cups cake flour
½ teaspoon baking powder
½ teaspoon salt
6 egg whites
1 teaspoon cream of tartar
1 cup sugar
¼ cup water
3 egg yolks
½ cup sugar
1 teaspoon vanilla
1 teaspoon lemon extract
   Chocolate Butter Cream (recipe follows)
   Caramel Brittle (recipe follows)
   Walnut halves

1. Grease bottoms of three 9-inch layer cake pans; line with wax paper; grease paper.
2. Measure cake flour, baking powder and salt into sifter.
3. Beat egg whites with cream of tartar until foamy-white and double in volume in large bowl of electric mixer at high speed; sprinkle in the 1 cup sugar, 1 tablespoon at a time, beating all the time until meringue forms stiff peaks.
4. Stir water into the egg yolks in small bowl of mixer; beat until thick at high speed. Beat in the ½ cup sugar, 1 tablespoon at a time, until fluffy, then beat in vanilla and lemon extract.
5. Sift dry ingredients over egg yolk mixture and fold in with wire whip, then fold into meringue until no streaks remain.
6. Measure 1⅓ cups of batter into each of the prepared pans; spread to edges to make thin layers. (Cover remaining batter with plastic wrap and keep at room temperature while baking first 3 layers.)
7. Bake in moderate oven (350°) 20 minutes, or until golden and centers spring back when lightly pressed with fingertip. Remove from pans; peel off wax paper; cool on wire racks.
8. Wash pans; grease and line with wax paper. Bake 3 more layers from remaining batter.
9. Make CHOCOLATE BUTTER CREAM. Put layers together with ½ cup between each on serving plate; keep remaining filling at room temperature. Chill cake while making candy topping.
10. Make CARAMEL BRITTLE. Pour slowly over top of cake, spreading quickly to edge. (It hardens fast, so be quick.) Frost side of cake with remaining CHOCOLATE BUTTER CREAM, making deep swirls with knife. Decorate with walnut halves. Chill until serving time. (Torte cuts more neatly if chilled overnight.)
11. When ready to serve, crack candy topping by tapping along cutting lines with a sharp, heavy-bladed knife, then slice into serving-size wedges.

CHOCOLATE BUTTER CREAM

Makes 3½ cups.

3 egg yolks
3 tablespoons rum
½ cup sugar
4 squares unsweetened chocolate
1 teaspoon vanilla
1 cup (2 sticks) butter or margarine
1 cup heavy cream

1. Beat egg yolks with rum until thick in small bowl of electric mixer at high speed; beat in sugar, 1 tablespoon at a time, until fluffy.
2. Melt chocolate in top of double boiler over simmering water; stir in egg mixture. Cook, stirring constantly, about 1 minute, or until mixture thickens; remove from heat. Beat in vanilla; cool slightly.
3. Beat butter or margarine in large bowl of mixer at medium speed; beat in chocolate mixture gradually. (Mixture will be thin, but will thicken as cream is folded in.)
4. Beat cream until stiff in small bowl with mixer at medium speed; fold into chocolate mixture until no streaks of white remain.

CARAMEL BRITTLE: Makes ⅓ cup. Melt ¾ cup granulated sugar over low heat in small heavy saucepan, stirring often with a wooden spoon just until golden. (Watch it, for sugar will turn brown quickly.) Pour over cake at once.

GÂTEAU AU CHOCOLAT

A torte-like cake that uses ground walnuts and breadcrumbs in place of flour.

Bake at 350° for 15 minutes.
Makes three 8-inch layers.

- 6 eggs, separated
- ¾ cup sugar
- ¼ cup water
- 1 teaspoon vanilla
- 1 cup broken walnuts, ground
- ⅓ cup packaged bread crumbs
- ½ teaspoon salt
  Chocolate Sour Cream Frosting
  (recipe follows)
  Whole walnuts

1. Line three 8-inch layer cake pans with a double thickness of wax paper. (Do not grease pans.)
2. Beat egg whites in large bowl of electric mixer at high speed, until foamy-white and double in volume. Gradually beat in ¼ cup of the sugar until meringue stands in soft peaks.
3. Beat egg yolks in small bowl of mixer at high speed until thick and lemon-colored. Gradually beat in remaining sugar until mixture is very light and fluffy and falls in ribbons from beaters across batter, about 5 minutes. Lower speed; beat in water and vanilla.
4. Fold walnuts, bread crumbs and salt into egg yolk mixture until completely blended. Fold yolk mixture into meringue until no streaks of white or yellow remain. Pour into prepared pans, dividing evenly.
5. Bake in moderate oven (350°) 15 minutes, or until centers spring back when lightly pressed with fingertip.
6. Invert pans over cake rack; let cool 20 minutes. Loosen cakes around edges with a small knife, then from bottom with small spatula. Be careful not to tear cakes (they are very delicate). Turn cakes out of the pans; peel off wax paper.
7. Reserve 1 cup CHOCOLATE SOUR CREAM FROSTING. Put layers together with a part of remaining frosting. Frost side with other part. Pipe reserved frosting through #16 star tip of decorating set onto top and side of cake. Decorate with whole walnuts, if you wish.

CHOCOLATE SOUR CREAM FROSTING

Makes enough to fill and frost three 8-inch layers.

- ¾ cup (1½ sticks) butter or margarine
- 4 squares semisweet chocolate, melted
- 1 package (1 pound) 10X (confectioners' powdered) sugar, sifted
- ¼ cup dairy sour cream
- 1 teaspoon vanilla

1. Beat butter or margarine and chocolate in small bowl of electric mixer, until thoroughly blended.
2. Add sugar, alternately with sour cream and vanilla, beating until mixture is of spreading consistency.

GÂTEAU SAINT-HONORÉ

Grandly French! A pastry round topped with tiny cream puffs, elegant enough to be named in honor of St. Honorius, Bishop of Arles and patron of bakers. The picture is on page 96.

Bake at 400° for 25 to 40 minutes.
Makes 12 servings.

Pastry
- 1 cup all purpose flour
- 3 tablespoons sugar
  Dash salt
- 6 tablespoons (¾ stick) butter or margarine
- 1 egg, slightly beaten
  Cream Puff Batter (recipe follows)

Filling
- ¼ cup sugar
- ¼ cup cornstarch
- 1 envelope unflavored gelatin
- ¼ teaspoon salt
- 3 eggs, separated
- 1½ cups milk
- 2 teaspoons vanilla
- 1 cup heavy cream
- ½ teaspoon almond extract
- ½ cup diced candied yellow and green pineapple
  OR: ½ cup candied mixed fruits

Caramel Syrup
- ¾ cup sugar
- 2 tablespoons light corn syrup
- 2 tablespoons water

1. Make pastry: Combine flour, sugar and salt in a medium-size bowl; cut in butter or margarine with a pastry blender until mixture is crumbly. Blend in egg with a fork, then knead a few times until smooth.
2. Roll out pastry to a 10-inch round on a lightly floured pastry cloth or board; place on an ungreased cookie sheet; trim edge, using a dinner plate as a guide, to make a perfect round. Prick all over with a fork; chill.
3. Make CREAM PUFF BATTER. Attach a #8B tip to a pastry bag; fill bag with part of the batter; press out all around edge of pastry circle. (It will take about ⅔ of batter for ring. When baked, batter will puff up to form a high rim around pastry.)
4. Shape remaining batter through tube into 14 small puffs on ungreased medium-size or small cookie sheet.
5. Bake ring and puffs in hot oven (400°) 40 minutes for ring and 25 minutes for puffs, or until all are puffed, crisp, and lightly golden. Cool pastry ring completely on cookie sheet on a wire rack. Remove puffs with a spatula; cool completely on wire racks. (This much can be done a day ahead, if you wish.)
6. About 3 hours before serving gâteau, make custard cream: Mix sugar cornstarch, gelatin and salt in a medium-size heavy saucepan. Stir in egg yolks and milk.
7. Cook over low heat, stirring constantly, or until gelatin dissolves and mixture coats a metal spoon. Strain into a large bowl; stir in vanilla.
8. While custard mixture cooks, beat egg whites until they stand in firm peaks in small bowl of electric mixer at high speed; fold into hot custard mixture; chill.
9. Beat cream and almond extract until stiff in small bowl of mixer at high speed; fold in candied fruits; fold into gelatin mixture.
10. Make caramel syrup: Mix sugar, corn syrup and water in a small heavy skillet. Heat, stirring constantly, just until sugar dissolves, then cook rapidly, without stirring, to 300° on a candy thermometer and until syrup is light golden; remove from heat at once.
11. Place pastry ring on serving plate. Dip cream puffs into caramel syrup and arrange on ring. Fill center with creamy filling. Spoon remaining caramel syrup over puffs and ring. Chill one hour before serving but do not chill for more than 2 hours, or pastry and puffs will be soggy.

CREAM PUFF BATTER

Makes one ring and 14 small puffs.

- 1 cup water
- ½ cup (1 stick) butter or margarine
- 1 cup all purpose flour
- ½ teaspoon salt
- 4 eggs

1. Heat water and butter or margarine to boiling in a medium-size heavy saucepan. Add flour and salt all at once; stir vigorously with a wooden spoon until batter forms a thick smooth ball that follows spoon around pan; remove from heat immediately.
2. Beat in eggs, one at a time, beating well after each addition, until batter is shiny and smooth.
BAKER'S TIP: Never substitute vegetable shortening or diet margarine for the butter or margarine in this recipe for cream puffs.

VIENNESE TORTE

It's a triple chocolate cake beauty with a coffee-cream filling. Serve on your loveliest plates with cups of demitasse.

Bake at 300° for 35 minutes.
Makes one 9-inch torte.

Filling
- 1 envelope unflavored gelatin
- ¼ cup cold water
- ¾ cup brewed coffee
- ½ cup (1 stick) butter or margarine
- ¾ cup sugar
- 2 eggs
- ⅓ cup cocoa powder (not a mix)
- 1 teaspoon vanilla
- 1 cup marshmallow cream

Cake
- 1 cup cake flour
- ¼ cup cocoa powder (not a mix)
- ½ teaspoon baking powder
- ½ cup (1 stick) butter or margarine
- ½ cup sugar
- 3 eggs
- ½ teaspoon vanilla
- ½ cup finely chopped walnuts

Frosting
- 2 tablespoons cocoa powder (not a mix)
- 2 tablespoons butter or margarine
- 2 tablespoons rum
- 1 cup 10X (confectioners' powdered) sugar
- Whole blanched almonds

1. Make filling: Soften gelatin in water in small saucepan; stir in coffee; heat slowly, stirring constantly, just until gelatin dissolves; cool.
2. Beat butter or margarine with sugar until fluffy in large bowl of electric mixer at high speed; add eggs, 1 at a time, beating about 3 minutes after each addition. Stir in cocoa and vanilla; slowly add cooled gelatin mixture; fold in marshmallow cream.
3. Pour into a wax-paper-lined 8-inch layer cake pan; chill 2 hours, or until filling is firm.
4. Make cake: Measure flour, cocoa and baking powder into sifter.
5. Beat butter or margarine with sugar until fluffy in large bowl of electric mixer at high speed; beat in eggs, 1 at a time. Sift in dry ingredients, stirring just until well blended with wire whip; stir in vanilla and nuts. Pour into a greased 9-inch layer cake pan, spreading evenly.
6. Bake in slow oven (300°) 35 minutes, or until cake begins to pull away from side of pan. Cool in pan on wire rack 10 minutes; remove from pan; cool completely.
7. Split cake crosswise with sharp thin-bladed knife to make 2 thin layers; place 1 on serving plate.
8. Run a spatula around edge of molded filling to loosen from pan; turn out onto cake layer on plate; peel off wax paper. Top with second layer. Chill while making frosting.
9. Make frosting: Heat cocoa, butter or margarine and rum in small saucepan until butter is melted; remove from heat. Stir in 10X sugar and vanilla; beat until smooth. (Frosting will be thin.) Pour immediately over top of filled cake, spreading to edge with spatula.
10. Chill until ready to serve. (Cake will hold well if made a day ahead.) Slice into thin wedges with a long, sharp slicing knife.

WELSH CHEDDAR CHEESECAKE

A suprisingly different cheesecake with the lively tang of Cheddar cheese and beer.

Bake at 475° for 12 minutes
then at 250° for 1 hour, 30 minutes.
Makes one 9-inch cake.

- 1 box (6 ounces) zwieback crackers, crushed
- 3 tablespoons sugar
- 6 tablespoons (¾ stick) butter or margarine, melted
- 4 packages (8 ounces each) cream cheese
- 8 ounces finely shredded Cheddar cheese (2 cups)
- 1¾ cups sugar
- 3 tablespoons all purpose flour
- 5 eggs
- 3 egg yolks
- ¼ cup beer

1. Combine zwieback crumbs, 3 tablespoons sugar and melted butter or margarine in a small bowl with wooden spoon. Press firmly over the bottom and partly up the side of a lightly buttered 9-inch springform pan. Chill briefly before filling.
2. Let cream cheese soften in large bowl of electric mixer. Beat with Cheddar cheese, just until smooth, at high speed. (Cheeses will beat more smoothly if they are at room temperature.) Add sugar and flour. Beat until light and fluffy. Add eggs and egg yolks, one at a time, beating well after each addition; turn speed to low; stir in beer; pour into crumb crust.
3. Bake in very hot oven (475°) 12 minutes; lower temperature to 250° and bake 1 hour, 30 minutes longer. Turn off oven; allow cake to remain in oven 1 more hour.
4. Remove from oven; cool completely in pan on wire rack; loosen around edge with a knife; release spring and remove cake from pan.
BAKER'S TIP: It is the nature of this cake to have a crack on the top, but it will not affect the delicious flavor.

CREAM HORNS PARISIENNE

An easy version of an elegant dessert.

Bake at 400° for 20 minutes.
Makes 16 horns.

- 3 cups all purpose flour
- 1½ cups (3 sticks) butter or margarine
- 1 cup dairy sour cream
- Water
- Sugar
- Pink Cream Filling (recipe follows)

1. Measure flour into a medium-size bowl. Cut in butter or margarine with a pastry blender until mixture is crumbly; add sour cream. Knead lightly just until pastry holds together and leaves side of bowl clean. Wrap dough in wax paper; chill overnight.
2. To make your own cream horn molds: Tear off eight 9-inch pieces heavy-duty aluminum foil from an 18-inch-wide roll. Fold each piece in half to make a square; fold square crosswise to make a triangle. Using center of longest side of triangle as tip of cone, start at one side and roll up to form a slim cone.
3. Divide pastry in half. Keep one half refrigerated until ready to use. Roll out evenly to an 18x10-inch rectangle on floured pastry board or cloth. Cut pastry lengthwise into 8 strips, each 1¼-inches wide.
4. Moisten each strip lightly with water. Starting at pointed end, wrap around cone-shaped foil, overlapping slightly. Place on ungreased cookie sheet. Chill 30 minutes; brush with water; sprinkle with sugar.
5. Bake in hot oven (400°) 20 minutes, or until puffed and brown.
6. Remove horns to wire rack to cool. As each horn is cool enough to handle, carefully remove from mold. Cool completely before filling. Use same molds for baking second batch.
7. Fill cones just before serving.

PINK CREAM FILLING: Makes 4 cups. Beat 2 cups heavy cream, 2 tablespoons sugar and ½ teaspoon almond extract until stiff in medium-size bowl of electric mixer at medium speed. Fold in 2 tablespoons finely chopped maraschino cherries and 2 teaspoons syrup from cherries. Add a drop of red food coloring.
BAKER'S TIP: If you wish to make only 8 horns, use only ½ of filling recipe. Shape second half of horns on molds. Place in a single layer in a pan; freeze. When frozen, wrap in aluminum foil. Bake as directed when ready to use.

BLACK BUN

From Edinburgh, Scotland, comes a recipe for fruitcake with a difference—it has black pepper in it, and the batter is baked in a rich pastry dough.

Bake at 350° for 30 minutes,
then at 300° for 2 hours, 30 minutes.
Makes one 9-inch square.

Pastry
- ¾ cup (1 ½ sticks) butter or margarine
- 2⅓ cups all purpose flour
- ⅛ teaspoon salt
- 2 egg yolks
- ⅓ cup cold water
- 2 tablespoons vegetable oil

Cake
- 2 tablespoons butter or margarine
- 1 cup chopped walnuts
- 1 cup all purpose flour
- ½ teaspoon baking soda
- ½ teaspoon cream of tartar
- 1½ teaspoons ground allspice
- 1 teaspoon ground cinnamon
- 1 teaspoon ground ginger
- 1 teaspoon ground mace
- ¼ teaspoon ground cloves
- ¼ teaspoon black pepper
- ¼ teaspoon salt
- 2 cups raisins, chopped
- 2 cups dried currants
- 1 cup chopped mixed candied fruits
- 1½ cups sugar
- ½ cup Scotch whisky
- ½ cup buttermilk
- 1 egg yolk
- 1 tablespoon water

1. Make pastry: Cut butter into small pieces in a large bowl; allow to stand at room temperature for 15 minutes.
2. Sift flour and salt into a bowl. Work in butter until the mixture resembles coarse oatmeal.
3. Beat yolks with water and oil. Add to the flour mixture and work into a ball. Dust the ball lightly with flour, wrap in plastic wrap and chill at least one hour. (It can be stored in the refrigerator several days or in the freezer two or three months.)
4. Sauté walnuts: Melt butter or margarine in a small skillet; add walnuts; sauté 5 minutes, or until golden.
5. Make cake: Measure flour, baking soda, cream of tartar, allspice, cinnamon, ginger, mace, cloves, pepper and salt into a sifter. Combine raisins, currants, candied fruits, walnuts and sugar in a large bowl. Sift flour mixture over and toss until well blended. Stir in Scotch and buttermilk with a wooden spoon to form a thick paste. (If batter is too thick, add a little more buttermilk.)
6. Roll out two-thirds of the chilled pastry to a 14 x 14-inch square on a floured pastry cloth or board. Line a 9x9x2-inch baking pan with pastry; let one inch hang over sides of pan. Pat dough down firmly.
7. Spoon cake batter into the lined pan and pat down firmly. Roll out the remaining pastry to a 10 x 10-inch square. Brush the overhanging edges with cold water; set pastry in place, fold over the edges, seal top and bottom together by crimping with a fork. Run a skewer right through to the bottom of the pan in four or five places. Cut pastry leaves to decorate the top. Brush the decorations with cold water to make them stick.
8. Bake in moderate oven (350°) 30 minutes, then reduce the oven heat to slow (300°) and bake two hours. Combine egg yolk and water in a cup and brush over the top of the pastry. Bake 30 minutes longer, or until a cake tester comes out clean. Set on a wire rack and allow to cool in pan. Remove from pan very carefully and wrap in aluminum foil; allow to mellow at least four days.

BAKER'S TIP: BLACK BUN can be kept for as long as several months if tightly wrapped.

BAKING BASICS

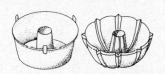

CHECK YOUR PANS

- A 10-inch Bundt® (fluted tube) pan and a 10-inch angel cake tube pan are *not* interchangeable; the Bundt® holds 12 cups of batter, the angel cake tube, 18 cups! Use a 9-inch angel cake tube pan as a substitute for Bundt®.
- For recipes using a 10-inch angel cake tube pan, you can use a 10-inch fluted tube pan, filling *only* two-thirds full, and pour remaining batter into an 8½x3⅝x2⅝-inch loaf pan.
- To determine amount of batter needed for odd-shaped pan, fill with measured water; use two-thirds that amount of batter.
- If you bake in glass pans, lower recipe temperature by 25°. Many new non-stick coated pans need a 25°-lower temperature, too—read label directions.
- Use heavy gauge metal pans for cake and cookie success.
- Cookie sheets should be at least 2 inches narrower than the oven.
- Always place cookie dough on cool baking sheet; it'll spread on hot one.

GÂTEAUX D'AMANDES

Tiny Génoise cakes, frosted with butter cream and coated with toasted almonds.

Bake at 350° for 20 minutes.
Makes 2 dozen tiny cakes.

- ¼ cup (½ stick) butter or margarine
- 6 eggs
- 1 cup sugar
- 1 teaspoon vanilla
- 1 cup cake flour
- 1 cup sliced almonds
- 1 jar (12 ounces) apricot preserves
- ¼ cup light rum
- Mocha Butter Cream (recipe, page 10)

1. Grease a 15x10x1-inch jelly roll pan; flour lightly, tap out excess.
2. Melt butter or margarine over low heat in a small saucepan; remove from heat. Pour into a cup; let stand until solids settle to bottom.
3. Beat eggs with sugar in top of double boiler; place over simmering water. (Do not let water boil or touch bottom of pan.) Heat, stirring constantly, 10 minutes, or until sugar dissolves and mixture warms slightly; pour into large bowl of electric mixer.
4. Beat at high speed 10 minutes, or until mixture is very thick and triple in volume; beat in vanilla.
5. Measure 3 tablespoonfuls of the clear liquid butter or margarine into a cup; discard solids.
6. Fold flour into egg mixture, a third at a time, alternately with the liquid butter, using a wire whip, just until blended. Pour into pan.
7. Bake in moderate oven (350°) 20 minutes, or until center springs back when lightly pressed with fingertip. Cool 10 minutes in pan on a large wire rack. Loosen around edges with a spatula; turn out onto rack, working spatula gently under bottom of cake, if needed, to loosen. Cool cake completely. Cut into 48 pieces.
8. While cake bakes, spread nuts in a shallow pan; toast in oven 12 minutes, or until light gold; cool. Place in a plastic bag; crush lightly with a rolling pin; spread in pan.
9. Press apricot preserves through a sieve into a small saucepan; heat slowly to boiling; stir in rum. Brush over tops and sides of each piece of cake.
10. Frost tops of half of the pieces with MOCHA BUTTER CREAM; top each, sandwich-style, with an unfrosted piece, apricot-side up. Frost sides of cakes; dip in toasted almonds; place in a single layer on a cookie sheet. Frost tops of cakes. Chill.

Chapter 5 continued on page 122.

There's hardly a child around who doesn't love to get his or her hands into something for the sheer pleasure of creating. Having your kids help you bake is an excellent way to meet that need. By making simple cakes and cookies now they'll not only have fun, they'll be learning the basics of sound nutrition and good cooking techniques so important for the rest of their lives. Our own panel of cookie lovers pictured on the following pages agree. They had a great time making and tasting some of the cookies in this chapter and are shown from left to right on pages 106 & 107 with their favorites: Ginger Softies, Oatmeal Crunchies, Tulip Cookies, Chocolate Rounds and Wheat Germ Drops. There are also some fun cakes for you and your kids to try together, or when a group of young friends comes for an after-school visit. The recipes begin on page 109.

Chapter 6
FUN IN
THE KITCHEN:

BAKING WITH KIDS

CHILDREN
will love to help you
bake this colorful,
easy-to-make
Circus Cake. Great
for party time.

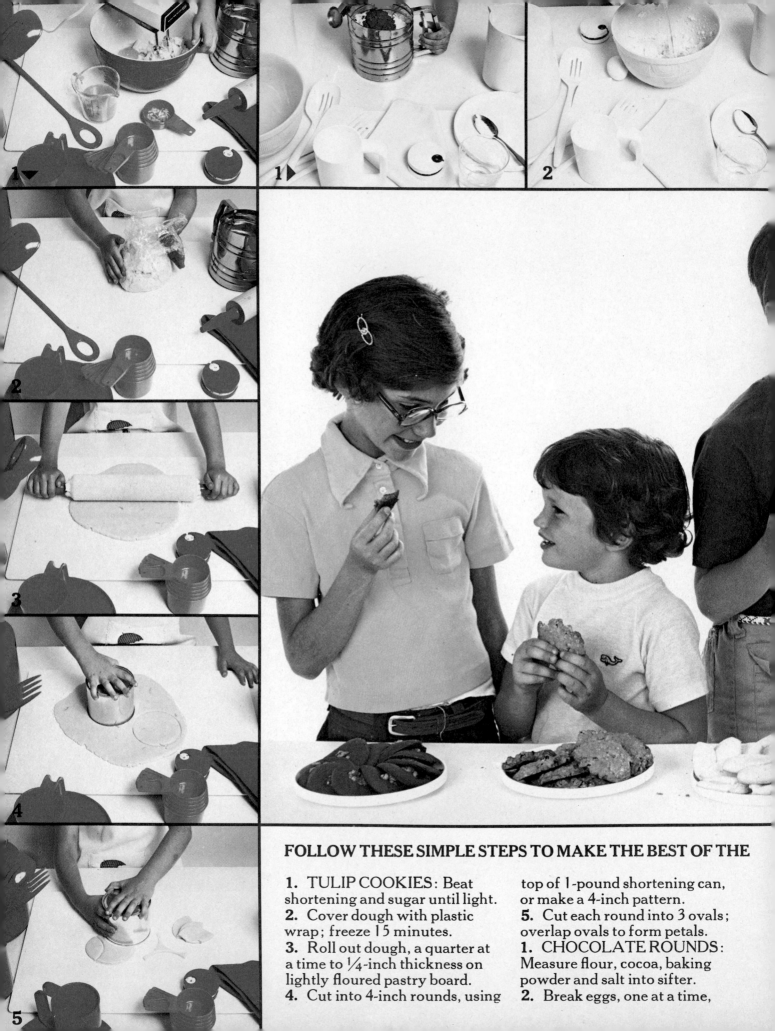

FOLLOW THESE SIMPLE STEPS TO MAKE THE BEST OF THE

1. TULIP COOKIES: Beat shortening and sugar until light.
2. Cover dough with plastic wrap; freeze 15 minutes.
3. Roll out dough, a quarter at a time to ¼-inch thickness on lightly floured pastry board.
4. Cut into 4-inch rounds, using top of 1-pound shortening can, or make a 4-inch pattern.
5. Cut each round into 3 ovals; overlap ovals to form petals.
1. CHOCOLATE ROUNDS: Measure flour, cocoa, baking powder and salt into sifter.
2. Break eggs, one at a time,

3

4

1 ▼

2

3

4

5

BATCH AS JUDGED BY OUR PANEL OF COOKIE EXPERTS

into shortening and sugar mixture and beat until smooth.
3. Roll dough, 1 teaspoon at a time, into balls between hands.
4. Flatten balls with the bottom of a glass dipped into sugar.
1. OATMEAL CRUNCHIES: Add milk to shortening and

sugar mixture and beat with spoon until smooth.
2. Stir in sifted dry ingredients until well blended with a spoon.
3. & 4. Add oats and raisins and stir in just until blended.
5. Drop batter by rounded teaspoonfuls onto cookie sheet.

107

DELICIOUS!
A member of our baking
panel approves
the Pumpkin Cake
she made along with
the other kids.

PUMKIN CAKE

What boy or girl wouldn't love to have a pumpkin for a birthday cake? It's baked in a bowl for the shape and there's pumpkin in the batter. The photograph is on page 108.

Bake at 325° for 1 hour, 15 minutes.
Makes one 9-inch round cake.

    2 cups all purpose flour
1½ cups granulated sugar
    1 tablespoon baking powder
    1 teaspoon salt
    1 teaspoon pumpkin pie spice
    6 egg whites
½ teaspoon cream of tartar
    6 egg yolks
½ cup canned pumpkin
½ cup vegetable oil
½ cup water
      Seven-Minute Frosting (recipe, page 6)
      Yellow, red and green food coloring
      10X sugar
¼ cup cocoa powder (not a mix)
    1 small banana

1. Sift flour, 1 cup of the granulated sugar, baking powder, salt and pumpkin pie spice into large bowl of electric mixer; reserve.
2. Beat egg whites with cream of tartar until foamy-white and double in volume in a second large bowl with electric mixer at high speed; sprinkle in remaining ½ cup granulated sugar, a tablespoon at a time, until meringue stands in firm peaks.
3. Stir egg yolks, pumpkin, vegetable oil and water into flour mixture until blended, then beat with mixer at medium speed, just until smooth.
4. Fold into meringue with wire whip until no streaks of white remain. Pour batter into an ungreased 9-inch deep metal or ovenproof ceramic bowl.
5. Bake in slow oven (325°) 1 hour, 15 minutes, or until top springs back when lightly pressed with fingertip.
6. Invert bowl, placing over edges of 3 custard cups to allow cake to hang above counter; cool.
7. Loosen around edge with knife; turn out onto a wire rack.
8. Prepare SEVEN-MINUTE FROSTING. Place ½ cup of frosting into each of two small bowls. Tint remaining frosting orange with yellow and red food coloring. Tint one bowl frosting green with food coloring. Stir 10X sugar and cocoa into frosting in second bowl to make a stiff dough.
9. Place cake on serving plate. Cover with orange frosting, making deep long swirls with spatula from bottom to top of cake to give pumpkin shape.
10. Cut a piece from stem-end of banana to make stem for pumpkin.

Place on top of cake into frosting. Cover banana with green frosting; spread remaining green frosting to indicate leaves, following the photograph on page 108.
11. Roll out chocolate frosting on a piece of aluminum foil to a ¼-inch thickness; cut into two triangles and a generous crescent, as shown in our picture. Press into side of pumpkin to make "jack o' lantern" face.
BAKER'S TIP: For non-party days, bake cake batter in a 10-inch angel cake tube pan and frost with whipped cream, if you wish. It's delicious served with warm cider.

HAVEN BARS

Top oatmeal pastry with semi-sweet chocolate pieces, walnuts and crumble topping to make a rich triple-decker bar.

Bake at 350° for 5 minutes, then at 350° for 35 minutes.
Makes 40 bars.

Dough
    2 cups all purpose flour
    2 cups old-fashioned rolled oats
    1 cup firmly packed brown sugar
½ teaspoon salt
½ teaspoon baking powder
    1 cup (2 sticks) butter or margarine, softened
      Crumble Topping
2½ cups all purpose flour
½ cup firmly packed brown sugar
¼ teaspoon baking powder
¼ teaspoon salt
½ teaspoon ground cinnamon
¾ cup (1½ sticks) butter or margarine
    1 package (12 ounces) semi-sweet chocolate pieces
    1 cup walnuts, chopped

1. Make dough: Combine flour, oats, brown sugar, salt and baking powder in a medium-size bowl; cut butter or margarine into mixture with a pastry blender or two knives until dough forms a ball.
2. Pat dough into an ungreased 15x10x1-inch jelly roll pan.
3. Bake in moderate oven (350°) 5 minutes; remove to wire rack.
4. Make crumble topping: Combine flour, brown sugar, baking powder, salt and cinnamon in a large bowl; cut butter into mixture with a pastry blender or two knives until crumbly.
5. Sprinkle chocolate pieces and walnuts over top; sprinkle crumble topping evenly over chocolate and nuts; press topping in lightly.
6. Bake in moderate oven (350°) 35 minutes, or until crumbs are golden.
7. Cool on wire rack 15 minutes; cut into 40 bars. Cool completely in pan.

OATMEAL CRUNCHIES

Chosen as a winner by our cookie experts. They're a favorite with kids of all ages. Photo is on page 106.

Bake at 375° for 10 minutes.
Makes 3 dozen.

1½ cups all purpose flour
½ teaspoon salt
½ teaspoon baking soda
      Dash ground mace
    1 cup vegetable shortening
1¼ cups firmly packed brown sugar
    1 egg
¼ cup milk
    1 teaspoon vanilla
1¾ cups quick-cooking rolled oats
    1 cup raisins
    1 cup chopped walnuts

1. Measure flour, salt, baking soda and mace into sifter.
2. Beat shortening with brown sugar in a large bowl with electric mixer at high speed until fluffy; beat in egg. Pour in milk and vanilla; blend well.
3. Sift in dry ingredients; mix with spoon until smooth; stir in oats, raisins and nuts until well blended.
4. Drop by rounded teaspoonfuls, 2 inches apart, onto cookie sheets.
5. Bake in moderate oven (375°) 10 minutes, or until golden. Remove to wire racks with pancake turner; cool.

CHOCOLATE ROUNDS

Here is a chocolate recipe for rainy days, when it's too nasty to play outdoors. The picture is on page 107.

Bake at 350° for 10 minutes.
Makes 3 dozen.

    2 cups all purpose flour
⅓ cup cocoa powder (not a mix)
1½ teaspoons baking powder
½ teaspoon salt
    1 cup vegetable shortening
    1 cup sugar
    2 eggs
    1 teaspoon vanilla
      Sugar

1. Measure flour, cocoa, baking powder and salt into sifter.
2. Beat shortening with the 1 cup sugar in a large bowl with an electric mixer at high speed until fluffy. Beat in eggs and vanilla.
3. Sift in dry ingredients; blend until well mixed. Shape dough into 1-inch balls, using hands.
4. Place balls, 3 inches apart, on cookie sheet. Dip a glass into sugar; press into balls to flatten.
5. Bake in moderate oven (350°) 10 minutes, or until cookies are firm. Remove to wire racks with spatula.

GINGER SOFTIES

Cookies like these have been making kids happy for generations. Shown on page 106.

Bake at 400° for 8 minutes.
Makes 3 dozen.

- 2¼ cups all purpose flour
- 2 teaspoons baking soda
- 1 teaspoon salt
- 1 teaspoon ground cinnamon
- ½ teaspoon ground ginger
- ½ cup (1 stick) butter or margarine
- ⅓ cup sugar
- ⅔ cup light molasses
- 1 egg
- ½ cup milk
- 2 teaspoons white vinegar
  Walnuts

1. Measure flour, baking soda, salt, cinnamon and ginger into sifter.
2. Beat butter or margarine and sugar until fluffy in large bowl with electric mixer at high speed. Beat in molasses and egg until well blended.
3. Combine milk and vinegar in a 1-cup measure. Sift part of the flour into bowl; stir, just to blend; stir in part of the milk mixture; sift in remaining dry ingredients, then add milk; stir just until smooth.
4. Drop by rounded teaspoonfuls, 2 inches apart, onto greased cookie sheets; top each with a walnut.
5. Bake in hot oven (400°) 8 minutes, or until centers spring back when lightly pressed with fingertip. Remove to wire racks with pancake turner; cool completely.

Suggested Variation: Add 1 cup raisins to cookie dough.

LEMON-CURRANT BARS

Crunchy bar cookies filled with one of those good natural cereals.

Bake at 350° for 30 minutes.
Makes 24 bars.

- ¼ cup (½ stick) butter or margarine, softened
- ½ cup sugar
- 2 eggs
- ¾ cup all purpose flour
- ½ teaspoon baking powder
- ¼ teaspoon salt
- 1 cup ready-to-eat-natural oat cereal (See Cook's Guide)
- 2 teaspoons grated lemon rind
- 2 tablespoons lemon juice
- 1 cup dried currants

1. Beat butter or margarine, sugar and eggs in bowl with electric mixer at high speed, until fluffy.
2. Sift flour with baking powder and salt; add to egg mixture. Stir in cereal with lemon rind and juice. Add currants; mix well.
3. Spread mixture in a buttered 9x9x2-inch baking pan.
4. Bake in moderate oven (350°) 30 minutes, or until golden brown around the edges. Cool in pan on wire rack for 15 minutes. Cut into 24 bars. These may be stored in pan, covered with aluminum foil or plastic wrap.

QUICK COCONUT COOKIES

Turn day-old bread into a nutritious snack-time treat.

Bake at 375° for 10 minutes.
Makes 2 dozen.

- 6 slices day-old white bread
- 1 cup chopped walnuts, pecans or peanuts
- 1 can (3½ ounces) flaked coconut
- 1 can (14 ounces) sweetened condensed milk (not evaporated)

1. Trim crusts from bread; cut into 4 pieces, lengthwise, to make sticks.
2. Combine nuts and coconut in one pie plate; pour condensed milk into a second pie plate.
3. Dip bread sticks into milk to coat well; roll in nut and coconut mixture; place on a greased cookie sheet.
4. Bake in moderate oven (375°) 10 minutes, or until golden. Remove with a spatula to wire racks; cool.

WHEAT GERM BROWNIES

The "heart of the wheat" takes the place of flour to make a nutritious snack.

Bake at 350° for 35 minutes.
Makes 16 squares.

- 3 squares unsweetened chocolate
- ¼ cup (½ stick) butter or margarine
- 2 eggs
- 1 cup sugar
- 1 cup wheat germ
- 1 cup chopped walnuts
- 1 teaspoon vanilla
  10X sugar

1. Combine chocolate and butter or margarine in a small saucepan; melt over low heat, stirring often; cool.
2. Beat eggs in medium-size bowl with electric mixer at high speed; slowly add sugar; beat until fluffy.
3. Add cooled chocolate mixture and beat until well blended; stir in wheat germ and walnuts, then vanilla.
4. Spread batter evenly in a greased 8x8x2-inch baking pan.
5. Bake in moderate oven (350°) 35 minutes, or until shiny and firm on top; cool in pan on wire rack.
6. Sprinkle 10X sugar over brownies, to coat evenly. Cut into 16 squares.

TULIP COOKIES

Use an empty one-pound shortening can as your cookie cutter. Photograph of these jumbo cookies appears on page 106.

Bake at 375° for 10 minutes.
Makes 2½ dozen.

- 2¼ cups all purpose flour
- 1 tablespoon baking powder
- 1 teaspoon salt
- ½ cup vegetable shortening
- ¾ cup sugar
- 1 egg
- 1 teaspoon grated California orange rind
- 2 tablespoons orange juice

1. Measure flour, baking powder and salt into sifter.
2. Beat shortening with sugar and egg in a large bowl until fluffy with electric mixer at high speed. Sift in dry ingredients; stir in with orange rind and orange juice until well blended. Wrap in wax paper. Chill in freezer 15 minutes, or in refrigerator 2 hours, or overnight.
3. Roll out dough, half at a time, to a ¼-inch thickness on a lightly floured pastry board. Cut into 4-inch rounds with the top of a 1-pound shortening can. Cut each round into 3 ovals with shortening can, following photograph on page 106.
4. Arrange ovals, 3 at a time, petal fashion, and place on cookie sheets.
5. Bake in moderate oven (375°) 10 minutes, or until lightly golden. Remove to wire racks with pancake turner; cool completely. Serve with orange-flavored cocoa or chocolate milk, if you wish.

TOASTY CLUSTERS

Nutrition-packed and bound to be popular with the milk-and-cookies set.

Bake at 325° for 15 minutes.
Makes 3 dozen.

- 2 cups natural oat-and-fruit cereal (see Cook's Guide)
- ⅔ cup sweetened condensed milk (not evaporated)
- 1 teaspoon almond extract
- ¼ teaspoon ground ginger
  Peanuts

1. Mix cereal, milk, almond extract and ginger in medium-size bowl.
2. Drop by teaspoonfuls onto foil-lined cookie sheets. Garnish each cookie with a few peanuts.
3. Bake in slow oven (325°) 15 minutes, or until firm. Cool on cookie sheets until cookies can be handled. Peel away foil; Cool completely on wire racks. Store in metal tin.

CIRCUS CAKE

Boys and girls will love having the circus at their house. Photo, page 105.

Bake at 325° for 1 hour.
Makes one 10-inch angel tube cake.

2¾ cups cake flour
 4 teaspoons baking powder
 1 teaspoon salt
 4 eggs, separated
1¾ cups sugar
 1 cup heavy cream
 1 teaspoon vanilla
 1 teaspoon lemon extract
⅔ cup milk
   Butter Cream Frosting (recipe, page 10)
   Yellow, green, red and blue food coloring
   Orange and white peppermint patties

1. Measure cake flour, baking powder and salt into sifter.
2. Beat egg whites until foamy-white and double in volume in small bowl of electric mixer at high speed; add ½ cup of the sugar, a tablespoon at a time, beating well after each addition, until meringue forms soft peaks.
3. Beat cream until stiff in medium-size bowl with mixer at medium speed; chill.
4. Beat egg yolks until thick in large bowl of electric mixer at high speed; add remaining 1¼ cups sugar gradually, beating well after each addition, until mixture is fluffy; beat in vanilla and lemon extract. Sift in dry ingredients alternately with milk; fold in meringue and whipped cream with wire whip; pour into greased 10-inch angel cake tube pan.
5. Bake in moderate oven (325°) 1 hour, or until center springs back when lightly touched with fingertip; cool on wire rack 15 minutes; loosen cake around edge and tube with knife and turn out; cool completely.
6. Prepare BUTTER CREAM FROSTING. Measure 1 cup into a small bowl and ¼ cup into a cup. Tint remaining frosting yellow with food coloring. Tint ¼ cup green with food coloring.
7. Place cake on serving plate; cover with yellow frosting. Stir enough 10X sugar into white frosting to make a stiff dough. Pat out on aluminum foil to a ¼-inch thickness. Cut into 8 clowns, using pattern on page 125 as a guide. Dip wooden picks into red and blue food coloring. Make dots on clowns for face and buttons, following picture on page 105. Cut out tiny ducks from remaining frosting dough. Tint a little remaining yellow frosting orange with a dot of red food coloring. Spread on ducks' tails

8. Alternate white or orange peppermint patties on top of cake. Press clowns evenly around bottom of cake, with 2 ducks between each. Pack green coloring into a cake decorating set, fitted with a #7 writing tip. Pipe a string from peppermint patties down to a hand of each clown.

GROUNDNUTTERS

Whole peanuts and peanut butter make chocolate shortbread high in protein.

Bake at 400° for 10 minutes, then at 350° for 20 minutes.
Makes 40 bars.

             Dough
 1 cup (2 sticks) butter or margarine
½ cup 10X (confectioners' powdered) sugar
½ teaspoon vanilla
⅛ teaspoon aromatic bitters
 2 cups all purpose flour
½ cup cocoa powder (not a mix)
¼ teaspoon salt
¼ teaspoon baking powder
¼ teaspoon baking soda
          Streusel Topping
 1 cup all purpose flour
½ cup firmly packed brown sugar
¼ teaspoon salt
½ cup peanut butter
¼ cup (½ stick) butter or margarine
 1 package (3 ounces) cream cheese, softened
½ cup salted peanuts
              Glaze
 1 package (6 ounces) semi-sweet chocolate pieces
 1 tablespoon vegetable shortening
¼ teaspoon vanilla

1. Make dough: Beat butter or margarine until fluffy in medium-size bowl with electric mixer at high speed; gradually add 10X sugar, then vanilla and aromatic bitters to blend.
2. Sift in flour, cocoa, salt, baking powder and baking soda, beating just until blended; press dough into a greased 15x10x1-inch jelly roll pan.
3. Make streusel topping: Combine flour, brown sugar, salt, peanut butter, butter and cream cheese in medium-size bowl; beat with electric mixer at high speed until well blended.
4. Crumble topping over chocolate dough in pan; sprinkle peanuts evenly over topping, pressing in lightly.
5. Bake in hot oven (400°) 10 minutes; lower oven temperature to 350° and bake 20 minutes longer, or until top is firm and streusel is golden.
6. Cool in pan on wire rack 15 minutes. Cut into 40 bars; cool.
7. Make glaze: Slowly melt chocolate with shortening in small heavy saucepan; stir often; add vanilla; drizzle glaze over bars in pan; recut.

WHOLE WHEAT COOKIES

A new twist to an old-fashioned favorite—whole wheat flour makes the difference.

Bake at 350° for 7 minutes.
Makes 2½ dozen.

¼ cup (½ stick) butter or margarine
¼ cup sugar
½ cup light molasses
½ teaspoon salt
 2 teaspoons baking soda
 1 teaspoon ground ginger
 1 teaspoon ground cinnamon
¼ teaspoon ground cloves
1½ cups whole wheat flour
 2 tablespoons vinegar

1. Melt butter or margarine with sugar and molasses in small saucepan over low heat. Cool.
2. Combine salt, baking soda, ginger, cinnamon and cloves with whole wheat flour in a large bowl. Stir in butter-molasses mixture. Mix in vinegar. Drop by teaspoonfuls onto greased cookie sheets.
3. Bake in moderate oven (350°) 7 minutes, or until cookies are set. Remove carefully with spatula to paper towels to cool. Store in covered jar.

WHEAT GERM DROPS

Snack time is nutrition time, too. The photo is on page 107.

Bake at 400° for 8 minutes.
Makes 4 dozen.

½ cup vegetable shortening
½ cup sugar
 1 egg
½ cup light molasses
2¼ cups all purpose flour
1½ teaspoons baking powder
½ teaspoon salt
¼ teaspoon baking soda
 1 teaspoon ground cinnamon
¼ teaspoon ground cloves
¼ cup milk
½ cup wheat germ
 1 package (6 ounces) semi-sweet chocolate pieces

1. Beat shortening, sugar and egg until fluffy in a large bowl with electric mixer at high speed. Add molasses.
2. Sift in flour, baking powder, salt, baking soda, cinnamon and cloves alternately with milk; stir in wheat germ, then chocolate pieces to blend.
3. Drop by teaspoonfuls, 2 inches apart, onto greased cookie sheets.
4. Bake in hot oven (400°) 8 minutes, or until golden; remove to wire rack with spatula. Cool completely. Store in metal tin with tight lid.

Chapter 6 continued on page 124.

1. To Make One-Bowl Cakes: Sift dry ingredients into large bowl.

2. Beat in shortening, eggs and liquid, scraping down side of bowl.

3. Divide batter evenly between layer cake pans.

4. To Make Butter Cakes: Add sugar to softened butter, beating well.

5. Add eggs and beat until well blended.

6. Add dry ingredients, alternately with liquid.

7. To Make Foam Cakes: Beat egg whites until double in volume; add sugar gradually.

8. Beat until meringue forms ribbons in bowl.

9. Fold dry ingredients into beaten egg yolks.

10. Fold egg yolk mixture into meringue.

And now, the rest of our cake collection. You may think with all to choose from in this book that there couldn't be any more, but you'll find in this section lots more just demanding to be baked. Americans have always loved cakes, and one reason may be the great versatility of this baking form: You can bake a cake in so many ways and there's always one for every taste. In the days when women had to cook on kerosene stoves and use coffee cups in the absence of more accurate measures, baking wasn't as easy as it is today. Many times a cake would fail and the exasperated cook had to try again. But now, with all our modern conveniences and detailed recipes you can be sure of success every time if you follow our directions carefully. The steps on the page at left will start you on your way to the perfect cake.

THE GRAND FINALE: A POTPOURRI OF SUPER
CAKES

BAKED ALASKA

This is it! A super-great version of the classic dessert that can't be rivaled.

Bake at 350° for 30 minutes,
then at 475° for 3 to 4 minutes.
Makes 12 servings.

Ice Cream Mold
- 2 pints coffee ice cream, slightly softened
- 1 pint strawberry ice cream, slightly softened

Torte Layer
- 1 cup all purpose flour
- 2 teaspoons baking powder
- ½ teaspoon salt
- ½ cup vegetable shortening
- ½ cup firmly packed brown sugar
- 4 egg yolks
- ⅓ cup milk
- ½ teaspoon vanilla
- 1 cup chopped walnuts

Meringue Topping
- 4 egg whites
- ¼ teaspoon cream of tartar
- ½ cup sugar

1. Make ice cream mold: Spoon coffee ice cream into 8-cup mixing bowl, spreading evenly over bottom and up side to line completely and leave a hollow in middle for strawberry ice cream. Freeze until firm, then spoon strawberry ice cream into hollow. Smooth top flat with a knife; cover with foil. Freeze overnight.
2. Make torte layer: Measure flour, baking powder and salt into sifter.
3. Beat shortening with brown sugar until fluffy in the small bowl of electric mixer at high speed; beat in egg yolks, 1 at a time, beating well after each addition, until mixture is blended.
4. Sift in dry ingredients, a third at a time, adding alternately with milk; stir just until blended; stir in vanilla and walnuts. Pour into a greased and floured 9-inch layer cake pan.
5. Bake in moderate oven (350°) 30 minutes, or until top springs back when lightly pressed with fingertip.
6. Cool in pan on wire rack 5 minutes. Loosen around edge with knife; turn out onto rack; cool completely.
7. Put BAKED ALASKA together this way: Place torte layer on a double-thick strip of foil on a cookie sheet. (This makes it easy to slide hot dessert onto its serving plate.) Loosen ice cream from mold by dipping mold in and out of pan of hot water, then invert onto center of torte layer. Lift off mold. Return to freezer while

making meringue.
8. Make meringue: Beat egg whites with cream of tartar until foamy-white and double in volume in a medium-size bowl with electric mixer at high speed. Sprinkle in granulated sugar, 1 tablespoon at a time, until sugar dissolves and meringue stands in firm peaks.
9. Spread over ice cream cake mold, swirling in peaks, to cover completely. (Work quickly so the ice cream doesn't melt.) Return to freezer until serving time.
10. When ready to serve, bake in very hot oven (475°) 3 to 4 minutes, or just until peaks are a toasty gold.
11. Slide cake onto a chilled serving plate; pull out foil strip. Use a sharp bread or carving knife to slice or cut into wedges.
BAKER'S TIP: You can make this dessert up to a week before serving. After meringue freezes, cover with plastic wrap. Bake meringue just before serving.

PARTY DATE CAKE

Dottie Thibodeau pleases students at Smith College, in Northampton, Massachusetts, with this fruit, nut and chocolate dessert.

Bake at 350° for 45 minutes.
Makes one 9-inch angel tube cake.

Topping
- ⅓ cup sugar
- ⅓ cup chopped walnuts
- ⅓ cup semi-sweet chocolate pieces

Cake
- 1 cup chopped pitted dates
- 1 cup boiling water
- 1 teaspoon baking soda
- ½ cup (1 stick) butter or margarine
- 1 cup sugar
- 2 eggs
- 1½ cups all purpose flour
- 1 tablespoon cocoa powder (not a mix)

1. Make topping: Combine sugar, nuts and chocolate pieces in a small bowl and reserve.
2. Make cake: Mix dates and boiling water in small bowl; cool; add baking soda and stir to combine thoroughly.
3. Beat butter or margarine and sugar until fluffy in medium-size bowl with electric mixer at high speed; add eggs, one at a time, beating well after each addition; turn mixer speed to low.
4. Add flour and cocoa, a third at a time, beating just until blended; stir in date mixture.
5. Pour batter into a greased 9-inch angel cake tube pan; sprinkle with chocolate-nut mixture, lightly press-

ing topping into batter.
6. Bake in moderate oven (350°) 45 minutes, or until top springs back when lightly touched with fingertip.
7. Cool in pan on wire rack 15 minutes. Loosen around edges and tube with knife; invert onto one wire rack, cover with second wire rack and turn right-side up; cool. Serve with whipped cream, if you wish.

SCRIPTURE CAKE

For generations American housewives have proven their knowledge of the Bible as well as their talent in the kitchen with this cake.

Bake at 325° for 1 hour, 30 minutes.
Makes one 9-inch angel tube cake.

- ½ cup (1 stick) butter or margarine
  (Judges 5:25)
- 1 cup sugar
  (Jeremiah 6:20)
- 4 eggs
  (Isaiah 10:14)
- 1 tablespoon honey
  (Exodus 16:31)
- 2 cups all purpose flour
  (1 Kings 4:22)
- 2 teaspoons baking powder
  (1 Corinthians 5:6)
- 1 teaspoon salt
  (Leviticus 2:13)
- 1 teaspoon ground cinnamon
  (1 Kings 10:10)
- ¼ teaspoon ground nutmeg
  (1 Kings 10:10)
- ½ cup milk
  (Judges 4:19)
- 6 figs, chopped
  (1 Samuel 30:12)
- ¾ cup golden raisins
  (1 Samuel 30:12)
- ½ cup sliced almonds
  (Genesis 43:11)

1. Beat butter or margarine until soft in large bowl of an electric mixer at medium speed; beat in sugar gradually until light and fluffy; beat in eggs, one at a time, until well blended; add honey. Turn beater to low.
2. Sift flour, baking powder, salt, cinnamon and nutmeg onto wax paper. Add to bowl, alternately with milk, just until blended. Stir in figs, raisins and almonds. Spoon into a greased and floured 9-inch angel cake tube pan or 12-cup fluted tube pan.
3. Bake in slow oven (325°) 1 hour, 30 minutes, or until a wooden pick inserted into center of cake comes out clean. Cool in pan on wire rack 15 minutes. Loosen cake around edge and tube with a narrow spatula; turn out onto wire rack to cool completely.
4. Wrap cake in cheesecloth soaked with sherry, if you wish; keep in a plastic bag for 1 week to ripen.

HOT APPLE PANDOWDY

For those chilly evenings in the country, with a mug of steaming cider on the side.

Bake at 350° for 50 minutes.
Makes one 9-inch square.

- 1¼ cups (2½ sticks) butter or margarine
- ⅔ cup sugar
- 1 egg, well beaten
- 2½ cups all purpose flour
- 1 tablespoon baking powder
- ½ teaspoon salt
- 1 cup milk
- 3 cups sliced pared apples
- ¼ cup firmly packed brown sugar
- 1 teaspoon ground cinnamon
  Sweetened Whipped Cream (recipe follows)

1. Beat butter or margarine in large bowl with electric mixer at high speed; add sugar gradually. When well beaten, mix in egg.
2. Sift together flour, baking powder and salt and add to butter mixture, alternately with milk.
3. Spread apples in bottom of a well buttered 9x9x2-inch baking dish.
4. Mix together brown sugar and cinnamon and sprinkle over apples. Pour batter evenly over the top.
5. Bake in moderate oven (350°) 50 minutes, or until golden. Let stand for 10 minutes on wire rack after removing from oven. To serve, invert on serving platter or serve directly from the baking dish. Pass SWEETENED WHIPPED CREAM.

SWEETENED WHIPPED CREAM: Makes 2 cups. Beat 1 cup heavy cream in small bowl of mixer at high speed, until almost stiff. Fold in 2 tablespoons 10X (confectioners' powdered) sugar and a few drops vanilla.

SAN ANTONIO PECAN CAKE

Sugar-frosted and studded with pecans.

Bake at 325° for 1 hour, 10 minutes.
Makes one 10-inch fluted tube cake.

- 1½ cups (3 sticks) butter or margarine, softened
- 2¼ cups firmly packed brown sugar
- 5 eggs, separated
- 3¼ cups all purpose flour
- 1 teaspoon baking powder
- 1 teaspoon salt
- ⅓ cup light cream
- 1 teaspoon vanilla
- 3 cups finely chopped pecans
  Snowy White Glaze (recipe follows)

1. Grease a 12-cup fluted tube pan. Dust with flour, tapping out excess.
2. Beat butter or margarine until fluffy in the large bowl of electric mixer at high speed; gradually add sugar. Beat until very light and fluffy.
3. Beat egg yolks until thick in a small bowl with a wire whip; fold into sugar mixture.
4. Sift flour, baking powder and salt onto wax paper; add to batter alternately with cream and vanilla. Mix well. Fold in pecans.
5. Beat egg whites until stiff, but not dry, in a medium-size bowl with electric mixer at high speed; fold into batter. Turn into prepared pan.
6. Bake in slow oven (325°) 1 hour, 10 minutes, or until center springs back when pressed with fingertip.
7. Cool cake in pan on wire rack. Remove from pan. Spoon SUGAR GLAZE over top of cake. Decorate with additional pecan halves and candied cherries, if you wish.

SNOWY WHITE GLAZE: Makes about ½ cup. Combine 1 cup 10X sugar and 1 teaspoon vanilla in a small bowl. Add enough milk (about 5 teaspoons) to make a thick consistency, beating with wire whip.

SPIRITED MARBLE CAKE

Everyone who tastes this cake, created by Mrs. Stephen Backity of Liverpool, N.Y., loves it. Don't pass it up.

Bake at 350° for 1 hour.
Makes one 10-inch angel tube cake.

- 3 cups cake flour
- 3¼ teaspoons baking powder
- ½ teaspoon salt
- 1 cup (2 sticks) unsalted butter or margarine
- 2 cups sugar
- 4 eggs, separated
- 2 teaspoons vanilla
- 1 cup milk
- ¾ cup canned chocolate syrup
- ¼ cup coffee liqueur
  Mocha Butter Cream (recipe, page 10)

1. Grease a 10-inch angel cake tube pan; dust lightly with flour; tap out any excess.
2. Sift flour, baking powder and salt onto wax paper.
3. Beat butter or margarine until soft in large bowl of electric mixer at high speed. Beat in sugar until fluffy. Beat in egg yolks, one at a time; stir in vanilla.
4. Stir in flour mixture, alternately with milk, just until blended.
5. Pour half the batter into a second bowl; stir chocolate syrup and coffee liqueur into one half. Spoon both batters into prepared pan, alternating layers of white and dark. Draw a knife or spatula through batter several times to marbleize.
6. Bake in moderate oven (350°) 1 hour, or until center springs back when lightly pressed with fingertip. Cool 10 minutes in pan on wire rack; loosen around edge with a knife; turn out onto wire rack; cool completly.
7. Frost top and side with MOCHA BUTTER CREAM.

OKOLE MALUNA CAKE

In Hawaiian, "Okole Maluna!" means "Bottoms up!" What better name could there be for this upside down cake.

Bake at 350° for 1 hour.
Makes one 9-inch square.

Topping
- ¼ cup (½ stick) butter or margarine
- ¾ cup firmly packed brown sugar
- ⅛ teaspoon salt
- 1 can (about 1 pound, 4 ounces) pineapple slices, drained
- 12 maraschino cherries, quartered

Cake
- 2 eggs, separated
- 2 cups cake flour
- 2½ teaspoons baking powder
- ½ teaspoon ground ginger
- ½ teaspoon salt
- ½ cup (1 stick) butter or margarine
- 1 cup sugar
- 1 teaspoon grated lemon rind
- ½ teaspoon vanilla
- ½ cup milk
- ½ cup finely chopped walnuts

1. Make topping: Melt butter or margarine in 9x9x2-inch baking pan; stir in brown sugar and salt; cook, stirring constantly, over low heat until bubbly; remove from heat.
2. Arrange pineapple and cherries on sugar mixture.
3. Make cake: Beat egg whites just until stiff in small bowl of electric mixer at high speed.
4. Sift flour, baking powder, ginger and salt onto wax paper.
5. Beat butter or margarine with sugar until fluffy in large bowl of mixer at high speed; beat in egg yolks, lemon rind and vanilla. Blend in dry ingredients alternately with milk; fold in walnuts and beaten egg whites with wire whip; pour over fruits in pan.
6. Bake in moderate oven (350°) 1 hour, or until center springs back when lightly pressed with fingertip.
7. Cool on wire rack 5 minutes; cover pan with serving plate; quickly turn upside down, then carefully lift off baking pan. Serve with whipped cream or ice cream, if you wish.

CHOCOLATE CHIP LOAF CAKE

A cake version of the old favorite, chocolate chip cookies. The loaf is topped with a sugar and chocolate frosting to give it a "shadow" effect along the edge.

Bake at 350° for 1 hour, 20 minutes.
Makes one loaf cake.

    2 cups all purpose flour
    1 cup firmly packed brown sugar
    ½ cup granulated sugar
    1 tablespoon baking powder
    1 teaspoon salt
    ½ teaspoon baking soda
    ½ cup vegetable shortening
    1 cup milk
    3 eggs
    ½ cup semi-sweet chocolate
       pieces, finely chopped
    1½ teaspoons vanilla
       Shadow Frosting (recipe follows)

1. Grease a 9x5x3-inch loaf pan; line bottom with wax paper; grease paper.
2. Measure flour, brown sugar, granulated sugar, baking powder, salt, baking soda, shortening and milk into large bowl of electric mixer. Add eggs, chocolate and vanilla.
3. Beat ½ minute at low speed, scraping side of bowl constantly. Increase mixer speed to high; beat 3 minutes, scraping side of bowl several times. Turn into prepared pan.
4. Bake in moderate oven (350°) 1 hour, 20 minutes, or until center springs back when lightly pressed with fingertip. Cool on wire rack about 10 minutes. Remove from pan; peel off wax paper; cool completely. Frost with SHADOW FROSTING. To serve, cut into slices with sharp knife.

SHADOW FROSTING

Makes enough to frost one loaf cake.

    2 cups 10X (confectioners'
       powdered) sugar
    ½ cup (1 stick) butter or margarine
    1 teaspoon vanilla
    4 tablespoons hot milk
    1 square unsweetened chocolate
    ½ teaspoon vegetable shortening

1. Combine 10X sugar, butter or margarine, vanilla and milk in small bowl of electric mixer. Beat at high speed, until frosting is very fluffy. Spread on top and sides of cake.
2. Melt chocolate with shortening in a small saucepan over very low heat; cool slightly. Drizzle down sides of frosted cake for "shadow" effect.

APPLE SUPPER CAKE

Goes together fast; great with coffee.

Bake at 350° for 45 minutes.
Makes one 9-inch square.

    2 cups all purpose flour
    2 teaspoons baking powder
    ½ teaspoon salt
    ¼ teaspoon pumpkin pie spice
    1 cup firmly packed brown sugar
    ½ cup (1 stick) butter or margarine
    ¼ cup dried currants or raisins
    2 eggs
    1 small can evaporated milk (⅔ cup)
    1 large tart apple, pared, cored and
       thinly sliced
    2 tablespoons granulated sugar

1. Sift flour, baking powder, salt and pumpkin pie spice into a large bowl; stir in brown sugar.
2. Cut in 6 tablespoons of the butter or margarine with a pastry blender, until mixture is crumbly. Measure out ½ cup and set aside for topping; stir currants or raisins into remainder.
3. Beat eggs slightly in a small bowl with a fork; stir in evaporated milk. Stir into flour mixture until well blended. Spoon into a greased 9-inch pie plate.
4. Arrange apple slices, overlapping, in 2 circles on top. Sprinkle with the ½ cup reserved crumb mixture; dot with remaining 2 tablespoons butter or margarine; sprinkle evenly with granulated sugar.
5. Bake in moderate oven (350°) 45 minutes, or until firm in center. Cool 10 minutes on a wire rack; cut into wedges. Serve warm.

BAKING BASICS

COOLING CAKES AND COOKIES

• Cool "foam" cakes—for example, angel food, chiffon and sponge—upside down, over a funnel or one-quart bottle; the walls cool and strengthen enough to support themselves when cake is placed right-side up.
• Cool butter cakes on wire racks.
• With especially fragile cakes, line wire rack with clean cloth and invert cake onto wire rack; top with second wire rack, and turn cake right-side up.

• If you don't have enough wire racks for cooling cookies, use a clean tea towel or paper towel.

CARDAMOM CAKE

Easy as pie! That's exactly what this is, made the way you make a pie.

Bake at 350° for 40 minutes.
Makes one 9-inch round cake.

                Dough
    1 envelope active dry yeast
    2 tablespoons warm water
    3 cups all purpose flour
    2 tablespoons sugar
    ½ cup (1 stick) butter or margarine
    3 eggs, slightly beaten
                Filling
    ½ cup (1 stick) butter or margarine
    ½ cup sugar
    1 teaspoon ground cardamom
    ½ teaspoon ground cinnamon
    ¼ cup dried currants
    3 tablespoons chopped citron
       Corn syrup
       Candied cherries
       Citron

1. Make dough: Sprinkle yeast and 1 teaspoon sugar into warm water in small bowl; stir until dissolved. ("Very warm" water should feel comfortably warm when dropped on wrist.) Allow to stand until mixture bubbles, about 10 minutes.
2. Measure flour and sugar in large bowl. Cut in butter or margarine with pastry blender until mixture is crumbly. Make a well in center; add eggs and yeast mixture; stir with wooden spoon until dough holds together. Knead a few times, using a little extra flour to keep hands and bowl clean. Let rest 10 minutes.
3. Make filling: Beat butter or margarine and sugar in small bowl until light and fluffy with wooden spoon; beat in cardamom, cinnamon, currants and citron.
4. Press two-thirds of dough onto bottom and about 1-inch up the side of a 9-inch springform pan; spread filling evenly over dough. Roll remaining dough on lightly floured surface into strips, about the thickness of a little finger. Arrange, lattice-fashion, on top of filling, pressing firmly around edge.
5. Cover pan with towel or wax paper. Let rise in warm place, away from draft, 1 to 1½ hours, or until doubled.
6. Bake in moderate oven (350°) 40 minutes, or until golden brown. Remove from oven; brush top with corn syrup; remove side of pan; cool on wire rack. Top with candied cherries and citron, if you wish. Serve warm.

LEMON SPONGE CAKE

Put springtime into winter meals with a fruit-topped lemon cake.

Bake at 350° for 30 minutes.
Makes one 9-inch square.

   3 **eggs**
   ¾ **cup sugar**
   1 **teaspoon vanilla**
   ⅓ **cup hot water**
 1½ **teaspoons grated lemon rind**
 1¼ **cups all purpose flour**
 1½ **teaspoons baking powder**
   ½ **teaspoon salt**
   1 **can (1 pound, 1 ounce) fruit cocktail**
   1 **teaspoon cornstarch**
   1 **tablespoon lemon juice**
      Dash ground cardamom

1. Beat eggs in large bowl with electric mixer at high, until thick and lemon-colored. Gradually add sugar. Lower speed; blend in vanilla, hot water and 1 teaspoon of the lemon rind.
2. Sift flour, baking powder and salt onto wax paper; fold into egg mixture.
3. Turn batter into buttered 9x9x2-inch baking pan.
4. Bake in moderate oven (350°) 30 minutes, or until center springs back when lightly pressed with fingertip. Cool on wire rack.
5. Drain juice from fruit cocktail into a small saucepan. Combine cornstarch and lemon juice; stir into fruit juice. Cook over medium heat until mixture thickens and bubbles 1 minute. Add remaining ½ teaspoon lemon rind, cardamom and fruit. Serve sauce warm over cake.

RAISIN SPICE CAKE

Everyone loves raisins, and here's a quick way to treat your family to them.

Bake at 350° for 40 minutes.
Makes one 9-inch square.

   ½ **cup (1 stick) butter or margarine, softened**
   1 **cup firmly packed brown sugar**
   1 **egg**
   2 **cups all purpose flour**
   1 **tablespoon baking powder**
   1 **teaspoon salt**
   1 **teaspoon ground cinnamon**
   1 **teaspoon ground nutmeg**
   ½ **teaspoon ground cloves**
   ¾ **cup cooled coffee**
   1 **cup raisins**
   ¼ **cup 10X (confectioners' powdered) sugar**
   1 **tablespoon lemon juice**

1. Beat butter or margarine, brown sugar and egg in the large bowl of electric mixer at medium speed, until well blended and fluffy.
2. Sift flour, baking powder, salt, cinnamon, nutmeg and cloves onto wax paper. Turn mixer speed to very low; add sifted dry ingredients, alternately with coffee. Mix just until blended. Stir in raisins. Turn batter into a greased 9x9x2-inch baking pan.
3. Bake in moderate oven (350°) 40 minutes, or until center of cake springs back when lightly pressed with fingertip. Cool in pan on wire rack.
4. Combine 10X sugar and lemon juice in a small bowl; add a few drops of water, if necessary, to make a spreading consistency. Spread over top of cake while still warm. Frosting will form a thin glaze.

BAKING BASICS

USING EGGS

• Eggs are more easily separated when cold, but they whip up more at room temperature.
• To whip egg whites, bowl must be free from any traces of fat and beaters must be clean.
• You needn't clean beaters *after* whipping egg whites if you'll be beating yolks or batter next.
• It's best to add eggs to batter one at a time, beating well after each.
• All recipes in this book use large eggs (about ¼ cup each). If you use small eggs, measure them.
• For smoother, fluffier cakes and cookies that are easier to mix, have all ingredients at room temperature.

HIGH ALTITUDE BAKING

• If you live less than 3,000 feet above sea level, you probably won't need to adjust recipes. Above that, follow the chart given below. Use smaller adjustment the first time you try a recipe; make larger adjustment only if necessary, or contact utility company.

Altitude (feet)	3,000-4,000	4,000-6,000	6,000-7,500
Reduce Baking Powder: For each teaspoon, decrease	⅛ tsp.	⅛-¼ tsp.	¼ tsp.
Reduce Sugar: For each cup, decrease	1 tbsp.	1-2 tbsp.	3-4 tbsp.
Increase Liquid: For each cup, add	1-2 tbsp.	2-4 tbsp.	3-4 tbsp.

• For all adjusted recipes, increase temperature 25°.
• For especially rich cakes, reduce the shortening by 1-2 tablespoons.
• For very high altitudes, increase the amount of egg in angel food, chiffon or sponge cakes.
  (These are only general guides.)

TOMATO SOUP CAKE

Tomato soup is not only good in a bowl.

Bake at 350° for 30 minutes.
Makes two 8-inch layers.

   2 **cups all purpose flour**
   1 **teaspoon baking powder**
   1 **teaspoon baking soda**
   1 **teaspoon ground cinnamon**
   ¼ **teaspoon ground nutmeg**
   ¼ **teaspoon salt**
   ¼ **cup (½ stick) butter or margarine**
   1 **cup sugar**
   1 **egg**
   1 **can condensed tomato soup**
   ½ **cup chopped walnuts**
   ½ **cup golden raisins**
      Lemon Butter Cream (recipe, page 10)

1. Grease two 8-inch layer cake pans; flour lightly; tap out excess.
2. Sift flour, baking powder, soda, cinnamon, nutmeg and salt onto wax paper.
3. Beat butter or margarine with sugar until fluffy in large bowl of electric mixer at high speed; beat in egg.
4. Turn speed to low; blend in flour mixture, half at a time, alternately with tomato soup, beating just until blended. Stir in walnuts and raisins. Pour into prepared pans.
5. Bake in moderate oven (350°) 30 minutes, or until centers spring back when lightly pressed with fingertip. Cool in pans on wire racks 10 minutes. Loosen around edges with a knife; turn out onto racks; cool completely.
6. Fill and frost with LEMON BUTTER CREAM, making deep swirls on top.

SPECIAL OCCASIONS (CHAPTER 3)

(Continued from page 79)

MEXICAN TORTE

Layers of crispy chocolate pastry are filled with chocolate butter cream and topped with chocolate curls. Truly a festive dessert.

Bake at 425° for 8 minutes.
Makes one 9-inch cake.

Pastry Layers
1½ cups all purpose flour
¼ cup sugar
½ cup dry cocoa powder (not a mix)
1 teaspoon salt
⅔ cup vegetable shortening
¼ cup cold water
Filling
2 squares unsweetened chocolate
2 tablespoons butter or margarine
1 cup 10X (confectioners' powdered) sugar
1 tablespoon instant coffee powder
½ teaspoon ground cinnamon
¼ teaspoon salt
1 egg
1 cup heavy cream
Chocolate Curls (recipe, page 76)

1. Make pastry: Sift flour, sugar, cocoa and salt into medium-size bowl; cut in shortening with pastry blender until mixture is crumbly. Sprinkle water over; mix lightly with a fork just until dough clings together and leaves side of bowl clean.
2. Divide in half; roll, one half at a time, into a 9-inch round about ¼-inch thick on lightly floured pastry cloth or board. (Use the stand-up ring, not base, of a 9-inch springform pan as a guide. Pastry shrinks a bit in baking and when rounds are spread with filling they should just fit into the springform pan.) Place on ungreased cookie sheets.
3. Bake in hot oven (425°) 8 minutes, or until firm; remove carefully from cookie sheets; cool on wire racks.
4. Make filling: Melt unsweetened chocolate with butter or margarine in top of double boiler over simmering, *not boiling,* water; beat in 10X sugar, instant coffee, cinnamon, salt and egg until smooth with electric mixer at high speed. Continue beating vigorously, keeping pan over simmering water, 1 minute; remove from heat.
5. Empty bottom of double boiler; fill with ice and water; return top. Beat mixture for about 1 minute, or until slightly cool, then beat in cream gradually until mixture is fluffy and spreadable. (This will take 5 minutes.)
6. Put cake together: Place one baked pastry layer in bottom of a 9-inch springform pan; spoon filling on top; spread evenly almost to edge; top with remaining pastry layer; chill overnight. (The filling will soak into pastry layers just enough to soften them.) Top with CHOCOLATE CURLS just before serving.

STRAWBERRY RIBBON CAKE

It's perfect for a birthday celebration.

Bake at 375° for 35 minutes.
Makes two 8-inch square layers.

3 cups cake flour
2½ teaspoons baking powder
1 teaspoon salt
1 cup (2 sticks) butter or margarine
2 cups sugar
4 eggs
1 teaspoon vanilla
½ teaspoon almond extract
¾ cup milk
⅛ teaspoon red food coloring
Strawberry Butter Cream (recipe, page 10)

1. Grease two 8x8x2-inch baking pans; dust with flour; tap out excess.
2. Sift cake flour, baking powder and salt onto wax paper.
3. Beat butter or margarine until soft in large bowl of electric mixer at high speed; beat in sugar gradually, until fluffy. Beat in eggs, one at a time, until fluffy, then vanilla and almond extract until well blended.
4. Stir in flour mixture, alternately with milk, just until blended. Spoon half the batter into one pan; stir food coloring into remaining batter; pour into second pan.
5. Bake in moderate oven (375°) 35 minutes, or until centers spring back when pressed with fingertip. Cool layers in pans on wire racks 10 minutes; turn out onto racks; cool.
6. Split each cooled layer, crosswise; put together, alternating pink and yellow, with part of the STRAWBERRY BUTTER CREAM; frost sides and top with remaining.

BAKING BASICS

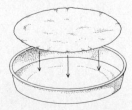

LINING PANS
• Line layer cake pans with wax paper for easier removal of delicate cakes.
• To give an even, golden crust to butter-type cakes, grease bottoms and sides of pans well with vegetable shortening, then dust with flour, shaking pan to coat well; tap out excess.
• Don't grease and flour foam cake pans. Cakes like angel food and chiffon have to cling to pan for rising.
• To grease cookie sheets, rub surface lightly with vegetable shortening. Don't grease sheets for cookies made with a cookie press.

REGAL STEAMED PUDDING

Here is a holiday steamed pudding that's not as rich or spicy as some of the traditional ones. Serve with hard sauce or whipped cream, if you wish.

Makes 12 servings.

2½ cups all purpose flour
1 tablespoon baking powder
½ teaspoon baking soda
1 teaspoon ground cinnamon
½ teaspoon ground nutmeg
¼ cup vegetable shortening
1 cup sugar
1 egg
1 can condensed tomato soup
Brandied Hard Sauce (recipe follows)

1. Sift flour, baking powder, baking soda, cinnamon and nutmeg onto wax paper or plastic wrap.
2. Beat shortening and sugar until fluffy in large bowl of electric mixer at high speed; beat in egg until smooth. Stir in flour mixture, alternately with tomato soup.
3. Grease an 8-cup steam pudding mold or 2-pound coffee can; sprinkle with sugar to coat well; spoon batter into mold; cover with mold cover or a double thickness of heavy-duty aluminum foil; tie in place.
4. Place mold on trivet or ring of foil in a large kettle. Pour in boiling water to depth of 1 inch. Cover kettle.
5. Bring to boiling; lower heat to just below simmering; cook 3 hours, adding more boiling water, if necessary, or until a long wooden skewer inserted in center comes out clean; cool in pan on wire rack 10 minutes; loosen pudding around edge of mold; turn out onto wire rack. Serve warm with BRANDIED HARD SAUCE.

BRANDIED HARD SAUCE: Makes ¾ cup. Beat ⅓ cup butter or margarine until soft in a small bowl; blend in 1 cup 10X (confectioners' powdered) sugar and 1 tablespoon brandy until smooth.

HOT CROSS BUNS

These are Eastertime favorites of "one-a-penny, two-a-penny" fame.

Bake at 350 for 30 minutes.
Makes 32 buns.

- 2 envelopes active dry yeast
- ½ cup very warm water
- ½ cup (1 stick) butter or margarine
- 1 small can evaporated milk (⅔ cup)
- ½ cup sugar
- 1 teaspoon salt
- 2 eggs
- 1 cup dried currants or raisins
- 4½ cups all purpose flour
- ¼ teaspoon ground cinnamon
- ¼ teaspoon ground nutmeg
  Lemon Icing (recipe follows)

1. Sprinkle yeast and 1 teaspoon sugar into very warm water in large bowl. ("Very warm" water should feel comfortably warm when dropped on wrist.) Stir until yeast dissolves; allow to stand until mixture bubbles, about 10 minutes.
2. Melt butter or margarine in small saucepan; remove from heat. Add evaporated milk, sugar and salt, stirring until sugar dissolves; stir into yeast mixture.
3. Beat eggs in small bowl with a wire whip; measure 2 tablespoons into a cup and set aside for brushing buns in Step 8. Stir remaining into yeast mixture; stir in currants or raisins until well mixed.
4. Sift 2 cups of the flour, cinnamon and nutmeg over yeast mixture; beat until smooth with a wooden spoon, then stir in just enough of remaining 2½ cups flour to make a soft dough.
5. Turn out onto lightly floured pastry cloth or board; knead until smooth and elastic, adding only enough flour to keep dough from sticking.
6. Place in greased bowl; brush top lightly with butter or margarine; cover with clean towel. Let rise in warm place, away from draft, 1 hour, or until double in bulk.
7. Punch dough down; turn out onto lightly floured pastry cloth or board; divide in half. Cut each half into 16 equal-size pieces; shape each lightly into a ball. Place 16 balls each in two greased 9x9x2-inch baking pans.
8. Cover with clean towel; let rise in warm place, away from draft, 45 minutes, or until double in bulk. Brush tops of buns with saved egg.
9. Bake in moderate oven (350°) 30 minutes, or until golden brown; remove from pans; cool on wire racks.
10. Drizzle LEMON ICING onto tops of buns to make crosses.

LEMON ICING: Makes ½ cup. Blend 1 cup 10X (confectioners' powdered) sugar with 4 teaspoons milk, ¼ teaspoon vanilla, and ¼ teaspoon lemon extract until smooth in small bowl with a wire whip.

GEORGE WASHINGTON COCOA ROLL

Celebrate the birthday of the father of our country with this delicious cake made with an appropriate filling of cherry ice cream.

Bake at 400° for 10 minutes.
Makes 8 servings.

- 4 eggs
- 1 teaspoon vanilla
- ¾ cup sugar
- ½ cup cake flour
- ⅓ cup dry cocoa powder (not a mix)
- 1 teaspoon baking powder
- ½ teaspoon salt
  10X sugar
- 1 quart cherry-vanilla ice cream
  Chocolate Whipped Cream (recipe follows)

1. Grease a 15x10x1-inch jelly roll pan; line with wax paper; grease.
2. Beat eggs with vanilla until fluffy-thick and lemon-colored in small bowl of electric mixer at high speed. Gradually beat in sugar until mixture is very thick.
3. Sift flour, cocoa powder, baking powder and salt into bowl. Fold in with wire whip until well blended. Spread batter evenly in prepared pan.
4. Bake in hot oven (400°) 10 minutes, or until top springs back when lightly pressed with fingertip.
5. Loosen cake around edges of pan with a sharp knife. Invert pan onto a clean towel lightly dusted with 10X sugar; peel off wax paper. Starting at one short end, roll up cake, jelly roll fashion; wrap in towel. Cool cake completely on a wire rack.
6. Soften ice cream slightly. Unroll cooled cake carefully; spread evenly with softened ice cream; reroll. Place on a cookie sheet. Freeze 1 hour.
7. Frost roll with CHOCOLATE WHIPPED CREAM. Freeze until serving time. Cut into 8 thick slices.

CHOCOLATE WHIPPED CREAM

Makes 2 cups.
- 1 cup heavy cream
- 3 tablespoons instant cocoa mix

Beat cream and cocoa mix in a small bowl until stiff, with electric mixer at high speed. Spread on cake roll.

EASTER EGG RING

Families in the province of Brindisi, Italy, have this delicious hot bread for breakfast on Easter morning. It's decorated with eggs (to symbolize life and death) that hardcook while the bread bakes.

Bake at 375° for 30 minutes.
Makes one 16-inch ring.

- ½ cup milk
- 2 tablespoons butter or margarine
- ¼ cup sugar
- 1 teaspoon salt
- 1 package active dry yeast
- ¼ cup very warm water
- 1 egg beaten
- 3 cups all purpose flour
- 3 drops oil of anise
- 6 uncooked white-shell eggs
  Easter egg coloring
  Butter or margarine

1. Heat milk with the 2 tablespoons butter or margarine in small saucepan; stir in sugar and salt; cool.
2. Dissolve yeast and 1 teaspoon sugar in very warm water in large bowl. ("Very warm" water should feel comfortably warm when dropped on wrist.) Stir in cooled milk mixture and beaten egg.
3. Beat in 1 cup flour until smooth with a wooden spoon; beat in oil of anise. (Buy it at your drugstore.) Gradually beat in enough of remaining flour to make a stiff dough.
4. Turn out onto lightly floured pastry cloth or board; knead until smooth and elastic, adding only enough flour to keep dough from sticking.
5. Place dough in greased large bowl; cover with clean towel; let rise in warm place, away from draft, 1 hour, or until double in bulk.
6. Tint uncooked eggs with Easter egg coloring, following label directions; let dry while dough is rising.
7. Punch dough down; turn out onto lightly floured pastry cloth or board; divide into sixths. Roll each sixth into a rope, 12-inches long. Braid 3 ropes together on one side of a large cookie sheet; braid remaining ropes on other side. Form braids into one large circle, pinching ends together to seal tightly.
8. Place each egg, large end up, in braid, spacing eggs evenly around ring. (The tiny air space in the large rounded end of the egg will keep it from cracking open during baking.) Cover with clean towel; let rise in warm place, away from draft, 1 hour, or until double in bulk.
9. Bake in moderate oven (375°) 30 minutes, or until golden brown; brush top with butter or margarine.

DESSERTS IN A HURRY (CHAPTER 4)

(Continued from page 91)

SUNBURST

Chocolate and cinnamon, the distinctive flavors of Mexican cooking, are combined in this festive coffee cake.

Bake at 350° for 20 minutes.
Makes 1 large coffee cake.

- 1 package hot-roll mix
- ½ cup sugar
- 2 tablespoons vegetable shortening
- 2 eggs
- ¾ cup warm water
- 1 envelope (1 ounce) liquid unsweetened chocolate
- 1 teaspoon ground cinnamon
- 3 tablespoons butter or margarine, softened
- ½ cup chopped walnuts

1. Combine hot-roll mix, 2 tablespoons of the sugar and shortening in a large bowl; prepare with 1 of the eggs and water, following label directions. Cover with a clean towel. Let rise in a warm place, away from draft, 1 hour, or until double in bulk.
2. While dough rises, blend chocolate, remaining sugar, cinnamon and butter or margarine in a small bowl.
3. Punch dough down; turn out onto a lightly floured pastry cloth or board. Knead 50 times, or until smooth; cover again; let stand 10 minutes.
4. Roll out dough to a 20x10-inch rectangle; spread chocolate mixture evenly over top; sprinkle ¼ cup of the walnuts over chocolate layer. Cut rectangle in half lengthwise; starting at a long side, roll up each half tightly, jelly roll fashion.
5. Cut one roll into 6 equal pieces; cut 4 pieces, the same size, from second roll. Twist remaining piece into a coil and place in center of a large cookie sheet. Pinch ends of all pieces to seal, then arrange around coil to form a sunburst design.
6. Beat remaining egg slightly in a small bowl; brush all over dough. Sprinkle remaining ¼ cup walnuts over top; cover.
7. Let rise again in a warm place, away from draft, 45 minutes, or until double in bulk.
8. Bake in moderate oven (350°) 20 minutes, or until golden and loaf gives a hollow sound when tapped. Remove from cookie sheet to a wire rack.
BAKER'S TIP: Check cakes and cookies that smell done, even if baking time given isn't up. The oven thermometer could be inaccurate.

VIENNESE CHOCOLATE CAKE

Mixes work their magic to save you time when you prepare this luscious dessert.

Bake at 350° for 30 minutes.
Makes 2 nine-inch layers.

- 1 package (about 18 ounces) chocolate cake mix
- 2 eggs
  Water
- 1 jar (12 ounces) apricot preserves
- 3 tablespoons brandy
- 1 package (about 1 pound) chocolate frosting mix
  Whipped cream

1. Grease 2 nine-inch layer cake pans; dust with flour; tap out any excess.
2. Prepare cake mix with eggs and water, following label directions; pour into prepared pans.
3. Bake in moderate oven (350°) 30 minutes, or until centers spring back when lightly pressed with fingertip. Cool in pans on wire racks 10 minutes. Loosen layers around edges with a knife; turn out onto racks; cool completely. Split each layer crosswise, using a sawing motion with a knife.
4. Heat apricot preserves slowly in a small saucepan until melted. Press through sieve into a bowl; add brandy and stir to blend.
5. Place one split layer on serving plate; brush generously with apricot mixture. Place a second split layer and brush. Repeat with remaining split layers. Brush remaining apricot mixture over side and top of cake.
6. Prepare chocolate frosting mix, following label directions. Spread over top and side of cake. Refrigerate until serving time. Garnish cake with whipped cream and top with a maraschino cherry, if you wish.

PLANTATION PINEAPPLE CAKE

The broiled-on topping makes quick work of frosting a cake.

Bake at 350° for 30 minutes.
Makes one 9-inch square.

- 2 cups biscuit mix
- ½ cup granulated sugar
- 2 eggs
- ½ cup milk
- 1 teaspoon vanilla
- 1 teaspoon grated lemon rind
- ⅓ cup butter or margarine, softened
- ¼ cup firmly packed brown sugar
- 1 can (8¼ ounces) crushed pineapple, drained
- ¾ cup flaked coconut

1. Combine biscuit mix, granulated sugar, eggs, milk, vanilla, lemon rind and 3 tablespoons of the butter or margarine in the large bowl of electric mixer. Beat at low speed ½ minute to blend ingredients. Increase speed to medium; beat 4 minutes. Scrape bowl often with rubber spatula.
2. Turn batter into a buttered 9x9x2-inch baking pan.
3. Bake in moderate oven (350°) 30 minutes, or until center of cake springs back when lightly pressed with fingertip. Cool cake a few minutes on a wire rack.
4. Combine brown sugar, pineapple, coconut and remaining butter in small bowl of mixer; beat until well mixed. Spread on cake. Broil, with top 3 inches from heat, just until topping begins to brown, about 2 minutes. Cool cake on wire rack. Cut into squares to serve.
BAKER'S TIP: One large lemon yields 2 teaspoons grated rind.

YANKEE PARTY CAKE

Tangy cranberry sauce and crisp apple chips add a festive touch to this distinctive dessert that's so easy to make.

Bake at 325° for 50 minutes.
Makes one 10-inch angel tube cake.

- 1 package (14½ ounces) angel food cake mix
- 1 teaspoon ground mace
- 2 medium-size baking apples, pared, quartered, cored, and thinly sliced
- 1 can (8 ounces) whole berry cranberry sauce
- 2 tablespoons sugar
- 1 teaspoon grated orange rind
- 1 envelope unflavored gelatin
- ¼ cup water
  Few drops red food coloring
- 1 cup heavy cream

1. Prepare cake mix with mace, following label directions. Pour batter into an ungreased 10-inch angel cake tube pan.
2. Bake in slow oven (325°) 50 minutes, or until top springs back when lightly pressed with fingertip.
3. Invert pan, placing tube over a quart-size bottle; let cake cool completely. Loosen cake around edge and tube with a spatula. Cover pan with a serving plate; turn upside down; gently lift off pan. Cut cake into 4 layers.
4. Combine apples, cranberry sauce, sugar and orange rind in a medium-size saucepan. Bring to boiling; reduce heat; cover. Simmer about 10 minutes, or until apples are tender.
5. Soften gelatin in water in a cup; stir into hot apple mixture. Add food coloring to tint pink. Pour into a

medium-size metal bowl.

6. Set bowl in a larger bowl partly filled with ice and water to speed setting. Chill, stirring often, until as thick as unbeaten egg white.

7. Beat cream until stiff in a medium-size bowl with electric mixer at high speed; fold 1⅓ cups into mixture.

8. Spread a third of the filling between each layer. Frost top of cake with remaining whipped cream. Chill until ready to serve. Decorate with mint leaves, if you wish.

BAKER'S TIP: If oven heat is uneven, experiment by putting racks at different levels. When cake rises evenly and is a uniform golden, rack is in best position.

BUTTERSCOTCH APPLE CAKE

Apple rings make a delicius topping for a colorful and spicy upside-down cake.

Bake at 350° for 45 minutes.
Makes one 13x9x2-inch cake.

2 large baking apples
¼ cup cinnamon red-hot candies
   Water
½ cup (1 stick) butter or margarine
1 cup firmly packed brown sugar
8 maraschino cherries
⅓ cup chopped pecans
1 package (about 18 ounces) yellow cake mix
   Eggs
   Whipped cream

1. Core apples, but do not pare; cut each into 4 thick rings.

2. Combine cinnamon candies and ½ cup water in a large skillet. Heat, stirring constantly, until candies melt; add apple rings. Simmer, turning once, 3 minutes; remove with a slotted spoon and drain on paper towels.

3. Melt butter or margarine in a 13x9x2-inch baking pan; stir in brown sugar. Place apple rings in two rows over sugar mixture; top each with a maraschino cherry; sprinkle pecans between apples.

4. Prepare cake mix with eggs and water, following label directions; pour evenly over apples in pan.

5. Bake in moderate oven (350°) 45 minutes, or until golden and top springs back when lightly pressed with fingertip. Cool in pan on a wire rack 10 minutes. Loosen around edges with a knife; invert onto a large serving plate. Let stand 5 minutes; carefully lift off pan. Serve warm with whipped cream, if you wish.

BAKER'S TIP: When testing if a cake is done, watch for pulling from sides of pan. (Not for foam cakes.)

OATMEAL SUNDAE CUPS

Festive desserts don't have to be fussy. Start with the new oatmeal cookie mix and you'll have a new way to serve ice cream.

Bake at 350° for 15 minutes.
Makes 16 cups.

1 package (18 ounces) oatmeal cookie mix
½ cup finely chopped walnuts
1 teaspoon pumpkin pie spice
¼ cup water
   Vanilla ice cream
   Bottled chocolate sundae sauce

1. Combine oatmeal cookie mix, walnuts and pumpkin pie spice in a large bowl. Stir in water and mix with a wooden spoon 1 minute, or until mixture is well blended.

2. Grease 16 muffin tin cups generously. Press 2 tablespoons of mixture into each cup to line bottom and side. (Or, use half the mixture to make 8 cups and drop remaining batter, by teaspoonfuls, onto cookie sheet.)

3. Bake in moderate oven (350°) 12 minutes; press down puffed-up cup centers with the back of a spoon. Remove cookie sheet from oven, if some cookies were made.

4. Return muffin tin to oven. Bake 3 minutes longer, or until cups are golden. Press down a second time with spoon, if necessary. Cool in pans on wire racks 5 minutes. Loosen cups around edge with a sharp knife; turn onto wire racks to cool completely.

5. To serve: Fill cups with vanilla ice cream and top with chocolate sauce.

BAKER'S TIP: Cups will store for several days if packed in a metal container with a tight-fitting lid.

BAKING BASICS

Beat: to stir
vigorously with a
spoon, egg beater,
wire whip or
electric mixer
as in ...

DICTIONARY OF BAKING TERMS

• Bake: To cook with dry heat, usually in an oven.

• Batter: A combination of flour, liquid and other ingredients of dropping or pouring consistency.

• Beat: The term formerly referred to as "cream," meaning to stir vigorously with a spoon, egg beater, wire whip or electric mixer, as in combining sugar and butter.

• Blend: To thoroughly combine two or more ingredients until very smooth.

• Boil: To heat until bubbles rise continuously and break on surface of liquid (212° at sea level); a rolling boil has rapidly forming bubbles.

• Brown: To cook until food changes color, as with butter or nuts.

• Caramelize: To heat sugar slowly in a heavy pan until it turns brown in color and caramel in flavor.

• Chop: To cut food into pieces with a knife, mechanical chopper, or other sharp tool, holding blunt end of knife tip on board with one hand and moving blade up and down with the other hand.

• Chill: To make cold by refrigerating at least several hours.

• Cool: To allow to come to room temperature.

• Cut in: To distribute solid fat in dry ingredients by chopping with two knives or pastry blender.

• Fold: To combine ingredients, using an up-over-and-down motion with a wire whip or rubber spatula.

• Dissolve: To combine dry and liquid ingredients in solution.

• Dough: A mixture of flour, liquid and other ingredients; stiff enough to knead or roll.

• Grate: To cut into tiny particles, using small holes of grater, as with lemon peel, chocolate.

• Knead: To work dough into smooth and elastic mass, using pressing and folding motion of hands.

• Mix: To combine two or more ingredients until mixture is of uniform consistency.

• Pare: To cut off outer covering of apples, pears and other fruit and vegetables with a knife, parer or other sharp tool.

• Peel: To strip off outer covering, as with fruit.

• Refrigerate: To place in refrigerator and make cold.

• Sift: To put dry ingredients through a sieve or sifter.

• Simmer: To cook a liquid or in a liquid at a temperature just below boiling; bubbles form slowly and break below surface.

• Sliver: To cut into long thin pieces, as with almonds.

• Stir: To combine two or more ingredients with a circular or figure 8 motion until all ingredients are distributed evenly within mixture.

• Toast: To brown in oven or toaster, as with nuts or coconut.

• Whip: To beat rapidly to incorporate air, increase volume and make a fluffier mixture.

EUROPE'S CLASSICS (CHAPTER 5)

(Continued from page 103)

PANETTONE

A traditional sweet fruit-filled bread from Italy. Delicious plain or toasted.

Bake at 375° for 1 hour, 15 minutes.
Makes 1 large round.

- ½ cup milk
- 2 teaspoons anise seeds
- ½ cup sugar
- 1 teaspoon salt
- 1 envelope active dry yeast
- ¼ cup very warm water
- 2 eggs, beaten
- 2 teaspoons grated lemon rind
- 3 cups all purpose flour
- ½ cup (1 stick) butter or margarine, melted and cooled
- 1 jar (8 ounces) mixed candied fruits, finely chopped
- ½ cup seedless raisins

1. Heat milk with anise in small saucepan; remove from heat. Let stand 5 minutes, then strain into a cup, discarding seeds. Stir in ¼ cup of the sugar and salt. Cool just until lukewarm.
2. Sprinkle yeast and 1 teaspoon sugar into very warm water in large bowl. ("Very warm" water should feel comfortably warm when dropped on wrist.) Stir until dissolved. Leave until mixture bubbles, about 10 minutes.
3. Stir in cooled milk mixture, eggs, lemon rind and flour. Beat vigorously, scraping down side of bowl. Continue to beat with a spoon 100 times, or until dough is elastic and forms a ball (about 5 minutes). Stir in cooled melted butter or margarine. Dough will become stringy, so beat again until it forms a ball.
4. Place in greased bowl; cover with clean towel. Let rise in warm place, away from draft, 1 hour, or until double in bulk.
5. While dough rises, prepare a 6-inch springform pan or 6-cup straight-sided baking dish this way: Cut a piece of foil, long enough to wrap around pan and overlap slightly; fold in quarters lengthwise. Grease pan and foil strip, then wrap strip around top of pan to make a 2-inch stand-up collar; hold with paper clip and string.
6. Sprinkle saved ¼ cup sugar over raised dough; stir down with wooden spoon; work in candied fruits and raisins. Place in pan.
7. Cover with clean towel; let rise in warm place, away from draft, 1½ hours, or until double in bulk.
8. Bake in moderate oven (375°) 1 hour, 15 minutes, or until a deep rich brown and hollow-sounding when tapped. Cool 5 minutes on wire rack. Remove foil collar, then remove bread from pan. Cool completely.
BAKER'S TIP: If your electric mixer has a dough hook attachment, beat on speed recommended by manufacturer for 3 minutes, or until dough becomes elastic and forms a ball.

CHELSEA TEACAKES

Such delectable treats! Chocolate-ripple cake is topped with two frostings.

Bake at 350° for 40 minutes.
Makes 4 dozen.

- 2 cups all purpose flour
- 1 tablespoon baking powder
- ½ teaspoon salt
- 3 eggs, separated
- 1 cup (2 sticks) butter or margarine
- 1 cup sugar
- 1 teaspoon vanilla
- ¾ cup milk
- 3 squares semisweet chocolate, grated
- Vanilla-Almond Cream (recipe, page 37)
- 3 squares semisweet chocolate

1. Grease a 13x9x2-inch baking pan; line bottom with wax paper; grease paper.
2. Sift flour, baking powder and salt onto wax paper or aluminum foil.
3. Beat egg whites until they form soft peaks in small bowl of electric mixer at high speed.
4. Beat butter or margarine in large bowl of mixer at medium speed: add sugar gradually, beating until fluffy. Beat in vanilla.
5. Add sifted dry ingredients, a third at a time, alternately with milk, stirring with a wire whip or beating with mixer at low speed just until blended. Fold in grated chocolate, then beaten egg whites until no streaks of white remain. Pour into prepared pan.
6. Bake in moderate oven (350°) 40 minutes, or until top springs back when lightly pressed with fingertip.
7. Cool in pan on wire rack 5 minutes. Loosen around edges with knife; turn out onto rack; peel off wax paper; cool completely.
8. When ready to frost, make VANILLA-ALMOND CREAM. Spread on top of cake; chill until firm.
9. Melt 3 squares chocolate for topping in a metal cup over simmering water; spread on top of firm frosting; chill again until chocolate is firm.
10. Trim edges of cake: cut cake into 2-inch squares, then halve each diagonally to make 2 small triangles.

PORTUGUESE SWEET BREAD

This easy-to-make sweet bread will be a spectacular addition to your Sunday brunch.

Bake at 350° for 50 minutes.
Makes one 10-inch fluted tube cake.

- ½ cup milk
- 1 teaspoon caraway seeds, crushed
- 1 envelope active dry yeast
- ½ cup very warm water
- ½ cup (1 stick) butter or margarine
- ¾ cup sugar
- 4 eggs
- 2 teaspoons grated lemon rind
- 4 cups all purpose flour
- 1 teaspoon salt
- ½ cup raisins

1. Heat milk with caraway seeds in a small saucepan until bubbles appear around edge. Cool until lukewarm.
2. Dissolve yeast and 1 teaspoon sugar in very warm water in a small bowl. ("Very warm" water should feel comfortably warm when dropped on wrist.) Stir until well blended and allow to stand 10 minutes, or until mixture begins to bubble.
3. Beat butter or margarine, sugar, eggs and lemon rind until fluffy in large bowl of electric mixer at high speed for 3 minutes.
4. Strain cooled milk into bowl; add dissolved yeast; blend on low speed. Add flour with salt gradually; beat at high speed for 2 minutes. Cover bowl with a clean cloth or plastic wrap.
5. Let rise in a warm place, away from draft, 1½ hours, or until double in bulk; beat dough down and beat in raisins. Spoon into a well greased 12-cup fluted tube pan or 9-inch angel cake tube pan. Cover; let rise in a warm place, 45 minutes, or until almost double in bulk.
6. Bake in moderate oven (350°) 50 minutes, or until bread gives a hollow sound when tapped. (If top is browning too rapidly during baking, place a piece of aluminum foil lightly over top of pan for remainder of baking period.) Cool bread in pan on wire rack 5 minutes; loosen around edges of pan; turn out onto wire rack to cool. Dust with 10X sugar; decorate with candied fruits, if you wish.
Suggested Variation: For ORANGE-CURRANT COFFEE CAKE, follow directions for PORTUGUESE SWEET BREAD, substituting anise seeds for caraway seeds, orange rind for lemon rind and dried currants for raisins.
BAKER'S TIP: If your electric mixer has a dough hook attachment, be sure to use it with this recipe.

RIGO JANCSI

These Hungarian cakes are the last word in the art of pâtisserie. Rich chocolate layers hold a two-inch-thick chocolate filling!

Bake at 350° for 15 minutes.
Makes 12 servings.

Cake
3 squares unsweetened chocolate
4 eggs, separated
½ cup superfine sugar
¾ cup (1½ sticks) butter or margarine
⅔ cup cake flour
¼ teaspoon salt
1 teaspoon vanilla

Filling
10 squares semisweet chocolate
2 cups heavy cream
2 tablespoons coffee liqueur

Frosting
1 cup superfine sugar
½ cup hot coffee
6 squares semisweet chocolate
2 tablespoons light corn syrup
2 tablespoons butter or margarine
2 tablespoons coffee liqueur

1. Make cake: Melt chocolate in top of a double boiler over hot water; cool to lukewarm.
2. Grease a 15x10x1-inch baking pan; line with wax paper; grease paper.
3. Beat egg whites until foamy-white and double in volume in small bowl of electric mixer at high speed. Beat in ¼ cup of the sugar, 1 tablespoon at a time, until meringue stands in soft peaks.
4. Beat butter or margarine in large bowl of mixer; gradually add remaining ¼ cup sugar and continue beating until mixture is well blended. Beat in egg yolks until smooth, then blend in cooled chocolate. Sift flour and salt into chocolate mixture; stir to blend; add vanilla.
5. Stir ⅓ of the meringue mixture into chocolate mixture with wire whip; fold in remaining meringue mixture until well blended. Spread batter evenly in prepared pan.
6. Bake in moderate oven (350°) 15 minutes, or until top springs back when lightly touched with fingertip.
7. Cool in pan on wire rack for 5 minutes; loosen cake around edges of pan with a sharp knife; invert cake onto a large cookie sheet; peel off wax paper; invert cake onto a large cake rack; cool completely.
8. Make filling: Cut semisweet chocolate into small pieces. Combine with cream in a medium-size saucepan. Heat slowly, stirring constantly, until chocolate melts; remove from heat; stir in coffee liqueur. Pour into a medium-size bowl. Chill 1½ hours, or until mixture is completely cold.
9. Beat chilled chocolate-cream mixture until stiff and thick.
10. Cut cooled cake in half, crosswise. Place half on a small cookie sheet. Top with whipped chocolate cream, spreading to make a layer about 2-inches thick; top with second half of cake. Chill at least 1 hour, or until filling is firm.
11. Make frosting: Heat sugar and coffee in a medium-size saucepan until sugar dissolves. Cut chocolate into small pieces; add to saucepan with corn syrup. Heat to boiling, stirring constantly, then cook at a slow boil, 5 minutes, stirring constantly. Remove from heat; add butter or margarine and coffee liqueur. Beat 5 minutes, or until mixture begins to thicken. Quickly spread over cake layer, about ¼-inch thick. Chill at least 1 hour.
12. To serve: Cut cake into 12 squares with a heavy sharp knife.

MAYFAIR TEA RING

Similar to buttery pound cake, it needs only a shower of powdered sugar to make it the perfect tea-party cake.

Bake at 350° for 1 hour.
Makes one 6-inch angel tube cake.

1½ cups cake flour
1 teaspoon baking powder
½ teaspoon salt
½ cup (1 stick) butter or margarine
1 cup granulated sugar
2 eggs
½ teaspoon almond extract
½ teaspoon vanilla
⅓ cup milk
½ cup finely chopped pistachio nuts
10X sugar

1. Measure flour, baking powder and salt into sifter.
2. Beat butter or margarine and granulated sugar until fluffy in large bowl of electric mixer at medium speed; beat in eggs, 1 at a time, beating well after each addition. Beat in almond extract and vanilla.
3. Sift in dry ingredients, a third at a time, adding alternately with milk; stir with wire whip or beat with mixer at low speed just until blended. Fold in nuts. Pour into a well greased and floured 6-cup angel cake tube pan. (Or spoon into a well greased and lightly floured 9x5x3-inch loaf pan.)
4. Bake in moderate oven (350°) 1 hour, or until wooden pick inserted near center comes out clean.
5. Cool in pan on wire rack 5 minutes; loosen around edge with knife; turn out onto rack; cool completely.
6. Wrap in wax paper, aluminum foil or plastic wrap and store for at least a day before slicing.
7. When ready to serve, sift 10X sugar over cake; top with a ring of slivered pistachio nuts, if you wish.

BAKING BASICS

STORING CAKES AND COOKIES

• To keep cookies crisp, store in container between layers of wax paper. Keep in cool place.
• To keep cookies soft, store in tin with an apple wedge or piece of soft white bread to add moisture, but replace them often.
• To freshen soft cookies, put in casserole, cover and bake at 300° for 8-10 minutes.
• To freshen crisp cookies before serving, place on baking sheet and heat at 300° for 3-5 minutes.
• For cakes with fluffy frosting, slip knife under cake carrier so it won't be airtight.
• For whipped cream frosting cakes, keep in refrigerator, covered with inverted bowl.
• Cakes with butter frostings may be loosely covered with foil or plastic wrap or stored in a cake carrier.

MAILING CAKES AND COOKIES

• Choose the right cakes and cookies for mailing: Soft drop, bar and fruit cookies mail well; fruit and pound cakes are good travelers, too.
• For cookies, use empty metal coffee or shortening tins; cakes may be sent in strong cardboard boxes.
• Wrap cookies in pairs, flat sides together, with foil and seal with cellophane tape; use plastic wrap, then foil, for cakes.
• Use crumpled foil, wax paper, or shredded tissue paper to line bottom and top of container and fill in any spaces; shifting causes breakage.
• Wrap container in corrugated cardboard, then double layer of brown paper; tie with twine or heavy string; label on one side only, using the words, "Perishable" and "Fragile" and "Handle with Care."

BAKING WITH KIDS (CHAPTER 6)

(Continued from page 111)

HAPPY BIRTHDAY GIFT CAKE

Tiny cake "packages" for each child surround the big chocolate baby-chick cake.

Bake layers at 325° for 35 minutes; loaf cake at 325° for 1 hour, 15 minutes.
Makes two 8-inch layers and eight 2-inch squares.

- 2 packages (about 1 pound each) pound cake mix
- 1 can (about 1 pound) chocolate frosting
- 2 cans (about 1 pound each) vanilla frosting
  Yellow, green, red and blue food colorings

1. Prepare 1 package pound cake mix, following label directions. Pour batter into two greased and floured 8-inch layer cake pans.
2. Bake in slow oven (325°) 35 minutes, or until centers spring back when lightly pressed with fingertip. Remove cakes from oven and cool on wire rack 10 minutes. Loosen cake around edges with knife; turn out onto wire racks; let cool completely.
3. Prepare remaining package of pound cake mix, following label directions. Pour into a greased and floured 9x5x3-inch loaf pan.
4. Bake in slow oven (325°) 1 hour, 15 minutes. Cool 10 minutes on wire rack; turn out onto wire rack and cool.
5. Cut loaf cake in half lengthwise, then divide and cut into 4 even pieces crosswise. Trim so that you have eight 2x2-inch squares; brush off crumbs.
6. Put layer cake on serving plate large enough so that the "gifts" will fit around the cake. Put layers together with chocolate frosting. Frost top and side.
7. Divide vanilla frosting into small bowls or custard cups and tint ¾ cup yellow, ¾ cup dark green, ¼ cup pink, ¼ cup blue, ¼ cup purple (2 drops red and 2 drops yellow) and ¼ cup orange (2 drops red and 2 drops yellow).
8. With a cake decorator and #18 star tip, pipe rosettes of green frosting around top edge of cake. With a #7 writing tip, carefully write "Happy Birthday" on cake. With a #18 star tip, pipe small rosettes around bottom edge of cake and alternately on every other green rosette on top of the cake.
9. To decorate "gift packages": Frost each cube in any color you prefer.

Pipe contrasting "ribbons" of frosting, using a #104 petal tip. Pipe green "leaves" with a #67 leaf tip. Pipe tiny "flowers" and designs to decorate as you wish (see pages 66-67).

BIG RED APPLE

Too big an apple to bring to teacher, but one the whole class can enjoy.

Bake at 325° for 1 hour, 15 minutes.
Makes 12 servings.

- 1 package (about 1 pound) pound cake mix
- 1 package (17 ounces) date and nut mix
- 2 cans (about 1 pound each) vanilla frosting
  Red and green food colorings
- 1 two-inch piece stick cinnamon
  10X sugar

1. Grease and flour a 10-cup and a 6-cup ovenproof bowl; tap out excess flour.
2. Prepare pound cake mix, following label directions; pour into prepared 10-cup bowl. Prepare date and nut mix, following label directions; pour into prepared 6-cup bowl.
3. Bake both cakes in slow oven (325°) about 50 minutes for date and nut cake and 20 minutes longer for pound cake, or until centers spring back when lightly pressed with fingertip. Cool in bowl on wire rack 10 minutes. Loosen around edge with spatula. Turn out onto wire racks to cool completely.
4. Cut each cake horizontally into three layers. Assemble cake with frosting between layers like this: Bottom of date and nut cake; middle of pound; top of date and nut; top of pound; middle of date and nut; bottom of pound. (You should have a ball shape.)
5. Divide remaining frosting in half; tint one half green. Reserve 1 tablespoon for "leaves." Spread remainder on one side of cake. Tint remaining half bright red. Spread on other half of cake, overlapping and blending slightly with green side to resemble an apple. Stick the cinnamon stick into top as a "stem."
6. To reserved green frosting, add enough 10X sugar to make a firm, pliable mixture. Flatten to a 2x ½-inch rectangle; cut out two leaves; brush top of leaves with green color; curve slightly and place on top of "apple." If you wish, make a "Wallace, the Worm" from the green trimmings. Place on the "apple"; dip a wooden pick into green color and paint a "smiling face" on "Wallace."

STRAWBERRY SUNDAE CAKE

Bake cake, put together with its ice cream fillings and frosting a day ahead, then let your freezer do the rest.

Bake at 350° for 30 minutes.
Makes one 9-inch layer.

- 1¼ cups cake flour
- 1 teaspoon baking powder
- ½ teaspoon salt
- ⅓ cup vegetable shortening
- ¾ cup sugar
- 2 eggs
- 1 teaspoon vanilla
- ½ cup milk
- 2 pints vanilla ice cream, softened
- 1 pint raspberry sherbet, softened
- 2 cups heavy cream
- ¼ cup sugar
- 1 teaspoon vanilla
  Strawberry Topping (recipe, next page)

1. Grease a 9-inch layer cake pan; line bottom with wax paper; grease paper.
2. Sift flour, baking powder and salt onto wax paper.
3. Beat shortening in small bowl of electric mixer at medium speed; gradually beat in the ¾ cup sugar until mixture is fluffy, then beat in eggs, one at a time, and vanilla.
4. Add sifted flour mixture, a third at a time, alternately with milk, stirring just until blended; pour into prepared pan.
5. Bake in moderate oven (350°) 30 minutes, or until top springs back when lightly pressed with fingertip.
6. Cool cake in pan on wire rack 5 minutes. Loosen around edge with a knife; turn out onto rack; peel off wax paper; cool cake completely.
7. Split cake, crosswise, into three thin layers with a sharp knife; press bottom layer into an 8-inch springform pan. Spread with 1 pint of the vanilla ice cream; top with second layer; spread with all of the raspberry sherbet; top with third cake layer. Spread with remaining 1 pint vanilla ice cream.
8. Cover pan with plastic wrap; freeze several hours, or until very firm.
9. Beat cream with the ¼ cup sugar and 1 teaspoon vanilla until stiff in a small deep bowl.
10. Release spring from pan and carefully lift off side; place cake on a cookie sheet. Frost side and top with part of the whipped cream mixture; spoon remaining in puffs around top edge to make a rim. Freeze overnight.
11. Prepare STRAWBERRY TOPPING and cool. Just before serving, place frozen cake on a serving plate; spoon STRAWBERRY TOPPING in center. Cut cake in wedges with a sharp knife.

STRAWBERRY TOPPING: Makes 1¼ cups. Thaw 1 package (10 ounces) frozen sliced strawberries. Stir a little of the syrup into 2 tablespoons cornstarch until smooth in a small saucepan, then stir in remaining berries and syrup. Cook, stirring constantly, over low heat until sauce thickens and bubbles 1 minute. Cool in bowl at room temperature, then cover with plastic wrap; chill.

BIG ORANGE

Our giant orange never grew in a grove, but it has all the flavor of a real one.

Bake at 325° for 50 minutes.
Makes one 10-inch round cake.

1 package (14½ ounces) angel food cake mix
2 cans (about 1 pound each) orange frosting
  Red, yellow and green food colorings
  10X sugar

1. Prepare cake mix, following label directions; pour into an ungreased 16-cup ovenproof mixing bowl, about 10 inches across top.
2. Bake in slow oven (325°) 50 minutes, or until top springs back when pressed with fingertip.
3. Invert bowl, placing rim on 3 or 4 cans of equal size, so cake can hang while cooling. (This may be done a day or so ahead, if you wish. Wrap in plastic bag; keep on counter.)
4. When cake is cool, loosen from bowl with a long spatula. Brush off loose crumbs. Place cake, rounded-side down, on serving plate.
5. Place about ⅓ cup frosting in a cone made from wax paper and 1 tablespoon frosting in each of 2 small bowls. Turn remaining frosting into a medium-size bowl; add enough red and yellow food coloring to make it bright orange; spread over top and side of cake. Cut about ¼ inch from tip of cone; pipe the frosting onto top of cake to resemble the segments of a cut orange.
6. To make "strawberry," add enough 10X sugar (about 1 tablespoon) to 1 tablespoon of reserved frosting to make a firm, pliable "dough"; form with fingers into a strawberry shape; paint with red food coloring. Tint remaining 1 tablespoon frosting green; place in cone made of wax paper. Pipe onto "strawberry" to resemble hull. Place in center of "orange" as a festive garnish.
7. Cut into wedges to serve. Serve with sherbet or ice cream and orange juice, if you wish.

Patterns for Circus Cake, page 111

BANANA SPLIT CAKE

The children will love this cake version of a soda fountain special.

Bake at 350° for 50 minutes.
Makes one 8-inch square.

3 tablespoons butter or margarine
2 large bananas
½ cup pineapple sundae topping
½ cup strawberry preserves
1 package (11¾ ounces) yellow cupcake mix
½ cup milk
1 egg
1 teaspoon vanilla
  Frozen whipped topping, thawed
  Walnut sundae topping

1. Melt butter or margarine in an 8x8x2-inch baking pan in oven, while oven is heating.
2. Peel bananas; cut in half, lengthwise and crosswise, to make 8 pieces. Arrange bananas, cut-side down, in melted butter, to resemble spokes on a wheel.
3. Spoon pineapple sundae topping in every other space between banana pieces. Spoon strawberry preserves in alternate spaces. Spoon pineapple sundae topping into center of pan to level of banana pieces.
4. Prepare cupcake mix with milk, egg and vanilla, following label directions. Pour over prepared fruits.

5. Bake in moderate oven (350°) 50 minutes, or until center springs back when lightly touched with fingertip. Remove pan from oven and cool on wire rack 5 minutes; loosen cake from sides of pan with a knife; invert onto serving plate.
6. Cool cake slightly. Just before serving, spoon thawed whipped topping into center of cake and garnish with walnut sundae topping.

STRAWBERRY SUNDAE PIZZA

Teens will get a kick out of this sweet new twist to their old favorite.

Bake at 400° for 12 minutes.
Makes one 14-inch "pizza" cake.

1 package piecrust mix
¼ cup sugar
1 egg, beaten
½ gallon vanilla ice cream
1 package (10 ounces) frozen sliced strawberries, thawed
1 tablespoon cornstarch
2 tablespoons cold water
¼ cup semi-sweet chocolate pieces
1 teaspoon vegetable shortening

1. Combine piecrust mix and sugar in a medium-size bowl; stir in beaten egg to make a stiff dough.
2. Roll out to a 16-inch round on a lightly floured pastry cloth or board; fit into a 14-inch pizza pan; trim overhang to ½ inch; turn under, flush with rim; flute to make a stand-up edge. Prick well all over with a fork.
3. Bake in hot oven (400°) 12 minutes, or until pastry is golden; cool completely in pan on a wire rack.
4. Spoon ice cream, petal fashion, into cooled pastry shell; freeze until firm, at least 2 hours.
5. Heat strawberries slowly, mashing berries well with back of spoon, until bubbly-hot in a small saucepan.
6. Blend cornstarch with water until smooth in a cup; stir into hot strawberries. Cook, stirring constantly, until sauce thickens and bubbles 1 minute; cool completely, then chill.
7. Melt chocolate pieces with shortening in a cup over simmering water; spread in a thin 6x5-inch rectangle on a cookie sheet; chill until almost firm.
8. Cut into twenty ¼-inch-wide strips; using tip of knife, roll each strip to look like a rolled anchovy; chill again until firm.
9. When ready to serve, spoon strawberry sauce in rings on top of pizza; garnish with chocolate rolls. Cut into wedges with sharp knife.
BAKER'S TIP: If you don't have a pizza pan, press dough into a 12-inch pie pan; bake, then fill.

BUYER'S GUIDE

Page 1: "Pearson's of Chesterfield" earthenware cookie jar by Denby Ltd., Inc., 10880 Wilshire Blvd., Los Angeles, Calif. 90024.

Page 5: "Friendly Village" 14-inch round chop plate by Johnson Bros. (Hanley) Ltd., 41 Madison Ave., N.Y., N.Y. 10010.

Pages 8-9: Background in red, white and blue Crystal Sugar, available at H. Roth and Son, 1577 First Ave., N.Y., N.Y. 10028.

Page 14: "Desert Rose" earthenware dinner plate, tea pot, sugar bowl and creamer by Fransiscan®, Interface Corporation, 2901 Los Feliz Blvd., Los Angeles, Calif. 90039; rectangular cake stand by Fostoria Glass Co., Moundsville, W. Va. 26041.

Page 18: "Looking Glass Collection" tea set, Scanlook "Gourmet Teak" wooden boards and "Pearson's of Chesterfield" earthenware roasting dish, all by Denby Ltd., Inc., 10880 Wilshire Blvd., Los Angeles, Calif. 90024.

Page 32: "Counter Saver" (#1, 2 and 4) by Corning Glass Works, Corning, N.Y. 14830; aluminum cookie sheets (#2, 3, 6, 7, 9 and 10) and "Super Shooter" electric cookie, canapé and candy maker (#3) by Wear-Ever Aluminum, Inc., 1089 Eastern Ave., Chillicothe, Ohio 45601; "Deluxe Tube Kit" for cake decorating by Wilton Enterprises, Inc., 833 West 115th St., Chicago, Ill. 60643; metal spatula (#9) by Foley Mfg. Co., Housewares Division, 3300 5th St. NE, Minneapolis, Minn. 55418.

Page 38: Nested ceramic bowl set (#2) and glass jars and containers (#3) available at B. Altman and Co., 5th Ave. and 34th St., N.Y., N.Y. 10016.

Page 39: "Patisserie" fluted pie plate by Pyrex; self-loosening cake pan, loose-bottomed cheese cake pan and others by Wear-Ever (#4), all available at B. Altman and Co., 5th Ave. and 34th St., N.Y., N.Y. 10016; "Toast 'N Broil" Toast-R-Oven (#5) (model #T26 3126-004) by General Elec-

tric Co., Bridgeport, Conn.; assorted specialty cake pans (#6) by Wilton Enterprises, Inc., 833 West 115th St., Chicago, Ill. 60643; "Super Shooter" electric cookie, canapé and candy maker (#7) by Wear-Ever Aluminum, Inc., 1089 Eastern Ave., Chillicothe, Ohio 45601.

Page 45: "Cake Taker" carriers, measuring cup set and coffee-tea canister set by Tupperware Home Parties, Orlando, Fla. 32802; metal spatula by Burns; wire whip, rubber spatula and rolling pins available at B. Altman and Co., 5th Ave. and 34th St., N.Y., N.Y. 10016.

Page 52: Cake pans (#1) by Wear-Ever Aluminum, Inc., 1089 Eastern Ave., Chillicothe, Ohio 45601; deluxe portable hand mixer (#2) (model #M68) by General Electric Co., Bridgeport, Conn.; nested dry measuring cups by Foley, nested stainless steel bowl set by Volrath and earthenware bowl by Mason Cash, all available at B. Altman and Co., 5th Ave. and 34th St., N.Y., N.Y.; special cookie cutters by Wilton Enterprises, Inc., 833 West 115th St., Chicago, Ill. 60643.

Page 59: Assorted muffin tins (smallest is a Gem Pan) by Wear-Ever Aluminum, Inc.; sugar shaker and 5-cup sifter by Bromwell, all available at B. Altman and Co., 5th Ave. and 34th St., N.Y., N.Y. 10016; small sifter by Foley Mfg. Co., Housewares Division, 3300 5th St. NE, Minneapolis, Minn. 55418.

Page 65: Cake Stand (#1, 2, 3 and 4) by Fostoria Glass Co., Moundsville, W. Va., 26041; Deluxe Tube and Cake Decorating Set and Syringe and Plunger Kit (#6, 9 and 10) by Wilton Enterprises, Inc., 833 West 115th St., Chicago, Ill. 60643; aluminum cookie sheets (#7, 8 and 9) by Wear-Ever Aluminum, Inc., 1089 Eastern Ave., Chillicothe, Ohio 45601; "Counter Saver" (#10) by Corning Glass Works, Corning, N.Y. 14830.

Page 69: Card from the Hallmark Historical Collection, Hallmark Cards, Inc., Kansas City, Mo. 64141; "Ashling" Continental champagne glasses by

Waterford Glass, Inc., 225 5th Ave., N.Y., N.Y. 10010; cake decorating equipment by Wilton Enterprises, Inc. (book, "Basic Cake Decorating, the Wilton Way," available for $1), 833 West 115th St., Chicago, Ill. 60643.

Page 70: Card from the Hallmark Historical Collection, Hallmark Cards, Inc., Kansas City, Mo. 64141; Stuart Crystal footed cake stand, Royal Worcester, 11 East 26th Street, N.Y., N.Y. 10010.

Page 71: Card from the Hallmark Historical Collection, Hallmark Cards, Inc., Kansas City, Mo. 64141; Spirit Decanter (#217) and "Ashling" cordial glasses by Waterford Glass Inc., 225 Fifth Ave., N.Y., N.Y. 10010; "Runnymeade" 12-inch plate by Wedgewood, 211 County Ave., Secaucus, N.J. 07094; Christmas lights by General Electric Co., Bridgeport, Conn.

Page 72: Card from the Hallmark Historical Collection, Hallmark Cards, Inc., Kansas City, Mo. 64141; "Golden Renaissance" candlesticks, round tray and pie/cake server by International Silver Co., 500 South Broad Street, Meriden, Conn. 06450.

Page 74: Tiered round pans, pastry bag and tips and "Easy-Glide Cake Stand" by Wilton Enterprises, Inc., 833 West 115th St., Chicago, Ill. 60643.

Page 81: 10-inch rectangular dish by Waterford Glass Inc., 225 Fifth Ave., N.Y., N.Y. 10010; "Creative Glass" Flameglow Candleholder, Glass Flask, Small Stacker Set and Soufflé Plus (How-To's), all by Corning Glass Works, Corning, N.Y. 14830; polyethylene cutting slab by Joyce Chen and black rectangular baking pan (How-To's) by Stone Hearth, available at B. Altman and Co., 5th Ave. and 34th St., N.Y., N.Y. 10016.

Pages 82-83: "Strawberry" honey pot and round box by Wedgewood, 211 County Ave., Secaucus, N.J. 07094; How-To's: "Kitchen Center" food preparation appliance (model #986-05) by Oster Corporation Milwaukee, Wisc. 53217; metal measuring cup set and "Multi-Measure" cup by Foley Mfg. Co., Housewares

Division, 3300 5th St. NE, Minneapolis, Minn. 51418; polyethylene cutting slab by Joyce Chen, available at B. Altman and Co., 5th Ave. and 34th St., N.Y. 10016.

Page 84: "Pearson's of Chesterfield" earthenware mineral bottles and mustard pots, and Scanlook "Gourmet Teak" wooden board, both by Denby Ltd., Inc., 10880 Wilshire Blvd., Los Angeles, Calif. 90024; How-To's: plastic measuring cup sets by Tupperware Home Parties, Orlando, Fla. 32802; metal spatula by Burns, "Multi-Measure" by Foley, jelly roll pan by Wear-Ever, all available at B. Altman and Co., 5th Ave. and 34th St., N.Y., N.Y. 10016; "Homestead Collection" bowl set by Pyrex, Corning, N.Y. 14830.

Page 94: "Hunt Scenes" 10-inch plate by Wedgewood, 211 County Ave., Secaucus, N.J. 07094; "Hyde Park" round chop plate by Royal Worcester, 11 East 26th St., N.Y., N.Y. 10010.

Page 96: "Athlone Ruby Sheffield" dessert plates by Coalport, 211 County Ave., Secaucus, N.J. 07094.

Pages 106-107: Three-speed hand mixer (model #107) by Hamilton Beach, Inc., 100 Hope Ave., Byesville, Ohio 43703; red, white and yellow bowls, measuring cups, spoons, pitchers, timers and cookie plates, all available at Design Research International Inc., 53 East 57th St., N.Y., N.Y. 10022; "Counter Saver" by Corning Glass Works, Corning, N.Y. 14830; cookie sheets by Wear-Ever Aluminum, Inc., 1089 Eastern Ave., Chillicothe, Ohio 45601; 5-cup sifter by Foley Mfg. Co., Housewares Division, 3300 5th St. NE, Minneapolis, Minn. 55418.

Page 108: "Edward" Danforth 13-inch pewter plate by Stieff Co., 800 Wyman Park Drive, Baltimore, Md. 2, 38, 39, 45, 52, 59, 81, 82, 21211; candles by Colonial Candle of Cape Cod, P.O. Box 670, Hyannis, Mass. 02601.

Page 112: "Deluxe Chrome Mixmaster" (model #1-80) by Sunbeam Co., 5450 West Roosevelt Road, Chicago, Ill. 60650.

All other photographed items are privately owned and not for sale.

COOK'S GUIDE

Page 10: Colored sugar-coated chocolates—M&M'S.
Pages 34 & 40: Frosting in a 4-ounce tube—Cake Mate Decorating Icing.
Page 55: Oven-toasted rice cereal—Kellogg's Rice Krispies.
Page 56: Marshmallow cream—Marshmallow Fluff.
Page 57: Chocolate-flavored crisp rice cereal—Post Pebbles Rice Puffs.
Page 85: Spirited strawberry-flavored beverage—Hereford's Cows.
Page 110: Natural-oat-and-fruit-cereal—Quaker 100% Natural Cereal with Raisins and Dates or Country Morning with Raisins and Dates; ready-to-eat-natural oat cereal—Heartland Natural Cereal, Plain.

ACKNOWLEDGEMENTS

The editors gratefully acknowledge the help of: Mr. George Latham, owner of The Orange Webb House, Village Lane, Orient, New York, where the pictures on pages 4, 5, 11 and 14 were taken. The Orange Webb House is an inn built in 1740 in Greenport, New York, and later moved by barge to Orient. It is open to the public from July 1 to October 15 on Tuesday, Thursday, Saturday and Sunday from 2 to 5 p.m. Sleepy Hollow Restorations own and maintain Philipsburg Manor in North Tarrytown, New York, a 17th Century farm house and gristmill trading center where the picture on page 108 was taken. It was once part of the 90,000-acre estate of Frederick Philipse, then New York's wealthiest merchant. It is open daily from 10 a.m. to 5 p.m. For further information, write or call Sleepy Hollow Restorations, P.O. Box 245, Tarrytown, New York 10591; 914/631-8200. Also thanks to: American Egg Board; Best Foods, a Div. of CPC, International, Inc.; Borden Kitchens; California Almond Board; California Bartlett Pears; California Fresh Nectarines; Campbell Soup Company; Kretschmer Wheat Germ Products; National Peanut Council; Nestlé Kitchens; Pacific Kitchens; Pacific Coast Canned Pear Service, Inc.; The Pillsbury Company; Pop-corn Institute; Wilton Enterprises.

CREDITS

Photography Credits—Bill Cadge: Pages 69, 70, 71, 72, 105, 106, 107, 108. Richard Jeffery: Pages 18, 19, 32, 65, 112. Bill McGinn: Pages 4, 5, 8, 9, 11, 14. Rudy Muller: Pages 93, 94, 95, 96. Gordon Smith: Cover, pages 1, 2, 38, 39, 45, 52, 59, 81, 82, 83, 84. René Velez: Pages 26, 27. **Cake Decorating Illustrations** (pages 66 & 67): Adolph Brotman. **Crewel Piece** (pages 26 & 27): Joseph Taveroni and Josephine Alessi. **Illustrations for Baker's Tips:** Maggic Zender.

INDEX